Levering and Urbanska earn rave reviews for *Simple Living*

"*Simple Living* is a delightful recollection that gaily skips along the mountain brooks amidst the wondrous smells of the vast orchards of Southwestern Virginia. . . . The book steadfastly proves emotionally gratifying and continuously productive."
 —*Richmond Times-Dispatch*

"Good-hearted and thought-provoking."
 —*Los Angeles Times*

"More journal than how-to manual, *Simple Living* is a thoughtful, gentle account of setting priorities, of picking—and discarding—options, and ultimately, of positive change."
 —*Greensboro News and Record*

"Levering and Urbanska have done with their tale of orcharding in Virginia what Scott and I have tried to do with our story of maple sugaring in Vermont. . . .They looked for a better life and found it.... Their hard work in the country became fun, for all the toil and setbacks. . . . I admire what they have done in the living and in the telling."
 —Helen K. Nearing, author with Scott Nearing of
  Living the Good Life

"This remarkable book offers eloquent witness to the rigors and rewards of simpler living amid our runaway consumer culture. In crystalline prose, the authors describe their own experiment in simple living. Full of wisdom, *Simple Living* provides both inspiration and guidance for those eager to leave the rat race behind."
 —David Shi, author of *The Simple Life*

"I enjoyed this lucid, honest book about how one couple (and others) left the hectic reach for material success to fashion far different lives with greater meaning and less luxury—and without sacrificing their work as writers. It is a wise and inspiring book and should have wide appeal."
 —Virginia Bell Dabney, author of *Once There Was a Farm*

P9-ARK-372

"Much of what Frank and Wanda share in this delightful book is similar to our own discoveries of enriched living through more time for ourselves, family, friends, and working for the betterment of those in need. *Simple Living* can give you confidence and courage to take steps to simplify your life, too."
                    —Millard and Linda Fuller, founders, *Habitat for Humanity*

"Deeply felt and warmly told, *Simple Living* is a beacon for anyone who has ever dreamed about a more serene, more self-chosen existence. Levering and Urbanska demonstrate that personal values are not incompatible with personal ambitions, that a move toward simplicity, far from being a retreat, can be a glad march toward meaning and contentment."
                    —Laurence Shames, author of *The Hunger for More*

"Frank Levering and Wanda Urbanska have produced a solid accomplishment in *Simple Living*. Its form is creative, and its message inspired and inspiring."
                    —*Winston-Salem Journal*

"Their honesty, sincerity, understanding of ambiguity, and plain good writing make this an engaging inquiry into values."
                    —*Booklist*

"*Simple Living* is a winner."
                    —*Minneapolis Star Tribune*

"To read *Simple Living* is to spend a long afternoon drinking herbal tea with a couple of sweet, pleasant, cheerful zealots."
                    —*The Houston Post*

PENGUIN BOOKS

SIMPLE LIVING

A former reporter for the *Los Angeles Herald Examiner*, Wanda Urbanska is the author of *The Singular Generation*. Her husband, Frank Levering, is a journalist, essayist, and screenwriter. They operate Levering Orchard in Ararat, Virginia.

FRANK LEVERING AND
WANDA URBANSKA

Simple
Living

*One Couple's Search
for a Better Life*

PENGUIN BOOKS

PENGUIN BOOKS
Penguin Books USA Inc.,
375 Hudson Street, New York, New York 10014, U.S.A.
Penguin Books Ltd, 27 Wrights Lane, London W8 5TZ, England
Penguin Books Australia Ltd, Ringwood, Victoria, Australia
Penguin Books Canada Ltd, 10 Alcorn Avenue,
Toronto, Ontario, Canada M4V 3B2
Penguin Books (N.Z.) Ltd, 182–190 Wairau Road,
Auckland 10, New Zealand

Penguin Books Ltd, Registered Offices:
Harmondsworth, Middlesex, England

First published in the United States of America by
Viking Penguin, a division of Penguin Books USA Inc., 1992
Published in Penguin Books 1993

10 9 8 7 6 5 4 3 2

Grateful acknowledgment is made for permission to reprint an excerpt from
"The Manifestation" from *The Collected Poems of Theodore Roethke*.
Copyright © 1959 by Beatrice Roethke, Administratrix of the estate of
Theodore Roethke. Used by permission of Doubleday, a division of
Bantam Doubleday Dell Publishing Group, Inc.

THE LIBRARY OF CONGRESS HAS CATALOGUED THE HARDCOVER AS FOLLOWS:
Levering, Frank,
Simple living : one couple's search for a better life / Frank Levering and
Wanda Urbanska.
p. cm.
ISBN 0-670-82893-9 (hc.)
ISBN 0 14 01.2339 3 (pbk.)
1. Farm Life—Virginia—Orchard Gap. 2. Orchards—Virginia—Orchard Gap.
3. Levering, Frank. 4. Urbanska, Wanda, 1956– . I. Urbanska, Wanda, 1956– .
II. Title.
S521.5.V8L48 1992
975.5'7–dc20 91–20960

Printed in the United States of America
Set in Caslon Old Face No 2
Designed by Kate Nichols

To our families

"Simple Living" would not have been possible without the support of many along the way. We are grateful to Pamela G. Dorman at Viking for her keen editorial eye and her strong guidance throughout. Paris Wald at Viking, too, has been a help and perenially upbeat presence. Elaine Markson, Geri Thoma, and Charlotte Sheedy deserve credit for their vital roles in the life of this project.

The following people we wish to thank for their loyalty and love—and in the case of the late Lois Levering Van Hoy for her gentle reminders that there is life apart from the computer screen: Marie Olesen Urbanski; Edmund and Zosia Zubalewicz Urbanski; Jane Urbanski Robbins; Sam and Miriam Lindsey Levering; Al and Elizabeth Smith Lindsey; Al and Betty Lindsey Wellons; Charles and Margaret Olesen Corbin; Bill Van Hoy; Ralph and Patty Webb Levering; Teresa Van Hoy; Montague Levering Kern; Betsy Levering Morgan; Merry Levering; Lou Lindsey; Virginia Levering Price and Tom and Sondra Upton Price. Thanks go to long-suffering and long-standing friends Liz Brody; Mal and Ellen Hoffs; Krysia Lindan; Bonni Kogen; Stephanie von Hirschberg; Tison Lacy;

Susan Christian; Jack Miles; Tony Gittelson; Jamie Cabot; Michael Levine; John Sacret Young; Howard Davis and Georgia Jones-Davis; Robin Brantley and Keith Love; Charlie and Susie Shaw Thomas; Tom and Sue Garrett Rickert; Tanya and Gene Rees; Bob and Helen Sekits; and Jamshid and Farzaneh Parvisi. We are delighted with the new friends the book helped us to make, and wish to thank the scores of people throughout the country who took us under their wing and into their confidence.

Contents

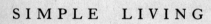

SIMPLE LIVING

CHAPTER ONE

The Beginning

The end of the journey was an old farmhouse set down in the middle of a cherry, peach, nectarine, and apple orchard in southwestern Virginia. Stuffing our Volkswagen to the gills and towing a U-Haul trailer behind our pickup truck, we had driven in tandem almost three thousand miles from Los Angeles, our home of seven years. This time we had come to Orchard Gap not to visit, but to live.

It was April 12, 1986, a fine spring day in the Blue Ridge Mountains. The sky was the color of faded denim above the timbered ridges that sheltered the sloping cave. As if powdered by a spring snow, the cherry trees lining the winding dirt lane were in full bloom. The hum of bees, the heady perfume of blossoms, drenched the air.

We were tired, but we were excited and didn't feel it much. Wanda Urbanska had recently turned thirty; Frank Levering, her husband, who had grown up here as the youngest of six children, was three months shy of thirty-four.

Frank's parents, Sam and Miriam Lindsey Levering, answered the horn blasts of two dusty vehicles. Wearing his customary overalls and frayed baseball cap, Sam strode from the house at a clip that belied his seventy-eight years. Five years younger and just as nimble, Miriam was at his side as she had been, in one activity or another, for fifty-two years of Quaker marriage. There were hugs all around, followed by lunch—barbecued chicken, baked potatoes, coleslaw, and chilled applesauce made from home-grown apples. This was a day of celebration.

It was also a day of change. As we had agreed the previous fall, Sam, Miriam, and Sam's older sister, June, were now to live a hundred yards up the hill from us where June and Sam had been raised—in the two-story, red frame house their parents built in 1910. Over the winter, the first phone line had been installed in what we called "The Red House," new and secondhand carpets laid, and insulation added. Shaded by holly and rhododendron trees, the ivy-covered brick house, built by Sam and Miriam in 1939 and their home ever since, would now be ours.

We entered it with open eyes. Lean times at Levering Orchard and years of child raising had taken their toll. The kitchen was still vintage 1939, with battered cabinets, covered over with weathered Con-Tact paper, and decrepit appliances. A threadbare green carpet covered the living room floor, and the once blond pine paneling had aged darkly, had endured visible termite damage, and was scored from the collisions of children and chairs. In both the downstairs and upstairs bathrooms, sinks and tubs drained slowly through narrow lead pipes. The four upstairs bedrooms needed spackling and new wallpaper or paint. And everywhere in the house, old windowpanes rattled loosely in their frames. Remarkably, the steep, shingled roof was the original one from 1939; but come a hard rain, Miriam said, we'd need three pots to catch the leaks.

Outside the kitchen windows, at the margin of the cherry orchard, one-hundred-foot-tall poplar trees were bathed in a faint green mist of infant leaves. In the piedmont below, a thousand feet lower than our cove, spring was two weeks ahead in a patchwork quilt of mint green forests and the earth tones of newly plowed fields. Above the rolling valley floor, a fifty-mile sweep of rounded peaks, stacked one against the other like soft blue pillows, tumbled at last into hazy nothingness on the southwestern horizon.

We felt both awed and grateful: awed by the natural magnificence of this place, just two miles below the Blue Ridge Parkway, which Sam's parents had moved to from Tennessee in 1908; grateful to Sam and Miriam for the opportunity to become partners with them in their orchard business and to live in this house, with all its space.

We also felt trepidation. In Los Angeles we had left behind Wanda's career as a journalist and author, Frank's as a screenwriter and free-lance writer. Here in Virginia, with the nearest city—Winston-Salem, North Carolina—fifty miles south, there was no assurance that we could continue to market ourselves as writers. Here there were few people of any sort—much less the editors and movie producers with whom we had established ourselves in Los Angeles. Here was the backwater culture of southern Appalachia—not the latest trends of urban living that are the favored subjects of magazines and movies. In our darkest moments we feared that in Orchard Gap—a community so small it appears on no map of Virginia—the writing careers to which we had devoted most of our adult lives would fade away.

What's more, hoping to combine writing with farming, we were getting involved in a business that had not shown black ink for more than a quarter of a century. From the time of Frank's childhood, Sam and Miriam had paid their bills and subsidized the orchard business from income generated elsewhere. For most of the 1960s, Miriam had been a high school and junior high school history teacher in nearby Mount Airy, North Carolina. During the same period, Sam had worked from time to time as a real estate appraiser. In the 1970s and early 1980s, Frank's parents had worked as political activists in Washington. At the time of our arrival in Virginia, their income derived from Social Security checks and Miriam's pension as a retired teacher. In a sense, Levering Orchard had long been an expensive hobby.

Even more disturbing, however, was the size of the debt that we would be assuming, first as partners, later as sole owners of the ninety-acre orchard and as majority owners of the forests and fruit packhouse. For as long as Frank could remember, his mother and most of his siblings had worried that someday its creditors would swallow Levering Orchard. Trained in horticulture at Cornell, Sam was passionate about the production of high-quality fruit—but not about salesmanship or the myriad details of managing a small business economically. It was Sam— not Sam and Miriam—who ran the business, and only during World War II and its aftermath, when prices for apples were high, had he ever made impressive profits. With the houses, packhouse, orchard land, and surrounding forests all mortgaged to two banks, and with the business steadily piling up more debt in the 1980s, family members wondered aloud what could be done to avoid losing the homeplace they loved.

Though Sam discounted such discussions as gloom-and-doom fantasies, in fact they were grounded in reality. In the mid-1980s foreclosures on family farms were making headlines nationwide. Many of those farms failed for the same reason ours was increasingly at risk: farmers had taken on a debt load in excess of their earning power and the value of their property. When we arrived in Virginia, we took a deep breath and stood ready within the next several years to shoulder a debt of almost $125,000.

It was the most sobering business decision either of us ever had to make. In the best-case scenario, we would meet our interest payments and, over the course of years, reduce and eventually eliminate the principal on the loans. In the worst case, the debt would grow so large that we would lose the place. Compounding our anxiety was the stark fact that neither of us had any experience in running a business.

For all these concerns, we entered our new lives with a tailwind of optimism. While our debt would be substantial, it was also true that the value of all the mortgaged property considerably exceeded $125,000. As orchard and forest, it was certainly worth less than as real estate for development—yet it was enough, at this level of debt, to keep the banks at bay. Like the rest of the family, we had no desire to test its property value in the lucrative vacation-home market. While gradually reducing our debt, we meant to spare these acres from the blade of the bulldozer.

We were also convinced that two gung ho young people could join Sam and Miriam in reviving the business. The first step was to end the deficit spending that had served Levering Orchard no better than it had the federal government. To do that, for the immediate future we had to be willing to work for little or nothing; we could cut expenses by doing more of the work ourselves, relying less on hired labor than Sam and Miriam had in the past. At the same time we had to risk conflict with Sam in making a new policy of refusing to borrow more money. Ever the optimist, Sam had borrowed for a quarter century on the theory that things could only get better, that next year would be different. Spending little on himself, Sam never hesitated to take out new loans that would buy the expensive equipment or the promising new varieties in an array of fruits that would turn the business around. His good-natured optimism was endearing—indeed, often seductive—but the deeper in debt the business sank, the harder it was to meet the interest payments over and above operating expenses—much less to pay off the loans. Concerned about Sam's pride in his own judgment, we were resolved nonetheless to stand our ground.

In one crucial respect, however, Sam's foresight stood the chance of saving the orchard he cherished. After more than a decade of low prices for apples—his primary crop—in late 1971 and early 1972 Sam rolled the dice. As orchardist neighbors raised their eyebrows, Sam instructed his crew to cut down a block of old apple trees in the cove and plant sweet cherry trees in the cleared ground. In the decade that followed he continued to replace old apple trees with cherries—until, at the time of our return, there were nearly thirty acres in cherry trees in two adjacent coves, many of them only beginning to bear. Roughly twenty-five acres were in sweet cherries, with the remaining five in tart pie cherries.

In a community dotted with apple and peach orchards, Sam's was a gamble no other grower had been willing to take. And no wonder: cherries are a fragile crop in the climate of the Southeast. In the spring their buds can withstand less cold than those of apples and peaches and are easily killed. Sweet cherries are ready to pick in June, but one hard rain when they're fully ripe can split them open, destroying their eye appeal for customers and leading to rot.

But Sam's gamble was calculated. Prior to 1971, the few sweet cherry trees on the place had generally come through with a crop. More often than not he'd been lucky in not having rain at the wrong time. And he'd noticed another thing: most of the customers who came liked to pick their own cherries. There was something about the experience of getting up on a ladder and filling your own bucket (and your belly, as you picked) that brought customers back year after year.

In 1986 Sam's cherry orchard appeared to be on the brink of success. With volume and sales increasing almost every year, cherries were the one fruit that had shown a consistent—if modest—profit in the recent past. And unlike his overhead on apples, peaches, and nectarines, fruits on which he continued to lose money, his investment in cherries was low: they were the first fruit to ripen, therefore requiring less care; and instead of hiring workers to pick and grade his cherries, Sam and a small crew set ladders for the customers to pick their own.

Looking out at the cherry trees in full bloom, we felt more optimism than apprehension on those luminous April days that followed our arrival. If we escaped a late freeze, the cherry crop this year would be the largest ever by far. Perhaps this would be the year Levering Orchard would begin to resemble the vigorous business it had been when Sam and Miriam were young.

As white petals drifted from the cherry trees and spring climbed the mountain forests in a darkening canopy of leaves, we settled into our new home. We set up our computers and wrote query letters to magazine editors; Frank began work in the field. We arranged with the bank to place our house under a separate mortgage, thus transferring a portion of the orchard debt directly to us.

With the transcontinental trek behind us, the longer journey of reinventing our way of life was only beginning. To meet our goals, we would have to be resourceful. In ways that were only beginning to dawn on us, we would have to change habits of thought, patterns of behavior ingrained from years of frenetic urban living.

What had brought us to Virginia was not merely the challenge of resurrecting a family business. Had the orchard alone beckoned us, we might never have left California. We were here, rather, because we wanted better lives. In Los Angeles we had lived fast but not well. Often short on cash, but always long on professional ambition, we'd saved little time for each other or for the day-to-day rewards of small but significant things—watching a sunset, keeping a journal. Moving to this mountainside offered us a new beginning.

But, like Sam in his decision to plant cherry trees, we knew we were gambling. We were betting that along with transplanting ourselves we could change the direction of our lives and enhance our marriage. We felt a sense of urgency—time was passing more rapidly every year. Amid the uncertainty and complexity of the new challenges we faced, we were determined to purge ourselves of needless entanglements and superfluous pursuits. Here was the place to learn what was essential. To learn what we stood for and—because how we lived expressed our values—to take our stand. In short, we were here in Virginia to simplify our lives. To find the time as well as the means to do the things that mattered most.

. . .

In the popular mind, the phrase *simple living* has often been associated with self-denial: with the image of Henry David Thoreau in a hermit's cabin at Walden Pond or Jimmy Carter wearing a sweater in the White House with the heat turned down.

In reality the phrase can just as easily be associated not with what is lost, but with what is gained. By living in a cabin for two years, Thoreau was able to "transact some private business"—namely, writing his first book, *A Week on the Concord and Merrimack Rivers*, and making a good start on *Walden*. By wearing a sweater and turning down the thermostat, Carter saved energy and scored a vital, if too often unheeded, point about the need for energy conservation.

But simple living as a philosophy has rarely been simple to practice or to define. "Simple pleasures," Oscar Wilde remarked, "are the last refuge of the complex." In real life, not only is it hard to avoid complexity and contradiction—even Thoreau, while living at Walden Pond, had his mother do his laundry—but there is no one formula, no laundry list, that pinpoints the meaning of simple living. Nor is there an absolute standard by which simplicity can be measured; what is simple for one person may for others be either Byzantine or hopelessly idealistic. The choices each person makes are conditioned by how he or she defines simplicity and by circumstances that are invariably singular.

Trying to remake ourselves in Virginia, we soon recognized that we would have to simplify our lives in our own way. No one else shared our quirky particulars. No one else could answer the questions: What is the best way to live, for us? How do we define what is valuable? Who are the people we want to be?

Like many Americans, we had been exposed for many years to what Davidson College historian David Shi calls "the ethic of plain living and high thinking" in American culture. Not only had we pored over *Walden*, but we'd read Helen and Scott Nearing's best-selling book *Living the Good Life* and witnessed the idealism of the back-to-the-land movement of the 1960s and 1970s. In addition, Frank had experienced firsthand from family life the Quaker practice of voluntary simplicity, of avoiding luxury, of keeping one's material desires to a minimum.

Still, we did not see ourselves as being aligned with any one religion, philosophy, or guru. It's true that, reflecting on our own lives in Los Angeles and those of our friends, we could agree with Thoreau's famous remark, "The mass of men lead lives of quiet desperation." But as a married couple with strong worldly interests, we did not wish to follow his footsteps into a cabin or to "live so sturdily and Spartan-like as to put to rout all that was not life . . . to drive life into a corner, and reduce it to its lowest terms," as Thoreau wrote in *Walden*. Unlike the socialist Nearings, in Virginia we had no desire to make a cult of self-sufficiency, and as orchardists and writers we would be trafficking regularly—and unashamedly—in the capitalist marketplace.

Not ascetics or ideologues, we were not embarking on a crusade against money. In addition to wanting to slash the orchard debt, we had distinct material ambitions, notably an extensive house renovation. And we wanted to furnish our home with pieces that were, if not new, at least inviting. That would require more than the skimpy savings we'd brought east with us from L.A. Still, we were convinced we could cut our cost of living sharply at the orchard and thereby reduce our dependence on the dollar.

As time went on in Virginia, the lure of personal freedom—freedom from the tyranny of never having enough time, freedom to do more things our own way, proved utterly compelling. A quest had begun in our lives, a search in all things, great and small, for that which could make us free.

That quest changed our lives forever.

This book tells our story. It tells of the choices we've made, of the changes in our lives. It tells of our successes and our failures in living the good life; of what experience has taught us and what we are still trying to learn.

This is a book about getting connected with natural rhythms and to life outside yourself. It's about buying an eight-year-old Chevy Malibu, as we did in 1988 when our Volkswagen gave out, and taking pride in maintaining it. It's about mending and caring for things rather than discarding them at the first sign of age or wear and the uplifting implications this ethic has on personal relationships. It's about the self-confidence gained by taking one's finances firmly in hand . . . and about working to make commitments rather than to guard options.

It's also a book about people, the stories of others who share in our orientation and quest. Ours is by no means an isolated experience, nor is it defined by a move to the country. In journeys around America, we have discovered others, in a wide variety of circumstances, who are streamlining their lives. A few of these people are in our own families. Some are friends. Many were strangers when we met them. In our travels we have entered the lives of these people, learned from them, and brought something of their stories home. Though we cannot always apply another person's choice to our lives, the decisions that people make offer a chance for reflection on what is desirable for us.

This book is about the urban and the rural and the small town, the big changes and the small steps. It's about cabin dwellers in Maine and apartment dwellers in San Francisco and New York. It's not so much about where one lives as what one does.

What we did in Los Angeles, it seems especially in retrospect, was lead one-dimensional lives. It wasn't that we were spend-aholics who had to move to Virginia to reform from a binge of high living. It was that our careers robbed our lives. More accurately, it was our excessive devotion to the pursuit of success—so common among our circle of acquaintances—that made not only our working hours but almost all of our social hours revolve around "making things happen," as Frank used to put it.

It was fine to reach for the stars when we first got to the coast, but after seven years of earthbound aspiration, the glitter of possibilities—of juicy film deals and fat book contracts—had worn off. By then there was nothing heroic about the struggle to meet the $640 rent on a two-room apartment each month, as well as insurance and the upkeep on two vehicles. The almost daily chore of coming up with bottles of wine for dinner parties and meal tabs for restaurant dinners seemed more like an albatross than the good life. We were weary of having to make—and shell out—so much money, yet we understood that dropping out of our social circle would close doors to the writing and film community for which we'd originally come west.

Our arrival in Los Angeles coincided roughly with the start of the 1980s. A film buff and recent graduate of Harvard Divinity School, Frank drove out in 1979 with visions of writing dramas for heavyweight directors. Wanda followed the middle of the next year, after a stint in New York working at *The Paris Review* as an associate editor under George Plimpton. It wasn't long before we were working as a cabdriver and Kelly Girl respectively, but we were convinced that with the right combination of elbow grease and imagination, nothing could keep us from making a splash. After all, we were endowed with good health, ambition, a storehouse of grand dreams, and, we hoped, enough talent to make a mark.

In November of 1980 Wanda landed a job at the now defunct *Los Angeles Herald-Examiner*, working first as an editor on the Sunday magazine and later as a reporter in the business section. Off she would go, mornings to work—first from our funky digs in bohemian Venice and later from our apartment in Westwood—tackling grueling miles of eastbound freeway traffic, sometimes moving at a crawl, sometimes at a blood-curdling sixty miles per hour in bumper-to-bumper traffic.

Frank was a free-lancer, occasionally working out of a producer's or director's office, most often pounding out pages on his typewriter at home. In seven years he wrote or co-wrote fifteen movie scripts, seven "on spec" to put up for sale, eight on assignment for employers ranging from an Emmy-winning actor, to an Oscar- and Emmy-winning director, to a producer touted as the "new king of the B's." Of the fifteen, only one has yet hit the silver screen—in the Kafkaesque world of screenwriting, not a bad batting average. It was a typically fitting Hollywood irony that this was the project he cared least about. Billed by its distributor, Embassy Pictures, as "the first futuristic monster movie in 3-D," *Parasite in 3-D* was co-written with two other writers in a short burst of creativity. Starring Demi Moore in her first film, it became a campy hit, and the week it opened in New York, it was second in box office receipts only to a Richard Pryor movie. Eventually *Parasite* grossed more than twelve times its production cost, and before he was thirty Frank landed in *People* magazine's "Look-out: A Guide to the Up and Coming."

For all the hooplah, *Parasite* made only the producers rich. Still, we didn't run into chafing financial problems until Wanda quit her full-time newspaper job to accept a contract from Doubleday to write a book on young Americans in the 1980s. Though the advance seemed substantial, after we bought a word processor, financed extensive research travel, and rebuilt the engine on our Volkswagen, it proved increasingly difficult to keep our ship afloat. Enjoying good health and optimistic natures, we decided to forgo health insurance on the gamble we wouldn't get sick.

We were lucky. But by early 1985 we were also, we knew, secretly and utterly miserable with our lives. The days were long in Los Angeles. The nights—the fraction of them we saved for each other—were short and bittersweet. Often at midnight or later, we'd crash on our pink couch, home from the latest dinner out, hungry for simple intimacy after a day as professionals and an evening as good company for someone else. With the ceaseless rumble of San Diego Freeway traffic as background noise, we'd fight off drowsiness and try to make conversation, casting unkind glances at the glowing red light on the answering machine signaling calls that had to be returned the next day. Minutes later we'd collapse into bed.

But it wasn't only our lack of time for each other or the money we were spending in order to keep up with colleagues. It was our entire way of living: just running in place, with no likelihood of being able to jump off the treadmill. We weren't saving money; our families weren't wealthy; and unless we improbably struck gold, two writers would never be able to afford a home—even a modest condominium—in Los Angeles.

Emotionally as well as physically, we felt cramped in our apartment, with two writers working sixty- to seventy-hour weeks in two close rooms. There were four desks, two computers, two typewriters, and five bookcases crammed in with furniture, clothes, and all the other paraphernalia of two pack-rats. While Wanda had a book to write, Frank grew increasingly restless as a screenwriter. All those scripts, most of them written with a high degree of idealism, and what did we have to show? In a business where the high-concept, high-budget movie reigned supreme, Frank was beginning to feel like a character in the "fish out of water" films that were big at the time.

Then lightning struck: at age seventy-seven, while walking in his apple orchard, Sam felt severe chest pains. As fate would have it, Miriam had only the night before arrived in Los Angeles for an extended visit.

Once the captain of the cross-country running team at Cornell, Sam had been in remarkably good condition his entire adult life. In his sixties he had climbed Mount Whitney in the Sierras and Longs Peak in Colorado on summer trips with Frank. A short, trim man with a full head of mostly black hair even in his seventies, Sam had always taken the Blue Ridge mountainsides in stride. He had never been hospitalized. Now, on a balmy day in May, he walked slowly downhill to the house of Virginia Levering Price, a widow and Sam's first cousin, who in the early 1980s had retired from her job as a nursing instructor in Mississippi and built a house in the cove. Virginia rushed Sam to the nearest hospital, twelve miles away in Mount Airy.

Frank took her call in Los Angeles. "Your father's had a heart attack," Virginia said calmly. "It appears to be serious."

Together with Miriam, we arrived by plane, then by car, late that evening to find Sam in intensive care, hitched to a battery of machines and tubes. His eyes were open. Taking turns, we held his hand, communicated with our eyes. Though he was not out of the woods yet, with time, his doctor said, Sam had a good chance of recovering.

Frank stayed for the cherry harvest that began three weeks later. A spring freeze had killed all the sweet cherries and spared only a partial crop of the sour variety. As Sam recuperated, Frank directed the operation, setting ladders in the cherry trees for customers and routing traffic. Those who were familiar with his brisk stride and the ease with which he spent strenuous days out in the orchard knew Sam was recovering at an agonizingly slow pace—walking only in small doses, flashing a weary smile to customers who had been loyal to him for many years. With all the peaches and nectarines killed by the same April freeze, Frank returned in July to Los Angeles, where he was scheduled to begin work for two producers on a screenplay and Wanda was still hard at work on her book.

We had some talking to do. Apple harvest would start in September, and even with a smaller crop than usual because of the freeze, Sam was not yet ready to take command of all the details. Perhaps he would never be.

Though Frank had repeatedly come home to help out in cherry, peach, and nectarine harvests, and we had expressed interest in coming to the orchard to live, the uncertainty of how that life would mesh with our writing careers had prevented us from making a binding commitment. Now, faced with Sam's disability and our own disenchantment with Los Angeles, we decided to make a trial run. After subletting our apartment for four months, we drove across the country in early September and settled into the vacant Red House up the hill from Frank's family. Wanda would work on the final draft of her book, hoping to finish it by year's end. Frank would work in the apple harvest until the last apple was picked, then continue work on his contracted screenplay.

It was a life we soon grew to love. Frank spent crisp autumn days with the pickers, hauling eighteen-bushel bins full of apples out from the trees with a tractor and offloading them onto a World War II army truck. Once he'd loaded six bins with the tractor's lift, he'd make the tortuous trip in the truck through the orchard to the packhouse, where, Sam, Miriam, and a small crew graded and sold the apples.

A tiger-striped cat sat on Wanda's lap as she wrote. Winnie—named for the Winn-Dixie supermarket where Wanda had found her abandoned on a fertilizer sack—was Wanda's sole companion, save for the glowing green letters on the computer monitor, until Frank's return each evening usually by sunset. We'd sit in the swing chair on the porch and watch the sun go down behind the mountains, then stoke the woodstove, draw a hot bath in the ancient, claw-footed tub, and soak away our saddle sores from long, productive days.

Free of the distractions of city living, Wanda marched her book rapidly toward completion. Though it was a financially strapped year at the orchard and Frank earned no money for his work, he'd had a sense of real, tangible accomplishment, harvesting first the cherries, then the apples. And Sam grew palpably stronger every day, pacing himself, seemingly invigorated by our youthful blood.

October passed in a riot of color in the woods; the apple harvest ended. When we weren't working on the book and the screenplay, we took long hikes in the woods, read for pleasure, and cooked heaping pots of pasta sauce that we froze for later use. Rather than drinking bottled water from a plastic bottle in Los Angeles, we drank cold spring water that flowed down the mountain and through our tap. Rather than jousting for position with Mercedes-Benzes and BMWs on our way to a crowded L.A. supermarket, we drove the twelve miles into Mount Airy once a week to do our shopping. And instead of lugging our clothes to a Laundromat, we washed them in Miriam's old washing machine and hung them out in the sun to dry.

Calling closure on months of conversations about our future, and setting aside our reservations, we declared the trial period over. The risk was worth taking. If we could forge a satisfactory business agreement with Sam and Miriam, we were going to make the commitment to move back to the orchard.

In November the details of the plan to ensure the continuation of Levering Orchard were hammered out among Frank's parents, his siblings, and ourselves. Within three years, in return for further labor and our commitment to the future of the business, we would own the orchard property and most of the surrounding forest. Frank's siblings would each receive woodland tracts, and the Red House and surrounding grounds would pass eventually from Frank's parents to joint ownership among all the siblings and their children.

Looking back at our decision to move east, we admit that it is perhaps too easy to overemphasize the fast-lane factor and underemphasize the fact that each of us, in a sense, was coming home.

When we met at a class at Harvard in 1977, we had more in common than we knew. Wanda was a twenty-year-old scholarship student, and Frank was a graduate student studying world religions. We both hailed more or less from traditions of simple living. In varying degrees, Wanda's parents, too, espoused a number of the values traditionally associated with simple living.

Wanda's father—a World War II–era Polish refugee who taught Spanish and Latin American studies at the college level— held the scholarly attitude that "you live in your mind." Home ownership was never an ambition of Dr. Edmund S. Urbanski, and when he had sufficient savings to purchase a place, he declined. Instead of seeing the tax advantages and investment opportunity, he saw the hassles of lawn care and maintenance as potential distractions from his academic pursuits. As a result, the Urbanski family always lived in rented houses and always drove cars until they dropped—stripped models that were bought new, for cash, late in the model year for bargaining leverage.

In part because of her father's refusal to join the middle class and make conventional steps toward financial security, Wanda's parents divorced when she was nine. Rather than taking a position teaching high school English, her mother enrolled in graduate school at the University of Kentucky at age forty-three and raised two daughters. Though it was the booming mid-1960s, a three-thousand-dollar stipend plus modest child support payments didn't stretch far. So Wanda learned early to take public transportation, to clip grocery coupons, and to frequent yard sales.

So while Wanda aspired to upward mobility, she wasn't all that comfortable with affluence. When she moved with her older sister and mother to Orono, Maine, where Marie Olesen Urbanski took a job teaching English at the University of Maine, her mother's interests reinforced Wanda's respect for simple living. Marie's specialty was nineteenth-century American literature, especially the transcendentalists and Margaret Fuller, an original thinker and author of the pioneering feminist work, *Woman in the Nineteenth Century*. As editor of *The Dial*, Fuller published Thoreau's early poetry and influenced his thinking on simplicity. For many years Marie edited the *Thoreau Journal Quarterly*. Intimately familiar with her mother's interests and growing up in the decidedly noncomformist culture of central Maine, Wanda was no stranger to the sort of offbeat man she first encountered in Monroe Engel's fiction-writing class in 1977.

By sleeping in his car that spring semester, Frank was taking to an extreme his father's tenet of shunning luxury. He was clearly his father's son. On family vacations Sam would abstain from motels and restaurants, choosing instead to sleep in the car or on the ground and eat a diet of bread, fruit, and powdered nonfat milk, which he would mix up in a jar with water from service station spigots. Quakers from the time of George Fox and William Penn had warned against attachment to material things, lest it interfere with time needed for social service and the spiritual life. Sam took the warnings quite literally, setting limits on a standard of living that smacked of radicalism even among fellow Quakers. As Frank was growing up, his father drove only battered old cars, ate a Spartan diet, and proscribed such conventional pleasures as movies, candy bars, Coca-Cola, and potato chips as needless luxuries to be avoided by his children.

Miriam Levering was never as extreme. Raised a Methodist, she became a Quaker after her own fashion. While as intent as her husband on reserving time for the spirit and social service, Miriam was not averse to buying a new sweater and matching scarf every now and then or splurging on a restaurant meal. In the main, though, by stretching meals and mending and recycling clothes, Miriam saved enough to give generously to family members or favorite causes. Frank's parents shared an unlikely characteristic: it seemed to pain them to spend a nickel on themselves.

With those years well behind us, it's tempting now to view Frank's time in Hollywood as a rebellion against his background, as a taste of the kind of life he had been denied growing up. It's an obvious theory—made more plausible by the analogous choices of his siblings, all but one of whom rejected the life of austerity for material comforts.

As for Wanda, who had lived "simply" growing up (though it was more by accident than design), New York and then Los Angeles had signaled—for a time—not only the possibility of success, but also the hope for a more materially abundant future.

The truth was, though, that our urban lives had changed us both immeasurably. In coming to live in Virginia, we were not simply coming home to embrace the values prescribed in our backgrounds. We were coming home, to be sure, but in our own way—certain that not one of our four parents had blazed precisely the trail we wanted to follow.

On January 1, 1986, Wanda finished the final draft of her book. The next day we sent it Air Express to Doubleday in New York from Knoxville, as we headed west on I-40 to live out our lame-duck days as Angelenos.

Los Angeles seemed strange during our last three months there. Wanda noticed for the first time that nothing that was commonly available was good enough. Public schools didn't make the grade; private schools are preferable. The police won't adequately protect you, so you install private security systems. You don't buy a car that you would ever dare lend to a friend; you buy one that, with its tinted-glass windows, sound system, and air-conditioning, carefully buffers you from the unexpected and the world at large.

Thrown back into the maze of freeways, under the shroud of smog, we found Los Angeles more like an unengaging movie than real life as we wanted to live it. We felt displaced, at a distance from friends who were going on with their business as usual, who had no feel for the kind of life we had lived the previous autumn. Holing up in the apartment, Frank stared out the window at a palm tree and finished his screenplay. Wanda wrote free-lance magazine articles and began dividing our belongings into those things we would take with us and those we'd leave behind.

Around Saint Patrick's Day we said good-bye to our friends by throwing a bash at our apartment. It was billed as "the Green Theme party." There the usual Hollywood weirdness: friends brought an actress who had recently been nominated for an Oscar, who freaked out at the sight of the crowd and went into hiding for half an hour in our bedroom. We played rock music and danced. We said good-bye a hundred times, tried to explain what we were doing, and fought back tears at two in the morning when the last of our friends departed.

Many of these people—the ones we'd gotten to know best— we would sorely miss. A good friend worried that our minds would atrophy away from the stimulation of the city. A few stopped just short of suggesting we were making a terrible mistake. Others voiced one of our keenest anxieties—that it would be hard to find friends who shared our interests out in the country.

We had a weekend garage sale. We sold the pink couch. We sold our computer table. We sold the patio table and chairs that had been bought with wedding money. Reluctantly we parted with a few books. We experienced the disturbing sensation of strangers appraising objects that had been fixtures of our everyday existence and trying to talk us out of things we'd decided to keep.

We loaded up the rest. Pulling away from Westwood, rolling east on I-10 past the Hollywood sign, past downtown where Wanda had worked at the *Los Angeles Herald*, out of the City of Angels, we watched a part of ourselves and familiar ways of living fade to memory in the rearview mirrors.

CHAPTER TWO

The Orchard

As family legend has it, Ralph Griffith Levering was tired of having to stoop for a living. A sweet potato and strawberry farmer near Knoxville, Tennessee, he wanted to reach for the sky as he worked. So in 1907 Frank's grandfather wrote the Department of Agriculture in Washington, D.C. Where in the South, he asked, was the best place to plant an apple orchard? Where would apples grow best? Where, in the fragile stages of bud, blossom, and embryonic fruit, would apples most likely escape the spring freezes that could destroy an entire crop in a few hours?

On the southeastern slope of the Blue Ridge conditions are most favorable for planting apple trees, came the reply. There the soil is fertile and deep, the sunlight abundant. There—because of something called the thermal belt—temperatures on cold spring nights are usually warmer than on the crest of the range or in the valley below.

The thermal belt, the department explained, is a zone created by a pattern of air movement on a cold, still night. Each day after a cold front has pushed through, the sun heats the earth. At night the warm air rises and the cold air sinks along the range, leaving a layer of colder air on the valley floor, a warmer layer on the slopes, then another colder layer at the crest. On a still night, an apple crop is more likely to survive on the side of the mountain than in the valley below, while apple trees planted on the crest of the range are consistently exposed to lower temperatures during the risk period from late March to late May.

Then thirty-six, a vigorous man of medium height with a close-cropped dark beard, Ralph Levering decided to take a walk. A long walk. Leaving his wife, Clara Osborne Levering—almost three months pregnant—and two young children in Maryville, Tennessee, in August of 1907, he caught a train to Asheville, North Carolina, then climbed high into the Blue Ridge, heading northeast along the southeastern exposure of the range. Following the Department of Agriculture's recommendations, he was looking for his own promised land—for just the right place to start an orchard.

Days turned into weeks as Ralph made his way over steep ridges, across isolated mountain coves. In moonshine country, he was several times mistaken for a revenue agent by suspicious mountaineers with rifles. Sometimes he camped at night; more often he stayed with strangers whom he insisted on paying for room and board. Commercial apple orchards, he discovered, were nonexistent in these Carolina mountains; but almost every mountain family had an apple tree or two. Everywhere he went, Ralph asked the same questions: When was the last time spring cold had killed the apples? How many years in living memory had apple crops been lost?

In late September Ralph crossed the Virginia line and reached the Carroll County community of Fancy Gap, just six

miles southwest of the next major gap between the peaks—
Orchard Gap. He had walked over two hundred miles, been
away from home for six weeks. It was time to see his family.
Descending out of the mountains to Mount Airy, North Carolina, he boarded a train for Knoxville.

But though he had found good sites and land was available
to buy, Sam Levering's father was not yet satisfied that he had
seen enough of the Blue Ridge to make a decision. After a
week's sojourn in Tennessee, he took a train to Roanoke, Virginia.

Now he walked southwest, again in the direction of Carroll
County. This time he found commercial orchards at Bent
Mountain, but in a letter he wrote home to Tennessee, he
reported that too many crops had been lost there to suit him.
In a few weeks he reached Friends Mission, a tiny Quaker
settlement in Patrick County, only ten miles from Carroll. This
was a good omen: Ralph Levering and his wife, Clara, were
devout members of the Society of Friends.

In early November, on the western edge of Patrick County,
Ralph found the first place he really wanted. Unlike many coves
he'd seen, this one tilted gently between two unusually high,
protective ridges; the soil was deep, loam rich, and drought
resistant. And the family wouldn't be far from a Quaker community.

But it wasn't to be. Garland Marshall, the land's owner,
had no interest in selling.

Where Patrick and Carroll counties meet, the front wall of
the Blue Ridge turns northward for several miles, veers south-
westward again past a gap in the peaks, then dips southward
briefly, forming a horseshoe in the range that sends long spur
ridges down to the valley floor. At the eastern edge of this

horseshoe that forms the community of Orchard Gap, Ralph came upon the Coveland Orchard, its trees not yet of bearing age. Henry Woods—an experienced apple grower originally from Crozet, Virginia—was the orchard manager. Though Woods could not yet report on crop production, Ralph was pleased that Woods was willing to help him get started should he buy land in the community.

Just over the next two spur ridges from Coveland Orchard, Ralph discovered two superb sites. He preferred the one farthest to the southwest, where the Shadrick family had two acres of Buckingham apple trees that had not lost a crop since 1878. But the Shadricks weren't selling, either.

In the adjacent cove to the northeast, a man in his late fifties lived with his wife and younger children in a two-story, one-room log cabin amid the November stubble of a cornfield. The cove was steeper and not as wide as the Shadrick cove, but tall ridges offered shelter from the wind. The porter-loam soil—though in spots badly eroded —was generally black and deep. And Ralph remembered what Clara had told him: "Ralph, if thee can find a place where I can see for fifty miles from the front porch, that would be good, too." Of all the sites that Ralph had seen in a three-month, 375-mile trek, this was the only one that had a view for Clara. Two additional factors fueled Ralph's interest. Twelve miles south, in Mount Airy, was a thriving Quaker meeting that the family could attend. And Mount Airy was a railhead—he hoped to ship many of his apples by train.

But Alex McMillian was a shrewd mountaineer. Yes, he was willing to sell—but it wouldn't come cheap. For "40 acres, more or less," as the deed read, Ralph Levering paid six hundred dollars, more than twice the going rate for that amount of mountain land. Later an accurate survey revealed that in fact Ralph had purchased almost fifty acres. But no matter. Living out his days at the foot of the mountain, McMillian was heard to boast that he had really gotten the best of that young "fur-e-ner."

In February 1908 Ralph, Clara, their seven-year-old son, Griffith, and their three-year-old daughter, June, arrived by horse and wagon at their new home. They were 1,860 feet above sea level, in the heart of the thermal belt. Two weeks later, in what had been the McMillian family's log cabin, Samuel Ralph Levering was born. Delivered by a legendary country doctor, Sam was to remain the youngest member of the family—and would outlive them all in a lifetime spanning the more than eighty-year history of Levering Orchard.

Orchards started from scratch take a long time to bear fruit. Ralph Levering was fortunate to have his new neighbor Henry Woods advise him as to which varieties to plant, to teach him grafting techniques. But Ralph could expect a decade or so between the time of planting—1909 and 1910—and his first significant harvest. In the meantime he had a young family to feed.

To clean up his land, Ralph gathered thousands of loose stones and laid stone walls along the contours of the cove. Then, with his father, who came to help from Tennessee, he built the barn that still stands east of our house, with ample room for a horse and a milk cow. Next came a large chicken coop and the "corn crib"—a wooden building for corn storage. Finally, Ralph and his father and men from the community built the spacious house into which the family moved in 1910. Painted with a mixture of linseed oil and iron oxide powder, the facades of the Red House faced precisely north, south, east, and west— Ralph had designed the new home on the points of a compass. Down the hill, just twenty yards east of where we live now, was the log cabin, which stood empty until the early 1940s, when Sam and Miriam had it razed.

Until the apple trees started bearing, Ralph and Clara made their living primarily by selling eggs laid by their chickens. From home they mailed as many as sixty dozen eggs a week by parcel post to Washington, D.C., where Ralph's sisters sold them on a regular route. To supplement their income—and as a service to an isolated community that had few public schools— Clara taught school in their home. Among her many pupils were Sam and his siblings.

In the early 1920s, at the time the orchard was coming into its own, Sam moved in with his two aunts and attended a Washington, D.C., high school. In 1926 he enrolled at Cornell University, where he studied and taught pomology for seven and a half years, intending eventually to return home and take over the family orchard. Most summers Sam could be found back at Orchard Gap, where there was plenty of practical orchard experience to complement his new training in plant physiology, plant nutrition, and the like.

Ralph's long walk was paying off. Rows of twenty-five-foot-tall apple trees stood regimentally across the cove, as if guarding the Red House. Ever-increasing crops of Yorks, Albemarle Pippins, Magnum Bonums, and Winesaps were coming through the spring cold every year. To grade and store his apples before selling them, Ralph and hired hands built an "apple cellar" across the road from the barn—a sixty-foot-long, forty-foot-wide underground room with concrete and stone walls. Like a cave, the apple cellar stayed cool even on the hottest days.

Sales were good and getting better. Ralph had never needed to ship apples by rail; the age of the internal-combustion engine had arrived. From September until Christmas trucks climbed Orchard Gap Road, winding down the orchard lane and loading up at the apple cellar. And Ralph had established a regular route of customers in Winston-Salem, to whom he home-delivered apples twice a week in his Model A truck.

Equally satisfying to Ralph and Clara was what having a productive business meant to their community. Both prior to and during the Depression, their orchard provided jobs for dozens of mountaineers, among whom was Ralph's crew fore-man, a hickory-tough neighbor named Arthur Dawson. By all accounts Ralph's long-standing relationship with Arthur was forged in mutual respect and affection. Each of the two men was a hardworking, staunch Christian; each was devoted to the art of fruit growing.

But in a community where formal education was scarcer than hen's teeth, Ralph Levering remained a curiosity. Before he'd married Clara and become a farmer in Tennessee, Ralph had gotten a master's degree in international law at Columbia University. His interests ranged far beyond Orchard Gap and growing apples. A lover of Romantic poetry, he was regularly heard reciting Keats and Shelley to his cow as he milked her in the barn. Once a week, for more than twenty years, he wrote a letter to the *Winston-Salem Journal*, usually on a subject of national or international concern. These letters—along with his regular apple route in Winston-Salem—brought him a measure of regional renown. Even now, almost half a century after his death, Ralph Levering is remembered by old-timers in the

region as the "old Quaker gentleman" who delivered apples
door to door and who wrote all those letters to the *Journal*.

To earn its keep, an orchard must constantly be replenished
with new trees, must adapt to changing consumer tastes, new
technology, and new methods of production. In the late 1920s
and 1930s, while Sam was in school and later working for the
Farm Credit Administration in Washington, he and his father
often disagreed about the direction the family orchard should
take. With age Ralph had grown conservative, a man for whom
the tried-and-true was almost always best. Even the new Blue
Ridge Parkway, built as a Works Progress Administration project in the 1930s—which ran just north of Ralph's land along
the crest of the range—was not to his liking. Sam, with his
Cornell education and exposure to state-of-the-art orchards, was
on the cusp of change. Luckily for the future of the orchard,
in dealing with his father he had a mind of his own.

For Sam the future was in newer varieties that consumers
would prefer when they saw and tasted them. The future was
also in increased production, packing apples in trays to ship
rather than selling them loose to local buyers, refrigerated storage, and an expanded work force. From money saved while at
Cornell and in Washington, D.C., he purchased land adjoining
Ralph's fifty acres and planted Red Delicious, Golden Delicious,
and Staymen Winesaps, varieties requiring the refrigerated storage facility that Ralph opposed. Against his father's wishes, he
returned home to plant part of the home cove in these same
varieties, even as Ralph was replanting a block in Winesaps—
an apple that soon became obsolete. In 1939 Sam, Miriam and
their infant daughter, Lois, moved from Washington, D.C.,

to an orchard with varieties reflecting the different strategies of father and son.

But Ralph Levering turned sixty-eight in 1939, and for him the race was now to the swift. Soon playing only an advisory role in the conduct of the business, he wrote his letters, enjoyed the birth of Sam and Miriam's next three daughters, and remained active in local and Quaker affairs until his death in 1945. Until she died in 1961, Clara continued to live in the Red House with Frank's aunt June.

To grade, store, and market the swelling volume of apples, Sam abandoned the apple cellar and built a two-story packhouse along Orchard Gap Road at the foot of the mountain. With two large grading machines, cavernous rooms where apples could be refrigerated, additional storage space for thousands of empty bushel-size crates, retail facilities, and a loading dock, the packhouse was a community showcase. For four months every fall, as many as twenty-five women and men worked in Sam's packhouse, eager for the paychecks that supplemented often meager yearly incomes.

Sam did not disappoint them. The 1940s and early 1950s were a time of record prosperity at the orchard, with Levering apples being trucked throughout the Southeast. Sam spread the wealth—bestowing generous bonuses on employees and paying higher than standard wages in the community. But labor was still cheap, and Sam could afford to hire more workers than he needed, to keep mediocre hands on the payroll because he wanted to help them and their families. To this day stories of Sam's generosity abound in the community: of making loans to men he knew would never pay him back, of helping illiterate people fill out government forms and receive benefits, of hiring workers who—for a variety of reasons—had been fired or were unemployable elsewhere. A tenderhearted Christian, Sam was always willing to give a prospective employee a second chance at his orchard.

From 1922, when he was ten years old, Arthur Dawson's oldest son, Garnet, had worked summers and, later, full-time at the orchard. With Sam's return to Virginia, Garnet replaced his father as foreman of the year-round field crew. Thus close ties between the Dawson and Levering families continued into a second generation, with Garnet every bit a match for his father in physical toughness and orchard smarts.

In the mid- to late 1940s, Sam expanded his operation once more, first by purchasing and planting the Shadrick Cove, later by partnering with Garnet and a third man in High Cliff Orchard, which they purchased from a neighbor. A few years later Sam acquired a young orchard started by a cousin of Miriam's who'd gotten cold feet about the apple business. These additional orchards increased the volume of apples passing through Sam's packhouse to an early 1960s peak of seventy-five thousand bushels. In number of bushels produced, he had become one of the leading apple growers in Virginia.

But even amid this cornucopia, Levering Orchard was in decline. In the conflict between Christianity and capitalism that continues in Sam to this day, the former—in something approaching its most idealistic form—usually won out. Though labor was becoming increasingly expensive, Sam was reluctant to lay off workers who needed a job. And there were other factors. The 1940s and early 1950s had seen years of windfall profits. Now margins on apple orchards—even under the most efficient management—were close to the bone. Competition from the Pacific Northwest—particularly with the popular Red Delicious apple—had lowered prices, while overhead expenses ranging from fertilizers to new equipment continued to rise. It was a time for belt tightening, but Sam's heart was not always in it. At the same time, he and Miriam chose not to pare down the significant amount of volunteer time they spent away from the orchard as peace activists. In their absence worker productivity could only decrease.

On December 10, 1965, a stunning event brought to a head the question of whether Levering Orchard should continue. For reasons that remain mysterious, the packhouse caught fire in broad daylight and burned to the ground, despite the best efforts of firefighters from four counties. Luckily, all of Sam's twenty-five packhouse employees escaped unscathed— though the lights in a grading room abruptly went out, and the pitch-black room filled with smoke before the exit door was opened and the room evacuated.

With thousands of bushels of premium Christmas apples burned to a crisp and the building not fully insured, the fire was a financial as well as an emotional shock to the family. Then the only child remaining at home, Frank remembers his mother suggesting that this might be an opportunity to bow out of the orchard business, a chance for his parents to concentrate on their peace and social concerns. But Sam would have none of it. For him it was a chance to modernize the business, to be a phoenix rising from the ashes to make things better.

The new packhouse went up the following summer—a long, blue, steel building with forklifts and a grading machine, two loading docks, and storage facilities. It belonged to the newly organized Parkway Apple Growers Cooperative—a group of local fruit growers, with Sam and Miriam the majority stockholders. To secure the loan, the two Leverings put their own assets at risk.

With apples not profitable, Sam purchased more land and planted peach orchards—his first major venture into the stone fruits that now comprise the majority of the orchard's roughly seven thousand fruit trees. Later he planted nectarines and cherries. He even planted an acre or so of plums. Levering Orchard, he was determined, was going to make its comeback with fewer apples and more summer fruits.

And it *was* coming back—to that end, Sam was willing to stake his reputation, his pride, and his own and Miriam's estate.

"Fruitopia," Frank's mother called Levering Orchard when he was a teenager. Once Miriam coined the word, she used it often, usually without irony. Despite its problems, the orchard was a good place to raise her family, what she called a "character-strengthening" environment for kids learning the value of working hard and getting along with others. "Fruitopia," she believed, had provided a rich family life and plenty of adventure for three generations, including that of her own parents. In the early 1940s Sam and Miriam built her parents, Earl and Lois Whitmarsh Lindsey, a small cottage fifty yards northwest of the brick house. There the Lindseys lived out their days after Earl's retirement as a Methodist minister in Pennsylvania. Both loved the rhythm of the seasons, the interaction of the family with the mountain community. Long wanting to be a writer, before his death Earl Lindsey completed a roman à clef he called *Smiling Cove*.

As Frank was growing up, there was no more vivid season than autumn, when carloads of professional black pickers from Florida arrived for apple harvest. These men were not migrant workers in the usual sense; for ten months every year they lived in their own homes and picked in the citrus groves near Wabasso and Vero Beach. Then—led by Darius Rigby, their crew chief—as many as a dozen pickers worked at the orchard for two months, eating and sleeping in the Red House. Six days a week they picked apples at a phenomenal speed—some up to 175 bushels in one day—for fifty cents a bushel. The coves echoed with the voices of men who seemed to love their work. Frank looked forward to being with them, to hearing the exotic flavor of their shouts, their gospel songs, and their animated conversation as they sped through the trees with their canvas picking bags slung over their shoulders, clambering up and down twenty-two-foot ladders. When a picker had finished a tree, he'd sing out across the orchard to Rigby: "Uh, tree man! Show me a tree!" Assigning every man a new tree, an always feverish Rigby would reply: "Right here, man! Hurry, man! Hurry!" Relatively quiet the rest of the year, the orchard was a hive of exuberant activity in the fall.

After the pickers left in late October, pruning began. Led by Garnet Dawson, a crew ranging from four to twelve men wielded pruning saws from late fall on through the winter to open up, shape, and top the trees. When pruning was finished, there remained the task of clearing out, by hand, the thickets of brush beneath the trees. On rainy or snowy days or in bitter cold, the men repaired broken apple crates beside a fire in the open-ended crate shed near the packhouse or did mechanic's work in the adjacent cinder-block garage.

Early to mid-March was the time for planting. Trees Sam had ordered from nurseries around the country arrived in thick bundles, packed in moss and wrapped in burlap. Usually two men would do the planting: one to dig the hole and fill it up,

one to nip overlong seedlings with snippers, making them pro-
portionate to the size of the roots to ensure a good start.

In late March, as the days lengthened and the tree sap rose,
the men dumped fifty-pound sacks into buckets and spread
fertilizer by hand in wide circles beneath the trees. Soon those
same trees erupted in blossoms—and with them came the bees.
For years a fearless soul named Ken Haynes was—among other
things—the orchard beekeeper, tending as many as 20 hives
east of the barn. Warm, sunny days—and Ken's year-round
care and feeding of the bees—ensured the pollination necessary
for most of our fruit crops. When Ken left the orchard for
another job, Sam contracted Herbert Joyce, an equally fearless
veteran "bee man" from whom we continue to rent hives every
spring.

Spraying started in early April and continued into the summer. In May came the first mowing, followed by a second
mowing in the dreaded heat of August. All summer long it was
all the men could do to keep up with the work: picking cherries,
hand-thinning peaches and nectarines and apples so that limbs
wouldn't break and the remaining fruit would grow bigger,
picking peaches and nectarines and plums and hauling them
into the packhouse to grade and sell.

For us, this cycle of the orchard year has continued largely
unchanged. Though the land we work is down to ninety acres—
Sam and his partners sold High Cliff Orchard, and a second
old apple orchard has been abandoned—the tasks that must be
done are essentially the same now as they were a generation ago.
But with increased mechanization as well as our efforts to cut

labor costs, the year-round work force has shrunk to zero. We're doing much of the work ourselves, with as little seasonal help as we can manage. With far fewer apples than when Frank was growing up, we no longer see, hear—or hire—the pickers from Florida. Autumn in the coves is quieter, and not as much fun, without them.

What apple trees we do plant these days are "specialty" apples—varieties not generally available in supermarkets that attract discriminating customers while not competing with the glut of standard varieties like red delicious. With apples—as with all our other fruits—the emphasis is now on retail sales at the packhouse, not on the costly packing and shipping of times past. In years when the stone fruits are scarce, the harder-to-kill apples are an "anchor to windward," as Sam likes to say, ensuring that the orchard will not go without fruit.

In the early morning hours of May 8, 1986, Ralph Levering's thermal belt lived up to its reputation. In the valley half a mile below us, the temperature dipped to 24 degrees and stayed there for a few hours—cold enough to destroy a cherry crop. But in the cove, the seven A.M. reading was 29 degrees—a near miss. Barring another, more devastating late freeze, Levering Orchard was back in the cherry business in 1986, after slim pickings the year before.

In anticipation of our largest crop ever, we sent out an extensive mailing list of postcards to Sam and Miriam's regular customers. The season would start on May 29. At 6:30 on the appointed day, the first car appeared at the "check-in station"— a card table near the barn where Miriam signed in customers, gathering names and addresses for future use, and issued buckets. There she would also direct traffic to one of four parking lots, open fields in two coves from which our customers could walk to the trees.

More cars appeared shortly. All day they kept coming— almost more people than we could handle, winding down through the cove on the one-lane gravel road. At the ripest trees, Frank and a muscular young helper named Joey Haynes received the customers and set ladders for them in the cherry trees, moving them to another location as needed. With metal hooks on their buckets to hang on a ladder rung or cherry limb, the customers picked—and picked. Large, dark red Viva cherries hung in bunches, irresistible both to the hand and to the mouth. All day people from as far away as South Carolina— most from cities and small towns in North Carolina and Virginia—toted twelve-pound buckets of cherries to their cars and continued down the one-way lane to the packhouse. At dusk dozens of pickers remained in the field with Frank and Joey, while at the packhouse Wanda, Sam, and Hattie Mae Love weighed the cherries, deducted the one-pound weight of the bucket, and were paid by the pound.

Word spread beyond our regular customers. Day after day, six days a week, the crowds came until, in four weeks, the trees were stripped bare. Ours was indeed a smiling cove: a small amount of rain had not damaged the crop, and gross sales exceeded the previous record, set in 1984, by more than a third.

For Sam particularly, the season was cause for celebration. For years he had hoped that one or both his sons would follow him into the business, as he had followed his father. Now that Frank was back home, it was harder than ever for Sam to fail: the dream of succession was vitally linked to Sam's thirst for success. Now he had proved to his son and daughter-in-law that there could be money in these trees—not just beauty and a way of life.

We knew how lucky we were. Hoping that we, too, could have a rewarding life here, Sam and Miriam had knocked themselves out for us, as well as for the orchard we shared in common. It was almost unimaginable: two people in their seventies—one who'd suffered a heart attack the previous year—working fourteen-hour days, collapsing into bed when darkness fell, only to rise again the next morning and do it all again. How many people our own age were capable of such effort?

But the days of their labor could not last forever. Not too far in the future, we knew, the long tradition of Levering Orchard would be entirely in our hands.

CHAPTER THREE

Taking Root

Many arrivals make us live: the tree becoming
Green, a bird tipping the topmost bough,
A seed pushing itself beyond itself,
The mole making its way through darkest ground. . . .
— THEODORE ROETHKE, "The Manifestation"

Ten yards up the hill in the next row of apple trees, seventy-four-year-old Garnet Dawson swung his scythe through the tall orchard grass in the August heat. Drenched with sweat, Frank hacked at the grass with a wide, lunging swing and then paused to watch. Garnet was forty years older than he almost to the day; the old man could not possibly be human. Beneath the shade of his John Deere cap, Garnet's lined face was as dry as deadwood in a drought. His overalls tied at his ankles against snakes and yellow jackets, he advanced swiftly down the row, his long blade slicing the grass in short, effortless strokes.

Try as Frank might to emulate Garnet's stroke, the longtime foreman of Levering Orchard would usually finish his row first and, rarely changing expression, come back to help in Frank's. Then they'd meet, often pausing to sharpen their blades with whetstones, and move on, day after day, week after week, down the endless rows where the tractor mower couldn't reach.

When Frank came in for the day at four-thirty after nine hours in the field, much as he had promised himself to settle into his office and start a novel, he usually sank down on the

couch in exhaustion. Not writing much was bad enough. Even
worse was a gnawing feeling that he had taken a giant step
down—that somehow he had failed. Committing himself to a
permanent regimen of orchard work, Frank realized, was not
the same as breezing in from California to help at harvesttime.
Was swinging a scythe or digging around young trees with a
hoe to be the measure of his worth? While Wanda was awak-
ening to her new environs and anticipating the October pub-
lication of her first book, Frank felt the boundaries of his
childhood world beginning to close in on him.

Though he had voluntarily traded wingtips for work boots,
asphalt for black soil, the mind does not so easily substitute
new patterns of thinking for old ones. There was keen envy
when a close friend in Los Angeles called to announce his new
job as a film executive at Disney. There were Frank's older
siblings, among them three Ph.D.'s with academic careers,
whose visits never failed to evoke his parents' pride and approval. During the June pick-your-own season, there was the
ironic chorus of dedicated cherry customers who seemed to
regard him as something of a curiosity and asked, "Aren't you
the one who went out to Hollywood?" Then, as Frank shoul-
dered their twenty-two-foot ladders, they added in disbelief,
"You mean you came back here to do *this*?"

Success was proving hard for him to conjure in a neatly
mowed orchard or a bucketful of dark sweet cherries. Frank
often found himself silently repeating his comforting litany
of acceptable achievements: the movie that hit the screen, the
producers with whom he'd worked. What tugged at him
was a sense that he'd pulled out too soon, without fulfilling
his early promise of writing films that made a difference.

Sometimes he wondered if this transplant back to Virginia was really going to take.

Wanda quickly relished much of her new life in Carroll County: settling into a home of her own after years of apartment living; cavorting with her long-lost cat, Cholla, a white-bibbed, white-socked wonder who had been evicted from the L.A. apartment and had lived during the interim at Wanda's mother's house in Maine. Wanda enjoyed physical safety in the country, a vegetable garden, and friendly neighbors.

Close as she felt to her in-laws, much as they'd welcomed her into the fold, she was still the daughter-in-law, the outsider with secular leanings and a foreign-sounding last name, moving onto their turf. There were enough differences to suspect problems might arise. Where Frank's family regarded marriage as a sacred institution, Wanda, a child of divorce, tended to see it as a more fluid arrangement. Where his parents were regular churchgoers, she'd dropped out in her teens.

Another long-standing issue nagged at her every day: the fear of losing control—control of her identity, her career, and her financial destiny. The specter of male chauvinism had cast its pall over Wanda all her life, the idea imparted by her mother that all men in some insidious way come to dominate their women, that even low-key Frank was capable of such behavior. And wouldn't living, quite literally, in his childhood home surrounded by the guideposts of his youth provide the ideal setting for the sublimation of her identity into his?

Although it was true that Marie Urbanski was something of a fanatic on the subject of feminism, Wanda had seen enough of the world to concur on many of her major points. Wanda had seen female friends wilt in marriage while their husbands thrived. She knew a legion of bright, talented women who had waged lifelong, uphill battles for confidence and esteem. She worried about the effect of violence against women and their objectification on television and in movies. Sexism remained a live issue for Wanda, something she would have to be vigilant of here in the South.

Without exception, all her L.A. friends were feminists, but in Carroll County, even in the home cove, Wanda's quiet brand of feminism went wanting for supporters. Neither Miriam Levering nor Sam's cousin Virginia Price was attracted to women's rights. What was most galling to Wanda about their antipathy was that as politically liberal "cause" people, they readily signed on to other progressive movements. But they did not or could not see the vital connection between the status of women and the great social issues. Not only among older women in the family, but in the community, as a married woman who'd retained her birth name, Wanda was an anomaly. (Actually her birth name was Urbanski, but after a 1977 visit to Poland, Wanda adopted the Polish feminine for her name, Urbanska.)

Wanda's fears of losing the reins of her life were compounded by an aversion to poverty. As a teenager her family had lived in a drafty, poorly insulated duplex, and her mother drove a low-slung, low-rent car that was ugly even when new. Back then she had vowed never to let herself get into her mother's fix. Marie had lived hand to mouth all her adult life, especially during those years when she was working on her Ph.D. at the University of Kentucky and later on before she became tenured at the University of Maine. Marie was sixty before she could scrape together a down payment on her first house. Without a financial cushion of her own, Wanda feared she would never have nice things or enjoy the kind of security that had so eluded her mother.

Scrutinizing her husband's parents, Wanda saw that lack of money was an accepted, even perversely cherished, tenet of the Levering life-style. It crossed Wanda's mind more than once those first months at the orchard that she was likely to sink into the straitened circumstances to which Sam and Miriam had grown accustomed. And now that he was back near his parents, what about Frank? Wasn't there a danger that her husband would lapse again into the indifference to money and material things that he'd expressed when she'd first met him as a divinity student who slept in his car?

Wanda couldn't be sure. Living in the house where he'd grown up, Frank could hardly be expected to perceive their new residence as she did. For him, the place—with all its deficiencies—was, after all, home. For Wanda, it seemed that unless enough income could be generated for major renovations, the walls would begin to close in on her. She could only wince in agreement when Frank's cousin's wife bluntly described the kitchen as "depressing" and Wanda's sister, after her first visit from California, pronounced the upstairs bathroom with its sloped ceilings "oppressive." Tactless though they were, for Wanda these words hit the nail on the head. And much as she wanted to rise above old demons, much as she had welcomed a change from the L.A. rat race, she was unwilling to take a vow of poverty that would send her back to the most vulnerable period in her life.

. . .

There is a photograph of us from that first summer that now seems a sort of idyll. A friend who flew in to visit from Los Angeles took it—a woman who had never before set foot on a farm. Work-hardened, Frank looks lean and muscular in blue jeans and a T-shirt; Wanda looks slender in a light cotton dress, her long blond hair set off by a tan. Barefoot, we stand arm in arm in the shade of the dark green cherry tree behind our house. We smile at the camera with what might pass to a stranger as deep contentment. To that stranger it might well appear that we had lived in this tranquil setting all our lives.

It's an appealing image—the kind that, if memory ever fails, might stand for the truth. But memory hasn't failed, not yet. Leaving Los Angeles did not in itself make life more satisfying. Change, we were discovering that summer, was not happening to us the way it happens to characters in a bad movie. Real change does not happen merely by cutting to a new location. It happens gradually, in fits and starts, in an internal tug-of-war between the deep-rooted claims of the old self and the yearnings to reach for something better.

What we knew in theory was not yet manifest in our lives. In theory we understood that success is not your profession or how many achievements you pile up, how much money you bank, or the security that money and things seem to provide. In theory success and security are intangibles, not your standard of living, but your standard of life; not the way others see you, but the way you see yourself.

In practice we had a long, steep climb up the side of our mountain, into pathless woods, across ravines choked with briars and rocky cliffs near the top, to make those brave words real in our lives. We had chosen to climb the mountain.

But the struggle to set standards of our own, to arrive where we wanted to be, was only beginning.

During our many travels subsequent to moving to Levering Orchard, we assumed a kind of mission: to meet others who were hashing out these same issues, climbing similar mountains, trying to make considered decisions about their lives. Three trips—one cross-country through Mississippi and Louisiana to California and back home through Missouri; a second to New York, Maine, and Vermont; a third to Georgia—were taken primarily to explore other people's thinking, with fun, relaxation, and friendship thrown in on the side.

Many of the lives we touched resonated with ours. Often we found that the issues with which people were struggling or with which they'd found clarity paralleled our own. Always we felt reinforced, as the Quakers would say, "held up into the light," by seeing the numbers of individuals who were thinking along our lines, who were bucking the blandishments of fast living and consumerism and defining their own wants, needs, and lives.

We discovered during the course of our travels that some people don't have the luxury of options in making the changes necessary for a more satisfying life; a Hobson's choice is forced upon them. Maybe a husband wants out of the marriage, or a wife issues an ultimatum. Maybe the company they own goes belly up. Or they're laid off from their jobs, or fired. Or maybe, as with a tall, striking woman in New York City, they simply can't go on anymore. So they do what Kathy Kent did: they fire their lives, hoping that "new" will mean "better."

. . .

On a bitterly cold winter afternoon, Kathy sat across from us drinking herbal tea at the Health Pub in Manhattan, a pastel oasis for those who eat and drink without sin. With her soft-spoken Texas accent, her flowing red hair, and her green eyes, it was difficult to picture this thirty-five-year-old woman in her Wall Street incarnation: working at the Commodities Exchange as an options manager for a brokerage firm and, later, for Shearson Lehman Brothers in retail brokerage.

Then she told us about her father.

"My father was raised during the Depression, and he was terribly poor," Kathy said. "For my father, happiness is financial security."

As Kathy grew up in Forth Worth, the oldest of three children, her father certainly must have been happy by his own definition. A workaholic executive in hotel and restaurant management, he was doing very well financially. That he had suffered the first of three heart attacks during Kathy's adolescence did not deter him from his course.

"My father's expectation for me was to be a success in business," Kathy said. "So that was extremely important to me."

In 1980, after waiting tables in New York and landing a few bit parts as an actress, she turned in earnest to the role her father had scripted for her. She went to work on Wall Street, working her way up from her first job as secretary to the chairman of the Commodities Exchange. "A lot of people," Kathy observed, "go through life living up to other people's expectations." She was one of that legion—or had been.

And so had we. We felt a pang of recognition at the characterization, both having traveled that route at one time or another. We both had parents who were only too willing to impart their philosophies to us and, if we let them, anoint us as disciples.

From early on, despite Marie's feminist politics and her scholarly interest in Margaret Fuller and Henry David Thoreau, she made no bones about her desire for Wanda to advance herself—through marrying well or pursuing a fast-track career or, even better, both. Her younger daughter was a special person and, therefore, entitled to all the finer things in life. In her adolescent years Wanda was convinced that this was what she wanted, too. Paradoxically, though Marie had followed her own drummer in an era in which it wasn't fashionable for women to do so, when Wanda decided in the summer of 1980 to leave New York City and put in with Frank Levering—who had announced he had $127 to his name and no work—her mother's disapproval might as well have been broadcast on the network news.

For Sam Levering, what his son should do in life was simple. Frank should follow in his footsteps: major in horticulture at Cornell and become an orchardist and leader among Quakers, devoting a large share of his time to public service. Frank had almost come to blows with Sam while still in high school over the Cornell issue, and he continued to separate himself from his father in his decision to become a writer and go to Hollywood. For Wanda, shedding the cloak of her mother's expectations came later, in her twenties, and not without tremendous pain and anguish. Was freeing oneself from the grip of these expectations an essential of simplifying one's life?

By 1986 Kathy's achievements had more than fulfilled her father's expectations. While her husband, a songwriter, was tasting the famine side of the feast-or-famine axis of his calling,

Kathy was pulling down $60,000 a year plus bonuses. "I had financial stability. And you get accustomed to a certain life-style—a certain car, clothes, trips to Europe. I took it for granted."

But as her father had before her, Kathy was buying her life-style at a bitter price. The relentless pressure and pace of being a floor operations manager was threatening her health. "I was burning out," she said. "I was feeling sick all the time, losing weight. I got so I couldn't sleep at night. I started having migraines. There wasn't really any relief. You'd get a little time away on weekends, then by three o'clock on Sunday afternoon, I'd start feeling anxious. By Sunday night I'd be throwing up in the bathroom. But," Kathy went on, "I still wasn't thinking about my future too much, because I felt trapped; I felt helpless to effect a change."

In December of 1986, having moved to an even higher-pressure job at Shearson Lehman, Kathy could no longer ignore the migraines that had increased in both frequency and intensity. The pain was most acute at the back of her head. Maybe she had a brain tumor, she worried. So she went to a neurologist, who put her through a pricey battery of tests. The neurologist's diagnosis: "Occipital neuralgia," Kathy said. "Head pain. I paid fourteen hundred dollars for this guy to tell me I had a pain in the back of my head."

The neurologist did have a possible remedy. A "procaine-type substance" could be injected at the base of her skull to deaden the nerves in the back of her head. One of the side effects of such a procedure, the neurologist warned, could be the deadening of nerves in Kathy's face.

That was a risk she refused to take. Kathy stayed with her job, enduring her pain. Then, in the spring of 1987, a friend told her about "this holistic guy." It wasn't easy to make the appointment. "All this new age stuff," Kathy said, "I thought it was total horseshit."

Figuring nothing would come of it, Kathy sat facing the man in his office. "Do you think you can heal yourself?" he asked. Kathy wasn't sure. "I can help you help yourself," he went on, "but you're going to have to take responsibility for your life. If you do that, I promise you your headaches will go away."

Though the new age approach sounded more sensible than she expected, Kathy remained skeptical. Then he got to the crux of the matter: "To what do you attribute your headaches?"

"My job," Kathy replied.

"That's simple. Change jobs."

"I can't do that," Kathy said.

The man looked at her. Then he gave her books to read on meditation, advice on how to change her diet. And a poem.

"It was about standing at the edge of a cliff and believing that when you jump, you'll fly," Kathy said.

Three months later, Kathy jumped.

"In a dark time," Roethke writes, "the eye begins to see." The year 1965 was a dark time for Millard and Linda Fuller, co-founders of Habitat for Humanity, the nonprofit organization dedicated to eliminating substandard housing worldwide with volunteer labor.

One morning in early spring, we drove through one-stoplight towns with grand old homes and tumbledown shacks, past miles of peach orchards in lush pink bloom, into Americus, Georgia, a modest city just eight miles east of Plains, home of

Habitat's most famous volunteers, Jimmy and Rosalynn Carter. A few blocks from Habitat's international headquarters, we parked the Malibu next to a crumbling sidewalk shot through with grass. In front of us, boards dangled loose on an old frame house; the front porch roof sagged on rotting pillars. Untrimmed bushes and vines choked the porch of the house next door.

The Fullers live across the street. In 1965, in Montgomery, Alabama, an architect was drawing up blueprints for a mansion, to be built on their new twenty-acre lot, complete with swimming pool and horse stables. The Fullers got swept up in a marital crisis, and that house was never built. Since 1977 the Fullers have lived in the tan, two-story frame house on Church Street for which they paid $12,500. With the last of their four children recently departed for college, the pair now live here alone.

As Linda and Millard talked about their lives, we sat around the kitchen table drinking coffee. The bars on the kitchen window had been installed, Millard explained, motioning behind him, after some guys broke in and scared their daughters.

When their marriage was shaken, Linda explained, speaking in slow, fervent tones, she was a homemaker in her early twenties with two young children and a husband who gave her whatever money could buy. The one thing that money could not buy—the thing she most desired—was time with twenty-nine-year-old Millard, who worked round the clock seven days a week amassing their fortune. The son of the owner of a small country store, Millard was a modern-day Horatio Alger, a lawyer and entrepreneur from Lanett, Alabama, who financed his college and law school educations by selling birthday cakes and printing desk blotters and campus telephone directories.

By 1965 the Fullers were millionaires, owning—in addition to their thirteen-room house and shares in various business interests, including a major cookbook publishing concern—a vacation retreat, two speedboats, and a Lincoln Continental. And Millard wasn't stopping there. His next goal was ten million.

It was the life Linda had thought she wanted. Her father, who owned an electrical appliance store, had never provided "any of the real luxuries in life. When I was growing up," remembered the tall Tuscaloosa, Alabama, native, "it seemed like my friends had prettier dresses than I did. I wanted more clothes and a bigger house."

Wanda nodded empathetically. She had harbored similar feelings while attending fifth through ninth grades on scholarship in private schools in Lexington, Kentucky. She was a clotheshorse back then, pumping every bit of baby-sitting money into her wardrobe; as for her mother's apartment it was such an embarrassment for years she refused to have friends over. Even Frank knew whereof Linda spoke. Though he'd attended public high school in Mount Airy, he'd often felt the inadequacy of his farmboy wardrobe.

When seventeen-year-old Linda first met Millard, the young law student at the University of Alabama seemed the answer to prayer. She loved him first, she said, laughing, "because he was tall. But I could see that he was going to be a lawyer and that would probably mean a lot of money, so I felt very good about getting hitched."

Linda married Millard the summer she graduated from high school. But as the years went on in Montgomery, Millard's colossal success began to take an unexpected toll. "I remember sometimes in the evenings," she said, "after I put the kids to bed, just how lonely I felt. Abandoned, you know?"

To feel better, Linda said, "any spare moment I had, I went shopping." She had bought so many dresses and her favorites—shoes—that they swarmed out of her huge closet and were colonizing Millard's. But Linda found that the thrill of acquisition could not fill the vacuum of her absentee husband indefinitely. "I reached the point where, even though I enjoyed wearing something when it was new, I realized I didn't have the companionship that I wanted from my husband."

Ironically, it was the plan for Linda's "dream house" that brought her feelings to light. "The more I thought about my life in that new house," she said, "the more I saw that house as a prison.

"Here was Millard knocking himself out to make all this money," she said, her voice down-shifting with emotion, "and it wasn't really making me happy anyway. One or two times I just went to him and I said, 'We don't have much of a relationship. I feel like I don't love you anymore.' And that kind of shocked him. And he would promise me that we would spend more time together. Then after a week or two, he'd be back in the same old routine, working all the time. I came to the realization that I was miserable, and it wasn't going to get any better. So one night I told him, 'I'm just going to have to leave and think for a while. Because I don't know what to do.' "

Though she was looking back a quarter century, tears shone in Linda's blue eyes. We were astonished that someone so much in the public eye would allow herself to become so vulnerable— that she hadn't swathed herself in a public persona to protect her from such outbursts of emotion.

Linda wasn't bluffing. The next day she departed for New York City, where she sought the counsel of a minister friend. She confided to him that she was considering divorce. After several sessions the minister said, " 'You've got to decide; I can't tell you what you're going to do,' " she recalled. "But the one thing that really gave me clear vision was when he said, 'If you've ever loved Millard, you can love him again.' "

A week had passed. "I called Millard to come up," Linda said. Millard jumped at the chance. His days had been hellish. With his support system gone and his future in limbo, he had been unable to concentrate at work. And a feeling of weight on his chest that made breathing difficult, along with chronic neck pain, had become even more pronounced.

In the foyer at Radio City Music Hall, the couple sat down together for a serious talk. Starting was hard. Linda began to sob. Arm in arm, they hit the streets of Manhattan. Linda wanted major change, but not, she hoped, divorce. Her discontent had stirred feelings deep inside Millard, loosing ambitions that had long lain fallow. He made a stunning proposal, an idea that had begun to brew during the days of Linda's absence.

Millard Fuller made a striking first impression. At six feet four, gaunt as a fencepost with craggy features and long arms and hands, he could be described as Lincolnesque (though he lacked the famed beard). Peering intently through wire-rimmed glasses at the two strangers in his kitchen, he would tip back and forth on his chair, hunch his shoulders under the red cardigan sweater, and twist his body this way and that as he listened or talked. He would pace to the barred window and back as his hands performed tricks in the air with invisible string, burning a seemingly bottomless supply of kinetic energy. This was the master salesman and leader of a large and growing organization, selling not cookbooks, but the theology of the hammer.

Millard remembered his wife's departure as a major watershed in his life. "It was a deeply spiritual experience because I realized that there is no security in material things—that you have the illusion of security, but that's not where real security lies."

That pivotal night on the town, Millard proposed to Linda that they sell their business, give away the proceeds, and start their life anew. No one could accuse the Fullers of timidity. Within a few months they'd sold their business interest to Millard's partner in Montgomery for roughly $950,000. They'd kissed the houses, the boats, the Lincoln Continental, goodbye. When all these assets were sold, Millard and Linda gave away well over a million dollars to churches, colleges, and charities, reserving only $25,000 for themselves.

"It was a very freeing thing," Millard said. "But a lot of people thought that we needed psychological counseling. Something must be wrong with you if you want to give away your wealth."

"A lot of our old friends thought we went off the deep end," Linda said. "A lot of our family did, too."

The grand adventure, as Millard called it, had begun.

That adventure would make a rich biography: how the Fullers piled their two young children into the car and took a long family trip to Florida; how, on the way back north, they stopped for a few hours to see a friend at Koinonia Farm, outside Americus; how, influenced by Clarence Jordan, Koinonia's leader, they ended up staying a month; how, after moving into an apartment over a gas station in New Jersey and working in New York as a fund-raiser for a black college in Mississippi, Millard returned with his family to live at Koinonia; how, working with Jordan, the Fullers started Koinonia Partnership Housing funded by Fund for Humanity, a precursor to Habitat; and how, in 1976, the Fullers founded the organization that now has, Millard estimates, one hundred thousand regular volunteers in the United States alone.

"We've found real treasure," Millard said. "Not in a big bank account, but in a wonderful relationship and a meaningful life. We finally started making some investments in the right places."

The Fullers' decision to divest themselves of the trappings of their lives and whittle them down to their essence sprang out of their commitment to a strong Christian faith. "A man's life," Jesus says in the Gospel According to Luke, "consisteth not in the abundance of the things which he possesseth." Throughout the gospels, Jesus stresses the virtue not of wealth but of unconditional love and compassion for all human beings. At Koinonia Farm, in a tightly knit, racially integrated Christian community, the Fullers had earned little income, spent little money on themselves while doing the daily work of the farm. Seeing poverty and suffering in the wider community around them, they had caught a vision of service to others, based on the life and teachings of Jesus.

Although we had no definitive biblical text as our guide, listening to the certainty the Fullers expressed lent us confidence in our course. As they talked about their work, our confidence deepened that from many different points on the compass, the same destination could be reached.

. . .

As president of Habitat for Humanity International, Millard draws an annual salary of $38,000. Performing a variety of tasks in an office at headquarters adjacent to her husband's, Linda makes $14,000. (With no apparent mindfulness of the wage discrepancy, Linda says her role is as Millard's "help-mate.") Millard some years pulls in $10,000 to $12,000 as a part-time attorney. All speaking fees—Millard noted that he was recently paid $10,000 for a speech in Rochester, New York—are donated to Habitat.

"We're just trying to make enough money to meet expenses," Linda said. "When we get all our kids through school, we'll probably cut our salaries down."

"Do you have any savings?" Wanda asked.

"We don't have any savings account," Millard said. "Zip."

"You feel that you could make more money if you needed it?" Wanda persisted. Somehow the idea of living without a financial cushion disturbed her.

"Making money," said Millard with a laugh, "has never been a problem."

That afternoon the Fullers were expecting a visit from a young Vermont couple whose business was on the brink of bankruptcy, Millard said. "They're coming at simplifying their life-style out of necessity. Lots of times people coming at it that way discover the joy of a simple life. But it is terrifying to most people."

"They don't realize," said Linda, "how wonderful it is."

. . .

Kathy Kent walked into the boss's office at Shearson Lehman. She was leaving the company.

"Oh?" he said. "Are you pregnant?"

"No."

"What brokerage firm are you going to?"

Kathy wasn't going to another brokerage firm. She was enrolling at the Swedish Institute of Massage Therapy on West Twenty-sixth Street. She was going into holistic medicine.

The boss's mouth fell open. "He thought it was a great joke."

It was no joke. Kathy had taken to heart the poem about leaping off the cliff. Three months after she'd read it, here she was, falling. Learning how to fly.

Following her mentor's advice, Kathy had started meditating. Her migraines were a thing of the past. She had, she said, taken full responsibility for her own health.

"It was part of a process of listening to yourself. I decided that you have to do what *you* want to do. Because if you don't, you're going to be very unhappy."

Kathy's father was not pleased. "When I told my father I was going to be a massage therapist," she said, "he gave me the same look my boss gave me. But that's the way it is. I had to stop talking to myself in the voice of my parents."

These days a certified massage therapist with a booming private practice, Kathy savors some delicious ironies. Her old boss called her to get her recommendation for an acupuncturist. And her mother, who recently moved with Kathy's father to Baltimore, is now herself studying to be a massage therapist. "We talk shop," Kathy said, grinning. "My father thinks she's out of her mind."

Kathy's triumph was not always assured. "When I first told

my husband what I wanted to do," she said, "I said, 'You're going to have to carry the ball for a while.' He was really scared. You run a lot of risks doing what you want to do. Not only economically, but emotionally. But it forced Jeff to go out on a limb. My changing my life brought him to a higher place."

Jeff's songwriting career has taken off. Bette Midler and Cyndi Lauper have recorded his songs. Among other things, Kathy said, he's been able to break into the lucrative advertising market, composing music for commercials.

"He's been very supportive," Kathy said. A number of Kathy's regular clients have come, courtesy of Jeff, from the music industry. "He's great PR," she said, laughing. "He hands out my cards and says to the guy, 'You know, Bill, I think you look a little stressed. You ought to see my wife.' "

Not long after Kathy broke the news to her boss at Shearson Lehman, she and Jeff threw what she described as a "party." "We had a glass of champagne. Then I started ripping up all my panty hose. It felt very liberating. I decided I wasn't going to keep anything that I didn't want. Nothing. I got all my Brooks Brothers suits together and gave them all to Goodwill. I thought, Some bag lady's going to see all those Brooks Brothers suits and go, 'Fantastic!' "

Unlike Kathy Kent or Linda and Millard Fuller, we faced no dark crisis that precipitated our move to Virginia. Once we arrived, change came slowly, not driven by disaster. That first year, 1986, the orchard did not set off the bank's alarm; it made a modest profit. Wanda found work as a free-lancer. As long as she was willing to travel on assignment and do telephone interviews, Virginia was proving to be as good a base for her as California (with living expenses down and distractions re-duced, maybe better).

Like most people we've talked to who have restructured their lives, Wanda had no sudden revelations. What she had was time, the kind of time she hadn't had since college. And as she'd done at Harvard, Wanda started keeping a journal, extensive entries that forced her to look at how she spent her days. No longer merely caught up in the flow of events, Wanda began—for the first time in her life—to shape events from her own point of view. It was her *life,* and she was starting to feel in control of it. In the process, ironically, she was starting to let go of old fears.

Wanda had written a book profiling a generation of young Americans, yet as the summer turned to fall and winter, her own voice had never been stronger. This life here was going to work. Frank's parents seemed thrilled to have her close by. It touched her when Sam brought in gifts of wildflowers or ripe fruit, a father-in-law's way of expressing affection. Miriam took a lively interest in Wanda's work and activities, and they frequently ran errands together in town. With her talents as a seamstress, cousin Virginia loved nothing more than to whip up a new blouse or dress any time Wanda needed one. Frank's family's delight in Wanda was almost too good to be true. Could this be the secure, loving family Wanda longed for as a child?

Wanda's disappointment in her new family's lack of feminist perspective was gradually replaced by the understanding that you don't always have to see things eye to eye to love, be loved, or even be close. Miriam, Sam, and Virginia had other things to teach her, other fruit to offer. As she observed the senior Leverings' marriage, she noted that a balance of power had been struck, that although Miriam was no feminist, she was strong, firm, and clear in where she stood. She was nobody's chump. Sam seemed to adore his wife, even if she crossed him.

As Wanda's posture relaxed, as she learned to relinquish the will to control life around her, she found that she was also poised—as the next few years would demonstrate—to improve relations with members of her own family.

Many friends mistakenly assumed that it was Frank, not Wanda, who had pushed the move to Virginia. In fact it was Wanda who'd first argued in Los Angeles that the moment had come to make a move, and Frank had agreed. So perhaps it should have been no surprise that it was Wanda who first felt at home at Levering Orchard.

For Frank, it was nice to make an impact, to help stop the orchard's flow of red ink. But Frank's Hollywood self—the quest for success—would not down. Like his stubborn father, proud of his tenacity, Frank was determined to stage a comeback. As soon as the apples were picked and sold, he started work on a new screenplay. The plan was to go out to Los Angeles, find a new agent, and try to sell it in the spring.

Because his prospects for a sale were iffy at best, and because she thought Frank's quest unhealthy, Wanda watched unhappily as events unfolded. She was determined to remain detached but supportive, to try not to interfere with his quest or attempt to exert control over his life.

In April we drove the pickup to Los Angeles in three grueling days. While staying with friends, Frank launched a frenetic campaign to sell the script or—if not that—land a screenwriting job. Early breakfast meetings. Ten o'clock appointments. Lunches. Drinks. Dinners. Not exactly a born salesman, Frank forced himself to sell. He pitched new ideas to producers, talked up his script, pinballed from one rejection to another. The pace, the parade of people, drove him to exhaustion. After three and a half weeks, no agent would take him on, no one nibbled at the script, no one offered him a job. It was a bust. A complete failure.

Work was pressing at the orchard. Two nights before leaving L.A., Wanda's friend Liz Brody asked Frank to stand in as her date at a famous director's son's bar mitzvah. Frank agreed. Besides, maybe he'd meet someone who could help him.

At the party afterward—with car-length, papier-mâché *Top Gun* model airplanes dangling from the ceiling and tens of thousands of dollars' worth of food and drink—he did. A young woman from Warsaw, married to a Polish film director, had been visiting Liz. The American Jew and the Polish Catholic had ties that predated them. Kasia Gintowt-Bajon's family had harbored relatives of Liz's close family friends from the Nazis during World War II. Kasia planned to return to Poland in due course. But, first, her dream was to see America—the Grand Canyon, Texas, whatever was out there between the two coasts. Could she make the trip with Frank?

Frank had wanted time alone, time to lick his wounds, time to take a hard look at his goals. But Kasia lacked transportation and money, and his heart went out to her. And Liz, who was eager for him to agree, assured him that she'd see to it that Kasia could cover half the gas money. The trip was fine with Wanda, who, with her book just published, had flown to Maine to address the annual meeting of state librarians.

Frank and Kasia hit the road. It was a strange journey. Kasia pinched pennies and seemed completely oblivious of Frank's inner struggle. It was a pleasure for Frank to watch

Kasia, who was a children's book illustrator, gawk at the Grand Canyon and describe the Painted Desert or a plains thunderstorm with childlike excitement and a foreigner's vocabulary. And once they arrived in Virginia, Kasia loved the orchard. She couldn't get enough of it and wandered through the trees most of a day before catching a bus for Washington, D.C.

A foreigner seeing things with fresh eyes proved the right tonic for Frank: it enabled him to look at his own life in a new way. He had come to realize that L.A.'s pace no longer agreed with him. He felt frazzled, thrown into fast forward, like Minnesota's freshman senator Paul Wellstone in his famous hyperkinetic campaign commercials. Frank was trying to fit himself, a square peg, into Hollywood, a round hole. Perhaps Hollywood was not him, never had been. Maybe he could find himself in Virginia. Maybe in Virginia new expectations could emerge, with the promise of new days.

Frank did not, however, forget Hollywood. Not entirely. But he put that script away in a closet and never wrote another scene.

CHAPTER FOUR

Work

Work is more fun than fun.
——NOEL COWARD

With remarkable frequency, it goes something like this. You're at a party, and someone— usually some guy in a high-paying, white-collar profession—asks what you do. "Oh," he cuts you off, apparently not wanting to learn the particulars, "writing, that's what I want to do. One of these days I'm going to start writing novels." And on he rolls, like a dump truck without brakes: his ideas for best-sellers, film scripts, or the great American novel; his master plan.

We know a doctor. We'll call him Jerry. Over the Christmas holidays a few years ago, Jerry squeezed out of his Jaguar and struck up a conversation with Frank on our front lawn. "You know, I've always wanted to be a writer," he said. "I have a million ideas in my head. Soon as I retire I'm going to write novels."

"Yeah," Frank said. "Soon as I retire, I'm going to be a doctor."

There's a moral to this story. It's not so much that writing is hard as hell and takes time to learn. It's the peculiar notion held by so many that you spend the lion's share of your life wanting to do something else, envying other people their work, before you get to the sliver reserved for the "real you." Or you work your tail off so you can retire early and do what you always wanted to do. Or you live for the weekend, where you do your "real work"—if you're not too exhausted. And then you're a writer, a painter, a musician, a carpenter, whatever. You're the person you always wanted to be.

Good luck.

For us, the moral of this story has a name: Judith Freeman.

We've known Judith for more than ten years. In 1988, the year she turned forty-two, *Family Attractions*, a critically acclaimed collection of short stories, was published—Judith's first work under her own name. A year later her novel *The Chinchilla Farm*, the quasi-autobiographical story of a Mormon woman from Utah who moves to Los Angeles after her husband leaves her, appeared to even wider acclaim, followed by her latest novel, *Set for Life*. At last Judith was doing the work she wanted to do, and she was doing it well enough to please both herself and many critics. Not bad for a writer who never earned a college degree.

We remember another, earlier time in her life.

With Judith, it wasn't working another job and, like Jerry with his Jaguar, fantasizing about being a writer. In fact, Judith was writing. When we knew her in Los Angeles, she had co-written a pseudonymous novel, was writing stories in fits and starts, and was making the rounds in Hollywood, pitching movie and television ideas to producers.

But with the exception of the novel, for which she and a partner were paid $15,000, and which, she said, "had a lot of offensive qualities," Judith did not appear to be bringing home much bacon as a writer. Nor did it seem there was any compelling reason for her to do so. Twice divorced, she lived, during our time in Los Angeles, first with her wealthy television-writer boyfriend in Beverly Hills, later by herself in a rented house in tony Santa Monica Canyon, a few blocks from the ocean. Since Judith only occasionally took part-time jobs that never seemed to pay much or last long, we could only assume that some other source was covering most of her bills.

From the outside it appeared to be a materially comfortable, if not lavish, west side existence, a life that held ample room for socializing, afternoon reading and walks, travel with friends. It was a life that many people would envy, that Judith herself did not appear eager to give up.

It's easy to oversimplify, to draw too facile a connection between the change in her life-style and work habits and the dramatic change in her professional fortunes. Yet the facts are striking. In 1985 Judith met Anthony Hernandez at a benefit auction for which the Mexican-American photographer was donating some of his photographs. They fell in love. In 1986, the same year we left Los Angeles, Judith married Tony in a simple, outdoor wedding ceremony and moved with some trepidation into his stucco apartment in Westlake, a section near downtown settled primarily by Mexican, Salvadoran, and Guatemalan immigrants. Set back high on a steep bank from the street, Tony's apartment, which he's had since 1970, rented for an incredible $98 a month. In its three rooms, Tony had one chair, a mattress on the floor, and nothing on the walls. In what is now both their bedroom and Judith's office was Tony's darkroom. The place, as Judith described it, "was like a monk's cell"—a monk's cell that she transformed into a spare but homey nest.

Since making the move, Judith has flourished as a writer.

She works hard but by no means obsessively, taking breaks during the day for swims, bike rides, and meditative walks to nearby MacArthur Park. She and Tony spend relatively little. The combination of their negligible rent and the fact that they prepare most meals in their small kitchen keeps their expenses extremely low. Earning $600 a month, Tony works half days in the mailroom at the Department of Water and Power, reserving the afternoon light and weekends for photography. When Tony is using their 1969 Volvo, which they bought used for $1,700, Judith takes the bus.

Is it accidental that Judith's writing career blossomed during the same period in which she simplified her life, conforming her time and her material needs to her desire to write? We think not.

Before, hers was a life full of distractions. "Now," she said, "it doesn't seem as though there are those distractions. I have a lot of time for writing, a lot of time for work. And so when you say to me, 'You're so extraordinarily prolific,' yeah, but the time has been created for it."

We were talking with Judith and Tony in the spacious house of friends for whom we were house-sitting in a swanky neighborhood in the San Fernando Valley. Though we'd been there for the better part of a week, having to punch out the right code to appease the elaborate security system put us on edge. It made us uneasy to live, however temporarily, in a place that needed so much protection, that had to defend itself so aggressively from the outside world.

Judith and Tony had come to this house as our guests for a dinner of pasta, salad, and the apple pie that Judith had baked that day. Now, late in the evening, she sat beside Tony on a cushion couch, an illuminated aqua swimming pool shimmering

through the sliding glass doors behind them. It was odd for us
to talk about simple living in a $400,000 home so dissimilar
from our own.

For Judith, the setting must have been especially jar-
ring, as she was the only one of the four of us who had ever
lived with such wealth. "I'm actually living much more in tune
with not only the way I was raised, but the way I really wish
to continue to be," she said, holding her body motionless, her
lips barely moving as she spoke, as if practicing meditation.
"And happily, it's a way that serves my choices very well as a
writer."

There was a double meaning in her last sentence. For not
only has the change helped her focus on work, but her new
neighborhood, which has surfaced in her writing, is an integral
part of what she calls her "more engaged existence." In *The
Chinchilla Farm*, narrator Verna Flake, a former Utah bowling
alley waitress who speaks in a voice remarkably like Judith's,
moves to a section of Los Angeles that is unmistakably Judith's
neighborhood. There Verna, like Judith, encounters daily a mix
of Spanish-speaking immigrants and—particularly in Mac-
Arthur Park—the homeless, many of them Anglos, a few of
whom she gets to know.

One homeless man whom Judith sees regularly calls her
"Sister." She calls him "Brother." "I know the people around
him," she said, "none of whom are as together as he is. I go
and sit on the bench. And it strikes me every once in a while
that here I am with Gabe and with Tom and with a variety of
other homeless people, talking to them. And it's a strange feeling
to realize that some of my most regular daily contacts are with
this group of people in the park that sit on the benches."

These lives—and the street scene in her neighborhood,

where women sell homemade *pupusas* and *chile rellenos* from shopping carts they push along the sidewalk, where kids play in the alleys, men cluster on street corners, and brassy mariachi music erupts without warning—give Judith a sense of community she never had on the manicured west side. Sometimes, however, the urban vitality that has energized her fiction is frightening. On her first New Year's Eve in the neighborhood, she told us, "there was about fifteen minutes of solid gunfire all around us. And we realized how many of our neighbors had weapons." For the foreseeable future, at least, Judith is where she wants to be, living the way she needs to live to do her work. Many of her old friends visit only rarely. Some refuse to brave the neighborhood at all.

"People are really afraid of urban environments," she noted. "You *can* live in these areas. One of the things that I've said to myself is that there's nothing I can't lose and do without. The only reason that we have a deadbolt to the bedroom is for Tony's cameras. That would be the greatest loss for us, because those are his tools."

Tony's tools—and his eye for the offbeat, for social flotsam and jetsam—have made him an increasingly esteemed photographer, winning grants and prestigious gallery showings. When we first met Tony, he was at work on an intriguing project on Rodeo Drive in Beverly Hills. Using a small camera handheld inconspicuously at his waist, he was photographing pedestrians as they passed by. The results were chilling: a motley parade of unposed, unaware, often compulsive faces, of wealthy matrons from Beverly Hills and tourists from Topeka and Tokyo, linked only by their common attraction for the street synonymous with conspicuous consumption.

Other projects have proved equally disquieting: a series of photographs of desert trash heaps outside Las Vegas, where people come regularly with guns to shoot bottles and cans for sport; photographs of the homeless in Los Angeles.

Tony is a slender man in his mid-forties. On this evening of borrowed luxury in the San Fernando Valley, he wore a white, starched, button-down shirt, pressed jeans, and deck shoes he slipped off after dinner. When Tony was growing up with his two brothers in East Los Angeles, his father, a former Colorado farmworker, had material aspirations for himself and the kids. From a very young age, Tony said, he had a sense of himself as an "oddball" in a family where "everybody wanted things, to show them off." One of his two brothers is now an attorney in San Gabriel; the other works full-time at the Department of Water and Power in field investigation. His brothers have an abundance of things. But Tony has a passion and an art.

"The main thing," he said, "was that I wanted to keep working doing photographs. And nothing else mattered. That's really what it comes down to. There are no guarantees, just a life, your own life. You just do it and don't stop it or interrupt it."

Tony's words were inspirational. And so was his life, one so powerful and clearly defined that he had attracted Judith to it and laid out for her the formula and foundation for getting on with what she wanted to do in life.

It was not difficult to find parallels in our experience and hers. At roughly the same time that Judith abandoned Santa

Monica Canyon, we left the west side of Los Angeles for what we hoped would be a better life. Like Judith, we wanted to hone in on the work that would be most satisfying, most meaningful. We wanted to make true in our lives Noel Coward's maxim about work being more fun than fun.

Of course, our situation was more complicated logistically than Judith's. Being orchardists *and* writers made for an unconventional work cycle. Frank was either on call or working full-time from March through October, with his busiest period running from June through August, when the summer fruits needed immediate harvesting. Wanda worked the cash register at the packhouse during cherry and peach harvests, about ten weeks altogether. In late fall, winter, and early spring, the orchard work slowed down. Although there remained never-ending management and financial responsibilities, this was our time for intensive writing. Our labors, quite literally, were tied to the seasons.

In part because of our need to generate income in *excess* of our living expenses, when we were able to write, we did not have the luxury of giving total focus to the writing that our hearts held. We were in the *business* of writing and, therefore, sought a wide range of money-making enterprises and opportunities, from writing for magazines and book review sections to selling publishers books from proposals. As the years went by, we branched out into teaching night courses at the community college and offering one-day writers' workshops throughout North Carolina. Consulting work also followed.

Our need for money was real, and so, too, were the often competing demands of our various editors and the urgent call of ripe fruit on the trees. This combination of demands made us workaholics of the first order in our early weeks and months at the orchard. In 1986, a typical summer scenario for Frank was putting in six twelve-hour days a week picking fruit and then on Sunday—his one designated day of rest—getting up at six A.M. to write a book review that might take the whole day.

The unhappy result was that dissatisfaction crept into Frank's orchard hours. He began to dread his days in the field. Once there, he watched the clock like an unhappy employee. Likewise, Wanda occasionally chafed at the bit over her long hours on her feet at the packhouse and winced when an orchardist neighbor teased, "This is not what your mother had in mind for you when you were growing up."

When it became apparent that we were driving ourselves just as hard—and often harder—here than we had out west, we had a talk. How could we create more balance in our lives without relinquishing our ambitions? How could we devote at least a portion of our time to something we'd long hankered to do? They were questions we would mull over for months.

Then, in October of 1986, we hit upon a plan. It was actually Frank's idea, though Wanda was casting about for a follow-up to her newly published book, *The Singular Generation: Young Americans in the 1980s*. Though logic and publishing wisdom would seem to dictate sticking with nonfiction, why not, Frank asked, return to fiction—Wanda's first love in college? And why not, he suggested further, write it together? He had a brainstorm for a novel to be set at a daily newspaper, tapping Wanda's knowledge of that business from her three years at the *Los Angeles Herald-Examiner*. Frank would contribute what he'd learned from screenwriting about advancing a plot. As long as we were working so hard, why not go at it as a team?

This was not a new idea. In the early days of our courtship, Frank had proposed ad nauseam that we collaborate on a screenplay, and Wanda had resisted with equal vehemence. Screenplays lacked the texture of good fiction, she said, and besides, the movie business seemed like a crapshoot, even riskier than the literary game.

To Frank's delight, though, Wanda fell for this scheme with little persuasion. After years of writing separately, we both welcomed the idea of joining creative forces. It was, he congratulated her, a measure of how much less she was worrying about money than when we'd first moved to Virginia.

We set aside time to develop the plot and characters. By the spring of 1987 we were hard at work on the blueprints for the novel. Scores of five-by-seven-inch cards, each summarizing a scene, marched in fifteen-foot rows up and down the green living room carpet. Ironically, once Wanda agreed to tackle the "on-spec" project, she plunged in with zest and confidence, while Frank wrestled with doubt. Though the plot moved briskly and the characters were becoming as real as family members, the aftertaste of Hollywood rejection was bitter in Frank's mouth. Now it was he, not Wanda, who was fretting over our shrinking bank balance and doubting that "this thing" would go anywhere. Though the friends who, upon hearing of our new writing collaboration, had jokingly recommended "a good divorce lawyer" were surprised by the mesh of our egos, though the inventive nature of the work was immensely satisfying, we were investing many hours of our time with no guarantee of return.

At last, in December 1987, apprehensive but proud of ourselves, we mailed the one-hundred-ten-page outline to Wanda's literary agent in New York. The work itself, as we had hoped, had knitted us closer together. A few arguments, an occasional ruffled feather, but no serious damage. What would the agent think? And could she possibly convert our pages into a sale?

Late on a cold afternoon in January 1988, our phone rang for the first time all day. Wanda was in Mount Airy running errands. Frank answered the phone.

It was Wanda's agent in New York. She had sold the outline for our novel to the higher of two bidders. The completed manuscript would be due in eleven months.

We dashed back to town in our pickup, bought a bottle of champagne, uncorked it, and let it flow. The advance wasn't a fortune, but it was enough to cover the bills while we cranked out the novel. We were as giddy as newlyweds. Not since college, when Wanda spent uninterrupted hours poring over her short stories, had she enjoyed "work" so much. And Frank dared to hope that the pall cast over his optimism by myriad Hollywood disappointments had finally lifted.

After the euphoria of the book contract wore off, reality set in. There was much work to do and—given the impending six-month fruit season—little time to do it. Still, we refused to rush it. Our work began with research in Washington, D.C., where the story takes place. We made the six-hour-each-way commute for seven weeks, returning from the capital on Wednesday afternoons to get ready for our Thursday-night creative writing class at Surry Community College and catch up on our messages, mail, and any other business. Then we headed back Friday mornings to Washington. We stayed for three weeks at Edmund Urbanski's Silver Spring, Maryland, apartment and later rented a room from a widow in Bethesda. We interviewed journalists and politicians and visited favored Capitol Hill watering holes to take notes on food, beverage, and decor.

After we finished our research, and staring at a December deadline, we agreed to a rough division of labor. While Frank took to the trees, Wanda accepted primary responsibility for moving the novel along. To make our partnership work, we had to be adaptable. In our different workplaces, we didn't always know when one of us would have to trade a tractor for a thesaurus. More than once, in the midst of a creative rush, Wanda was called to pick an emergency bucket of plums for a customer who had arrived early.

For Wanda, feeling indispensable both financially in our marriage and creatively in this particular undertaking paid deep dividends. Perhaps from her feminist upbringing, or perhaps from seeing friends whose low-paying jobs were trivialized by their husbands, whose contributions were marginalized when they married wealthier men, Wanda realized that she liked nothing so much as carrying the ball in a partnership collaboration.

We did, in the end, miss our deadline—but not by much. With Wanda's start on the novel and Frank's efforts once the apples were picked, we made rapid progress, sometimes writing together on the same scenes, usually writing separately, always abiding by the rule that if one of us didn't like what the other had written, he or she had license to rewrite or delete. The other partner would have the next crack at the edited material, back and forth, until both of us were happy. The rule was rough on writerly pride at times but, we agreed, fair and effective.

Our individual strengths emerged over the course of the project. Wanda was the copyeditor and Frank the "spell king," an ironic accolade with which he had been saddled in seventh grade after winning the county spelling bee. Wanda preached rewriting and seemed to thrive on it, while Frank favored the first rush of creativity and often clung tenaciously to what one writer has dubbed the "little darlings" of prose.

More significant, though, we looked forward to the work. There were thickets of disagreement and foul moods, but ultimately it was exhilarating to make our way through them. We were loving the process: inventing a world, coming to a mutual understanding about characters, imparting our values in the shape of the story. As never before, we were learning a common language as writers, breaking out of the isolation that plagues many who write alone.

The work carried Wanda back to the great pleasure of her youth, in those halcyon days before her parents' divorce, when she and her sister reveled in a fantasy world of Barbie and Ken. The dolls' extended family of fifteen, with their extensive wardrobes, soda shop, fashion shop, sports car, airplane, and motorboat, occupied at least one-third of the floor space in Wanda and Jane's attic bedroom. Wanda lived to play "B. & K.," as they called it, with its complicated plots, intricate family relationships, petty rivalries, and feuds. Wanda was Barbie, and Jane was Ken. Barbie was ahead of her time—a self-starter in early 1960s garb, an entrepreneur who led a reluctant Ken and the troop of Midge, Skipper, Alan, Tutu, and the rest on camping expeditions out of the house and down to the pond. Other times, Barbie, now the nightclub singer, donned her "solo in the spotlight" outfit and took up a microphone before an admiring audience of her plastic peers.

As nothing else, for Wanda, writing this novel with Frank brought back that sense of play.

While we were collaborating on the novel, each of us realized the importance of maintaining our individual identities as writers as well. We continued to work independently on magazine pieces and book reviews, and when we could steal the time, we would push along literary projects of our own. But we liked working together so much that when the novel was finished in January 1989, we were already at work on another joint project, eager to keep the home partnership fires burning.

While the orchard was proving a congenial setting for our creative work, we were also bringing in lessons from the field and the sales platform that were slowly changing our lives. Often the lessons did not come easily.

When Frank was growing up, he wanted mainly to escape "learning the value of physical work," or the other, similar homilies children are supposed to swallow. Like many rural kids who ultimately leave the farm for better-paying and more prestigious jobs in the city, Frank found his chores and orchard work monotonous, his father oppressive. Freedom and creativity were anywhere but here. And it was no accident that Frank passed up a full scholarship to nearby Wake Forest University and chose instead a college far from home, Wesleyan University in Middletown, Connecticut.

As an adult, he knew he should appreciate the value of manual labor: hadn't writers from Walt Whitman to Gary Snyder to Wendell Berry extolled the virtues of honest sweat? And wasn't he philosophically in accord? Yes, but none of those august thinkers had ever worked with Sam Levering. As endearing as Sam was most of the time, his wisdom could never be challenged. Both as boss man and father, Sam was always right. It was hard for a man in his late seventies and early eighties to change, to accept the new reality that his son and daughter-in-law were now his business partners. Some of Frank's unhappiness in doing grunt work he blamed on his father's lingering notion that Frank was merely taking orders. Having made all orchard decisions since 1939, Sam adjusted slowly and sometimes explosively to the democratic procedures of partnership.

Family businesses are notorious war zones, and in the years since 1986, Sam and Frank have incurred their full share of battle scars. But the battles—and Sam's life-threatening quadruple bypass—have brought father and son closer, each man coming to know the other in ways not possible before their lives were joined in work, before they shared a common stake. For Sam, along with the pain of diminished power and physical prowess has come the joy of sharing hard-won knowledge with a son. For Frank, the years here have brought the conviction that this is our place, too, along with a new appreciation of Sam's determination and grit.

In American culture, manual labor is reserved largely for recent immigrants, illegal aliens, blacks, poor whites, women, small farmers, teenagers, and leftover hippies. For Frank, who had made steady strides toward conjuring success in his new farmer fittings, the half-year diet of manual labor became easier to swallow as his investment grew in the orchard, as he helped decide what fruits to plant, what trees to cut, how to market four thousand bushels of peaches.

For Wanda, the everyday routine of making up a cash drawer, laying out bags and filling some with fruit, waiting on customers, and, at the end of a long day, clearing out and closing down, was exhausting. It was also exotic. Wanda liked to joke that she was the only member of Harvard's class of 1978 to end up in the produce business. She could lose herself in this, the most mundane of human enterprises. How much more basic can you get than selling a gallon of fruit to a budget-minded retiree? Or hearing about a customer's bunions as she slowly makes her way up the stairs to the loading dock platform? Or admiring a pickup truck newly purchased by a patron who wanted someone to notice?

Working at the packhouse provided a superb stage for a parade of humanity—everyone from those few who expected service on the double, or assumed you would slash the price of your fruit as if it cost you nothing at all to grow, to the thoughtful majority whose hallmark was courtesy. By and large, our cherry customers were attuned to simple pleasures—in coming great distances for fruit, in picking their own, and canning or freezing quantities to last for a year or two. Most of our customers were repeaters, longtimers who insisted they looked forward to receiving our annual mailing as if it were a treasured Christmas card. Occasionally a bicyclist from Spain might hop off his ten-speed and purchase half a pound of cherries to munch on as he pedaled up the mountain, but mostly Wanda dealt with the veteran customers who came back year after year, often week after week, bringing their friends and relatives and lingering to visit. For Wanda, the long hours at the packhouse carried a side bonus: making more precious the time she had for her writing.

Working on the orchard put us in daily contact with the extended Dawson family—Glenn, Randall, Mark, Esther, Bill, and Beth. No one, however, had more impact upon us—and especially on Frank—than Garnet Calvin Dawson.

Sometimes when Frank worked with him, that relentless old man with the scythe seemed a pretty good imitation of the Grim Reaper, come to take Frank's life away—at least his life as a writer. The image was not as farfetched as it might seem. When Frank was small, he found Garnet frightening. Garnet had massive forearms and was resolutely taciturn, with a hawk-like face and piercing eyes that made the boy want to hide behind his father's pant legs. Once, sensing Frank's fear, Sam took his son aside and told him that his foreman was a good, kind man who would never hurt him.

When Frank was a teenager, a day with Garnet in the orchard seemed like toiling on a chain gang. A ferocious worker, Garnet showed no mercy for youthful frailty or for the boss's son, driving furiously until dark if necessary to finish a job. Any activity other than work Garnet viewed with suspicion. Playing ball or reading a book were signs of sloth.

It was ideal preparation for high school and college athletics. After summers with Garnet, Frank showed up at football camp ready for battle. Savage war cries on the gridiron were nothing next to interminable days with the orchard foreman in the heat and rain. The man had a perverse sense of humor. In the midst of picking plums in an all-day downpour, he'd turn to a drenched Frank and say, "Ain't nothin' but a clearin'-off shower!"

These were scenes from the past. Getting to know Garnet

better as an adult, Frank came to feel that the older man had changed. Or was it that Frank had learned how to talk to him? Getting a job done was still supremely important, but now the silver-haired Garnet would stop for a few minutes to catch his breath. For the first time, Garnet would quit work on the hottest afternoons. Not only was he more vulnerable physically than before, but he was letting his emotions show, talking candidly about getting old, about the waning of strength and stamina.

And he was telling stories as he worked, vivid sketches of Frank's father and grandfather that made Frank feel part of a living tradition. Garnet knew every inch of this ground. Often triggered by the sight of something—an old rock wall Frank's grandfather had built, the stump of a tree someone had cut— memories of people long dead invaded him constantly.

"Well," Garnet would say at the end of the day, "we'll try it again tomorrow."

In his essay "Life Without Principle," Thoreau surely had Garnet in mind when he wrote: "Do not hire a man who does your work for money, but him who does it for love." Starting with summer jobs in his youth, Garnet has worked at Levering Orchard ever since, building a brick home and college-educating four of his five children from his earnings. Garnet and his homemaker wife, Esther Hiatt Dawson, have always lived simply: they rarely travel, never eat out. They can, freeze, or eat fresh much of their food from orchard fruit and an enormous vegetable garden. With ample savings and few expenses, it's been clear for more than ten years that money isn't what has kept Garnet toiling.

By the late 1970s Garnet could have retired, as family members have been urging him to do ever since. He could have spared himself cold winter days that aggravated the arthritis in his hands. But retirement was not a word in his Appalachian vernacular. When younger men, including Garnet's youngest son, quit for less strenuous work, when Sam was a peace activist spending weekdays in Washington, D.C., it was Garnet's steady work and dogged effort that kept the orchard going.

The longer Frank worked alongside the old man, the less preoccupied he was with the orchard's debt, the more he began to see the orchard as Garnet did: not as a collection of numbers to be crunched, but as a complex organism offering mentally challenging, intrinsically satisfying work. It was more complicated than it looked. In pruning a tree for maximum vigor, a worker had to consider a wide range of variables, such as cutting branches to bring fruit maximum exposure to the sunlight. In picking peaches—the job he'd once despised most— Frank began to appreciate the skill required to do the job well. It took a subtle eye for color to know which peaches to pick, which ones to leave a few more days to ripen. Not only was his attitude changing, but Frank was learning practical skills from Garnet, who had a wide range at his fingertips, everything from how to negotiate a tractorload of fruit down a rain-slickened hillside to repairing a broken water line.

But probably most impressive was Garnet's constancy, practically unheard of in this day and age. You couldn't replace him. Experience taught that if you hired a younger man, he could never be counted on to show up for work the next day. Garnet was directed, steady, committed. Nothing else seemed to matter, and there was no higher priority than tending the orchard. Garnet offered a striking contrast to Sam, who despite the voluntary nature of his public service work had nonetheless set out to change the world. Sam's were grand if intangible goals, an archetype writ large for what Frank had come to see as his own unhealthy quest for success.

Frank saw, too, that at the end of a day, Garnet put his work behind him and enjoyed a bone-weary sense of accomplishment that Sam never could or would enjoy. Sam's goals could never be achieved. But Garnet's goals almost always were. If Sam was thinking globally, Garnet was acting locally.

So when the 1987 season was over, the fact that we broke even on all the fruit even though an April freeze had killed three-quarters of our cherry crop made us feel grateful and lucky. That patience was a sign of progress. There would be better years ahead.

Garnet's way allowed Frank to see the value in smaller, more immediate things. Not only with orchard work, but in his writing, Frank began to find pleasure in a well-turned sentence; he began to perceive success in writing a single good review. In the past, his drive and discontent had been so enormous that he'd vowed not to rest until he'd won an Oscar.

Orchard work helped Frank put his worldly ambitions in perspective, a perspective he had lacked in Los Angeles. With time, with sweat, with the revolving wheel of the seasons, came a growing feeling of connectedness—not only to a tradition and to the people who kept it alive, but to natural cycles. There were youth and age here, blended together, each with its strengths and frailties. In the world of plants and animals were life and death, growth and decay. Forgetting himself, Frank began to feel like a creature among creatures, part of the larger scheme of things. At times, even on the hottest

days, swinging the scythe for hours on end, Frank lost all sense
of time, felt a nameless joy merely in being alive in creation.
Now that he was no longer begrudging his time, he was, just
possibly, taking a long cool drink from the timeless waters of
eternity.

Thomas Hosmer Price, Frank's second cousin, is one of two
pediatricians in Starkville, Mississippi, a town of a little over
fifteen thousand residents when Mississippi State University is
out of session. As a forty-seven-year-old, Ivy League–trained
doctor who earns $70,000 a year, Tom has made a choice that
parallels Garnet's, Sam's, and our own. In exchange for higher
personal return, he has opted to stay at the lower end of the
pay scale for physicians—far lower, given the fact that the
average American doctor earns over twice that annually. Tom's
choice precludes many of the amenities that often cushion the
lives of doctors: the vacation cruises, the luxury cars, and the
country club memberships.

Turning down—or not pursuing—more lucrative job prospects in other parts of the country, Tom Price has chosen to
remain in his native Mississippi to do the work he values most.
As a result, he is able to take only a one-week vacation each
year, when he and his family invariably visit his mother, who
is our neighbor and cousin, Virginia Price. The rest of the
year, if Tom isn't at work, more than likely he's on call. In
his east-central Mississippi county, which is heavily populated
with impoverished blacks, Tom is the only pediatrician who
will accept Medicaid patients, for which he's paid eighteen
dollars per visit.

Tom is a short, muscular man who lives with his wife,

Sondra Upton Price, and their two children, Rachel and Thomas Hale, in a modified A-frame near the edge of town. On the evening we arrived, we sat with Tom and Sondra beneath a high ceiling latticed with unfinished cypress beams, the kind of cypress, Tom told us, that grows in swamps and is immune to termites.

Tom's life changed forever during the 1960s civil rights movement in Mississippi. That era, along with his own lifelong exposure to racial inequality, gave him the sense of mission that defines his professional life today. With his sister and two brothers, Tom grew up in Meridian, less than a hundred miles south of Starkville. Tom was working at a hardware store in Meridian in the summer of 1964 when three civil rights workers were murdered near Philadelphia, Mississippi, a town between Meridian and Starkville. A good friend, he learned later, was on a crew resurveying a dam as part of an effort to conceal the bodies. At the time, Tom said, he was a Goldwater Republican, well aware that his father's ancestors had fought for the Confederacy in what Daddy Price used to call "the War Between the States." Though his mother had hosted meetings of civil rights workers in her home, received threatening phone calls, and had crosses burned in the yard, Tom had not been actively involved in the movement.

But with the advent of what he called "the civil war" in Mississippi, he began to ask himself what he, one man, could do to make conditions better. Tom's father, who died in 1962, had been a physician. Enrolled as an undergraduate at the prestigious University of the South in Sewanee, Tennessee, Tom decided that he, too, could make a difference in that profession. When he learned about the appalling infant mor-

tality rate in Mississippi—at the time the highest in the nation—
he found his mission: helping to reduce it.

"My favorite verse in the Bible," he told us, "is, 'As you
do unto the least of these, so you do unto me.' There's no 'leaster'
you can get than being a black teenage girl pregnant in Mississippi." As Tom recounted the trajectory of his life and the
emergence of his thinking, we realized that we too had always
identified and empathized with the disadvantaged: minorities,
outsiders, newcomers, immigrants, victims, even the underdogs
in ball games. But Tom was putting that perspective into hands-
on work.

It was not hard to see that Tom's empathy had in part been
born of personal experience. In the late 1960s and early 1970s,
it was Tom—a white Mississippian at the University of Pennsylvania Medical School—who was "the least of these." "One
reason I came back to Mississippi," he said, "was the prejudice
against me up north. At a party someone would say, 'Where
are you from?' If you said, 'Mississippi,' they'd literally turn
and walk off."

Though many were brave and some paid with their lives,
it had always been striking to hear Virginia Price's view of
white northern civil rights activists who came to Mississippi.
Hers was a story not told by Hollywood, in whose scenarios
white northern activists are the unqualified heroes, spurring
reluctant blacks to action. Native whites, almost without exception, are one-dimensional and racially venomous. Virginia's
account presented a more complex picture. The white northerners who came to two meetings in her home, she told us,
were suspicious of local whites and not interested in learning
the culture or in doing the spadework necessary to work co-

operatively for change. They tended to lump together all white southerners in a monolithically racist society to which they were morally superior. Southern whites like Virginia who endorsed racial progress, who knew blacks intimately from years of daily interaction, she said, were simply ignored.

Though it now has more elected black officials than any other state, and though the sheriff often associated with the three Philadelphia murders is now working for a black man, Mississippi continues to evoke simplistic images and painful derision. At dinner one evening, Tom joked about a recent poll of business executives in which Mississippi was rated as America's least desirable place to live.

"So let's move," chimed in teenaged Rachel. "I can pack in a day!"

Sondra, also a Meridian native, could only grimace. When she was a newlywed she had wanted to live somewhere else, but she has long since resigned herself to her husband's commitment.

For us, knowing his mother's version of history, Tom's story about being rejected up north simply because he was a white man from Mississippi conveyed the ultimate irony. In 1972, right out of medical school, Tom had gone to work in a clinic in Jackson, working almost entirely with black children. Since 1977 he's been in Starkville. Where now, we wondered, were those morally superior white northerners, those who preached racial equality and would have nothing to do with white natives?

To get to Tom's office, 1.8 miles from his home, you cross the main drag—Dr. Martin Luther King Drive—and skirt the edge of town, driving through pine woods and past a brick low-income housing project where black kids play in the streets. Sondra, who works with Tom as a nurse, described the Starkville Children's Clinic as "children-friendly." As if to illustrate the point, a young Thomas Hale immediately clambered up to the top of a large wood playhouse and, letting out a yelp, swung clear to the floor like a monkey. "Patients," noted Sondra dryly, "are not allowed to do that."

In addition to the standard features, to sunny colors and prominently displayed antismoking literature, the office has two waiting rooms, one for sick and one for well children. It was not hard to visualize the broad strokes of Tom's and Sondra's workdays or to hear the cries of impatient children as Tom and Sondra went about their tasks in the smaller rooms down the hall. For privacy, Dr. Tom—who wears a trademark bow tie because it can't be yanked by juvenile patients—retreats to his personal office with its framed diplomas and studio portraits of Rachel and Thomas Hale.

Directly across from the office is the one hospital in the county, where Tom makes regular rounds, doing emergency work and often putting in long hours, sometimes for little or no pay.

We piled into the elevator and rode to the upper-floor nursery, where Rachel and Thomas Hale pressed their heads against a glass panel. Behind it were tagged newborns in bassinets, black and white, some asleep and some awake, none of them much larger than the football Tom used to cradle in his hands as the center on the Meridian High School football team.

Since Tom first decided to become a pediatrician, the infant mortality rate in Mississippi has dropped significantly. It is now "better than a few other states," he observed happily. And then he sobered. "But I'd like to get it down a lot more."

Not that he's doing the job by himself—not by a long shot. But as future statistics are gathered from Starkville, Tom and Sondra Price will be a major force behind them.

The British writer and social reformer John Ruskin once wrote, "In order that people may be happy in their work, these three things are needed: They must be fit for it; they must not do too much of it; and they must have a sense of success in it."

In looking at our own work lives, we knew that we were fulfilling the first and last of Ruskin's three conditions—we were fit for our work and enjoying a modicum of success in it. But, like Tom Price, we were painfully aware that we fell dangerously short on the second condition: we continued doing too much work. And yet, as we settled into the orchard, listened to its seasons, learned its lessons, as we zeroed in on the work we most wanted to do, we understood that the time had come to modify the conditions surrounding our work, to become, if not less ambitious, at least less consumed with work.

It was little comfort that our workaholic condition was shared by millions of Americans and was, in fact, a hallmark of the "singular generation" that Wanda had identified in her first book. Indeed, many of our peers had paid a far greater price for overwork than had we. For although overwork was denying our lives of fullness, it had not affected our health or torn at our commitment to each other.

Our L.A. friend Michael Levine had suffered more deeply than we. He believes that workaholism cost him his five-year marriage. The New Jersey native and his wife were partners in crime. Both would come home from twelve-hour work days, "put something in the microwave, fall into bed, turn the television on, and each read our trade papers. We wouldn't talk to each other. The TV's going in the background—the blue glow, you know? And we're dying." Eventually the glue that held them together had dried up.

Dr. David Shi, chairman of the History Department at North Carolina's Davidson College and author of two books on simple living, said that "this sense of being in a rat race, of being out of control of time," is the central concern of many who attend his lectures on the topic. "I hear a lot, frequently from lawyers who raise their hands and say, 'I know I lead a harried and too complex life, and I know that I'm not doing justice to my family responsibilities, but I work in an environment where I cannot voluntarily choose to decelerate. The whole ethos of my firm is to bring in more hours, more clients.' They realize they're caught in a vise. And for them, getting out means leaving that prestigious law firm with its six-figure salary and perhaps hanging out a shingle—taking the risk of being a general lawyer in a small town, with a much more modest income."

Such a leap of faith would bring the side effects of slashing one's work hours and making less money, and it would place one squarely in the simple-living tradition. Wrote Richard J. Foster, Quaker theologian and author of *Freedom of Simplicity,* "Simplicity takes vigorous exception to both the slothful and the workaholic."

Optimum efficiency is one way of getting more done in less time. It was a concept cited frequently by those trying to simplify their lives.

"If I carefully organize my time every school day," said

Farnham Blair, a forty-nine-year-old English teacher at Orono High School in Maine, "and make a tight schedule in advance, I wind up having extra time on my hands. I can then use this time as I please."

No doubt time management was what we needed, too. But efficiency is a factor difficult to summon with the snap of the fingers for something as elusive as creative inspiration. But we did notice that when we were wearing our writing hats, being productive was almost always a function of feeling fresh and enthusiastic. As recently as five or six years ago, though, no matter what the job, we would grit our teeth and grind it out. We'd rarely take a break until the thing was done. This bulldoggish approach applied as much to peach harvest as to a writing project. Tough it out, the attitude was. No pain, no gain.

Since then we've decided to say "no" more often: to turn down tempting free-lance assignments when we're already at work on something else. We've also shortened our work hours while simultaneously focusing on the work we most love. To our surprise, with this new reduced work schedule, we have managed to remain as productive as before—possibly more so. And there have been other intangible rewards.

Half a mile down the mountain from us lives Emma Dawson, Garnet's aunt. Miss Emma, as everyone calls her, is 109 years old. Still of sound body and mind, she is the oldest person in Carroll County, perhaps in southwestern Virginia. Like Garnet, she is a link to another time, to the Blue Ridge culture before cars, TV sets, and the ubiquitous satellite dishes.

There's an expression among the mountain people of Miss Emma's generation, one we've heard repeated nostalgically by folks like her youngest child, Everett: when you're not working, when you're sitting on the porch in the cool of the evening or visiting neighbors on a Sunday afternoon, you're "enjoying time."

For us, given the pressing demands of our work, enjoying time—when not working—has been the hardest trick of all. Learning it just might be one of the keys to that longevity on which Miss Emma has the local patent. Or, if not to longevity, then at least to a life in balance.

Oddly enough, water helped to poke a chink in our work armor. Or, to be more precise, a swimming pool. In nearby Galax, Virginia, Wanda discovered an indoor public pool. Always a sucker for pools, she started swimming, guilty at first for the time away from work and for burning the fossil fuel needed to make the fifty-mile round trip. Frank simply refused to go. Too much lost work time, he growled.

These days Frank is the first to pack his trunks and towel. For six months each year, twice a week, he quits work at four forty-five to drive to Galax for a five-thirty swim with Wanda. Lap swimming has become a ritual, a mental break from work, and—we've both discovered—a means of making our work hours fresher.

Not long after we started swimming together, Frank put up a basketball goal on the side of the old barn. In his youth Frank and older brother Ralph had played basketball religiously, but the goal was long gone and so, Frank had told himself, was the childhood license to play.

Most work days now, we take several breaks to shoot hoops. There's still a residue of guilt: Aren't we supposed to be working? But we're overcoming it. Frank shoots with one ball, Wanda with a second. Sometimes the balls clang off the rim and go bounding over the fence and down the hill. We tear after them like kids, lest they roll clear to the foot of the mountain.

Mountain hikes on our property are easier in winter. In the pathless woods we don't have to worry about briars or snakes. Though we lack Garnet's knowledge of every topographical quirk in the area, we do have our favorite destinations: an abandoned mountaineer's cabin halfway up the mountain, an unmarked pioneers' cemetery at the top of an adjoining cove.

In short, we've blown the whistle on ourselves. "Time out," we've declared. Time out to write letters. Time to sit on the porch watching the sun go down, enjoying time. Time to visit with Sam and Miriam at midmorning or linger with the newspaper after lunch. To cook from scratch, to tend our two woodstoves, to make our beds in the mornings and clean our house on Saturdays. The simple sorts of things that unfrazzled people do.

Along with our new attitude has come some new ground rules: Sunday is a day of rest. This was a biggie. It would have been unimaginable in Los Angeles, and when we first arrived at the orchard, at least part of Sunday was always devoted to work. And except on our busiest harvest days, we now quit work the other six days by six-thirty and take time to cook dinner together. At long last Frank has shed the late-into-the-evening macho ethic of one of his former employers, a sort of who-can-work-whom-under-the-table contest.

We readily admit that this new balanced life of ours is still a work in progress. We have not arrived, but we are well under way.

For inspiration we look to those who've succeeded at striking a healthy balance in their lives—one of whom, given his executive status at a major sock manufacturing company in Mount Airy, would seem an unlikely candidate: Robert Merritt.

Robert Merritt makes socks—lots of them. In 1989 the U.S. hosiery industry produced 4.2 billion pairs, and Americans spent nearly $3 billion buying socks. As chairman of Renfro Corporation, which sells exclusively in the United States, Robert certainly did his part. "When Americans woke up this morning," he told us proudly, "one out of sixteen put on socks made here at Renfro."

The mind boggles. How to visualize? A huge crowd on the mall in Washington, D.C., one out of sixteen bodies wearing a pair of Robert's socks. Times Square in New York: one out of sixteen pedestrians wearing a pair of Robert's socks. It was easier to deal with the man than with his market share. Here Robert was, a trim, five-foot-six, sixty-four-year-old grandfather with a soft voice and a boyish smile, casually dressed in a golfer's shirt, sitting behind a desk in his office. Behind him, on the pale yellow wall, was his own painting of the deck of a house overlooking the ocean.

Frank's family has known Robert a long time. After World War II Robert's father and Frank's father worked closely together as supporters of the United Nations. But it wasn't until after we moved to Virginia that we got to know Robert and his wife, Cama Clarkson Merritt.

And, trying to develop our own business practices at Levering Orchard, we were interested in what Robert had done to give Renfro its reputation as one of the most profitable and worker-friendly companies in our area.

Not that we were drawing too close a parallel. With 1,600 employees in five plants and gross sales in 1988 of $56 million, we were not exactly in Renfro's weight class. Still, it was stimulating to talk with a man who, like us, produced a humble product. What could be more basic than a piece of fruit or a pair of socks?

Robert's attitude toward his work, his sense of humor about both making socks and himself—and his enthusiasm for life outside of Renfro—intrigued us. On the outside, he acknowledged with a grin, "making socks seems about as exciting as signing an alimony check."

Robert has managed to inject excitement into a calling that he fell into through what he calls "classic nepotism" and in which he advanced rapidly through the ranks. Since 1955, when he joined the company, he has challenged his ingenuity while benefiting the company as an inventor. One of his inventions, on which the company holds a patent, is "a device for measuring the coefficient of the friction of yarn, which allows you to measure how well lubricated the yarn is, which helps you knit more efficiently," he said. Likewise, as a manager, Robert has long been an innovator, instituting such pro-employee policies as profit-sharing and flextime and offering health-education programs like a smoking cessation clinic.

"When I came here," Robert said, "we paid minimum wage, and I wasn't proud of what we were doing. I saw a lot of long-service employees who retired humpbacked, without much savings to show for their labor."

Today, two-thirds of Renfro's employees are women and, along with their male counterparts, they are, Robert says, the only plant workers in Mount Airy—a town teeming with textile and furniture plants—to participate in profit-sharing. Renfro workers share 20 percent of the profits, before taxes, as well as receiving annual bonuses based on a percentage of their salaries.

Good management has meant good business, and Renfro's market share has grown from 1 percent in 1965 when Robert became president to the over 6 percent market share it now holds. But with his business victories well in hand, what is most striking about Robert today is his responsiveness to his own needs, the balance he has struck between work and other dimensions of his life. "There's only a limited amount of time and opportunity," he said. "I don't ever want to say I wish I'd done something."

So he does it. Robert has served or is serving on the boards of the local arts council, literacy council, and community college. He is a past president of the Mount Airy Rotary Club. And as a passionate amateur, he has tried his hand in a number of the arts. He photographs local topography and people and faithfully carries his camera when he and Cama travel abroad. He has offered photography courses at the community college, mastered hang gliding, and plays a mean guitar at the sing-along Christmas party the Merritts throw every year. At the community theater, he played an intense Clarence Darrow in *Inherit the Wind* and Merlin in *Camelot*.

We like Robert's nerve. We like the way he's always learning, always trying something new at an age when many of his peers are lounging at the country club. We like the way he approaches work and play with zest and confidence and combines the two.

It was not difficult for Frank to remember a time when movies seemed to hold the key to his happiness. It was all larger than life: the big screen, the big city, the big success. In that vision of work that was supremely important, apples, socks, and small writing achievements held little rank. But no more.

"I'm never satisfied," Robert told us the day we visited his plant. "I don't think we'll ever arrive at where we want to be but the trip is a lot of fun."

For our work, too, those seemed like words to steer by.

CHAPTER FIVE

Keeping Up with the Joneses

It wasn't Pearl Harbor. It wasn't the day John F. Kennedy was shot. But we remember Friday, March 11, 1988, as a day that will live—if in something less than infamy—in something more than the oblivion into which most dates soon fall.

In the Volkswagen Rabbit that we had bought used in 1982, we had just passed Front Royal, Virginia, an hour west of Washington, D.C. on I-66. Suddenly we lost power, and black smoke billowed from beneath the hood. We drifted to the side of the interstate and made a grim inspection. The engine was a cauldron of hot, hissing metal, blown-out oil, and acrid smoke. Hours later a Front Royal mechanic confirmed our suspicion: a leak had drained the oil from the motor, which had locked up. The four-cylinder engine was ruined.

For years we'd had trouble with the Rabbit's electrical system. Now it was small consolation that we weren't to blame—that no red light had flashed to warn us about the leak. The fact was that we'd lost our primary means of transportation. In a rented car we made our appointed rounds for the next few days in Washington, researching our novel. Then, returning to Front Royal, we sold our vehicular headache to an auto junkyard. To us, at least, the seven hundred dollars it would have cost to replace the engine was more than the car was worth.

The following weeks brought an unexpected emotion: not the pain of loss, but the excitement of a new option. The Rabbit's demise roughly coincided with the arrival in our mailbox of what for us was a small fortune: half the advance for our novel. Resolved to spend only as we earned, and not to borrow, we suddenly had the money to buy a new car outright.

We did need a car. Life in Virginia wasn't so simple that we didn't often need two vehicles at once. Frank used the pickup almost daily in the orchard from April through October, hauling fruit, tools, and supplies, and without a second automobile Wanda would have no way of getting into town or around the orchard quickly.

But in our excitement over the prospect of a new car, the distinction quickly blurred between our need for reliable transporation and our desire for something snappy and new. We feasted on possibility, studying a buyer's guide to the 1988 models. Off and on for more than two months, we stalked car lots in Mount Airy and Winston-Salem and Washington, D.C., scrutinizing sticker labels and peering inside at virgin upholstery. We scoped out Chevy Novas, Dodge Aries K's, and Ford Escort wagons, initially jolted by price tags pushing $10,000— without tax and license. The more cars we saw, the wider our eyes grew. Admiring his brother's Toyota Camry, Frank revised his fantasies upward. "As long as we're spending ten thousand dollars," he ventured, "why not go to twelve for a Camry or an Accord?" On the lot of a Honda dealer, in the tantalizing presence of a sleek Accord, Frank stopped just short of making an offer. Only Wanda's counsel to think it over held us back.

All but forgotten in the spring sunshine and the waxed gleam of car lots was what the money was slated for: house renovations. In our forty-nine-year-old house, the need was urgent. We were startled that we had come so close to buying a new car and eclipsing our goals.

It is tempting to demonize advertising. In *The Culture of Narcissism,* Christopher Lasch argues that mass advertising creates consumers who are "perpetually unsatisfied, restless, anxious, and bored." And it's true: we would have to live in a cave, without newspapers, magazines, a radio, and television to escape the incessant bombardment of advertising that stirs desire for new and prestigious products, that makes consumers feel that—without them—they are hopelessly out of step.

But surely advertising alone could not account for the intensity of our fantasies. The more we thought about it, the more we had to admit that we, too, had our eye on the Joneses. What we wanted was linked inextricably to what Frank's brother had, to what Wanda's sister had, to what many of our cherry customers had as they drove gingerly through the orchard. Seeing those expensive cars, we'd often felt the pang of envy; our tiny, tinny Rabbit with its flaking brown paint had long suffered by comparison.

"You drove across the country in *that?*" Frank's brother-in-law once asked, eyeing the Rabbit with disdain. The words stung. Not having a "better" car was a reminder that—for us, if not for him—money was tight. It reminded us that in a culture in which a "nice" car is a primary symbol of success, we didn't cut the mustard. Thinking about our two-month romance with the idea of a new car, it was hard to deny the suggestion that we, no less than others, craved the status a new car confers. We wanted a car that would keep us apace with the Joneses, that would tell both them and us that we had arrived.

The imperative to be like the Joneses is manifest in many aspects of American life: the way we dress, the restaurants we frequent, the foods we eat, even where we shop. It rears its ubiquitous head in the gifts we purchase and in the way we furnish our homes. Keeping up with the Joneses—the perceived need not to *be*, but to *have*—can be a full-time undertaking.

Sadly, the race usually begins at an early age. Time and again friends and family members have worried aloud about the pressure their kids feel to have what other kids have: the latest style of basketball shoes, the coolest cars. From early childhood, it seems, kids can fear being different, can dread the possibility of not conforming. Once we become adults, few things in our culture encourage us to change the conformist patterns of childhood and adolescence. Some of us nurse old wounds from the times when sticking out was painful, armoring ourselves with the new wardrobes or big houses that will protect us from ever feeling so vulnerable again. Others who never had hand-me-down clothes or secondhand cars may see no reason to respect those who did.

Money, we imagine, offers the freedom, contentment, and respect we crave. Spending it, we discover that what was new and better is soon old and inferior. To stay in the race, it's soon time for another purchase, time to discard what we haven't long possessed. Rather than acting of our own free will, we're making passive, predictable decisions. Rather than being comfortable with what we own and who we are, we become restless captives to a vicious cycle of earning enough bucks to buy what we think we want.

Webster's first definition of "freedom" is the "exemption or liberation from . . . the undue, arbitrary power and control of another." By that definition, our pursuit of a new car was not an exercise in freedom. In fact, we were renouncing liberty in our desire to emulate others. We weren't yet free to make our own rules for what we possessed.

To have that freedom—to break out of the cycle and be one's own person—requires the ability to resist the "wants"— the fourteen-karat gold earrings, the latest video camera—and affirm the real needs. For us, resisting the wants has meant learning to distinguish between the two, looking for products that meet our needs, not our compulsions. Above all, resisting the wants requires strength of conviction in what we value: not the expensive, the big, and the new, but quality, utility, economy, and —when possible—beauty.

That strength has not come overnight. For us, an unforeseen opportunity has become a reference point for those times when what the Joneses have looks better. In May of 1988 Wanda's mother asked if we'd buy a used car if one became available. "I mean, for instance, if I were to sell, would you be interested?" Marie continued.

At first Wanda was decidedly uninterested. Her mother's tan, four-door, 1980 Chevy Malibu sedan was boxy and looked like the unmarked police car it often is in many cities. Its standard, floorboard gearshift shifted only with difficulty— more like the gears in one of our ancient orchard trucks than a passenger sedan. Its lone frill was an AM radio.

But the more we talked about it, the more we had to admit

that buying the Malibu made sense. The car had been well serviced, repainted, garaged by Marie in Maine, and despite eight years of automotive life, it had only twenty-five-thousand-odd miles on the odometer. Marie was tired of arm wrestling the gearshift and was looking for a lighter, easier car to handle. Though our yearnings were still potent and it was hard not to contrast the Malibu with what might have been, we bought it at a reasonable price, and Wanda and Marie drove the car to Virginia in July.

No doubt our set of wheels is not the envy of friends, family, or neighbors. But it remains a good car for us. Since 1988 the "Golden Retriever," as Marie dubbed it, has carried us (and often Sam, Miriam, and Virginia) to all points on the compass. And remarkably, we've had only one minor repair: a muffler replaced. Though not beautiful, its squarish looks have grown on us. It's all we can ask for in quality and utility, and its overall costs from date of purchase have been remarkably low.

In letting the Joneses go their own way, time, we've discovered, is on our side. The longer you define what you need, and the more you affirm your own values, the easier it is to resist the wants. But success doesn't come without effort. And it helps to meet people who know what you're going through.

Ellie Young knew very well. Once, she had epitomized the struggle not to differ from the Joneses, but to go them one better. Now, at the western end of a Malibu-powered journey from Virginia, she seemed a compelling example of how—even in a wealthy city—one can break out of the cycle of getting and spending and live better than before.

We met her in San Francisco. A mutual friend had suggested we get acquainted. Now Ellie Young sat yoga-style on her ottoman, unconvinced that she had anything to offer us. After all, until recently she had worked as an upscale tour guide and was accustomed on the job to luxurious hotels and haute cuisine. Last year she'd made what she considered a good sal-ary—$18,000—and with her promotion to sales manager, which included training and overseeing tour salespersons, she expected to make considerably more this year.

"Not that I would live differently if I made a lot of money," she said matter-of-factly. "Not the way I feel now."

It took hours, on a foggy afternoon, to find out what she meant. By then this petite, youthful woman of fifty-one had taken the chill out of her eight-by-twelve-foot basement room.

With the possible exception of a male companion (she is ambivalent on that point), Ellie has, she said, everything she needs to live well. She doesn't need a car—Bay Area trans-portation is better than adequate; and when she wants to get away for the weekend, she simply hops on a plane or rents some wheels. She doesn't need a TV set—in fact, she returned the one her boss gave her, explaining she'd watched it three times in three months.

"I'm very comfortable here," Ellie said. "I've found that I love a small space."

For $275 a month, utilities and laundry privileges in-cluded, Ellie rents her basement room with its separate outside entrance. In the adjacent laundry room, next to the washer-dryer, she keeps a microwave and minirefrigerator. Her land-lords and their teenage son, whom she rarely sees, live upstairs in the large, Spanish-style house in a posh neighborhood.

Ellie entertains guests in her room, though never more than two at a time. The spotless white walls are bare except for a painting of a sun-drenched wheat field; she keeps an electric heater and, in addition to the ottoman, a chair, a single bed, a small bedside table with photos of her three grown children, and wicker bookshelves.

"I know good renters and bad renters," Ellie said in her clear heartland tone. "And I am a good renter."

Ellie ought to know. In the late seventies and early eighties she and her ex-husband owned as many as thirteen rental units—duplexes, quadriplexes, singles. Their own quarters were more commodious. They lived in a "huge" house in Shell Rock, Iowa, a small town in the northeastern corner of the state, where Ellie's husband was a sales manager for a publishing firm and Ellie was a regional manager for a wholesale food sales company, working a seven-state territory.

Yet Ellie had become the sort of person Mark Twain was describing when he wrote, "He is now fast rising from affluence to poverty."

"We needed all the things that we thought we needed," Ellie said. "A large house, two fancy cars—and more of everything. So I thought that my major concern in life was to make more money. But I wasn't enjoying my life."

Then, in 1984, Ellie returned home one weekend to hear a guilt-ridden confession: her husband of twenty-seven years was having an affair with his tennis partner.

"I was just completely crushed," she told us. It was the beginning of a four-year trek to Ellie's basement room in San Francisco, a rocky, circuitous route with stops in Virginia, a much longer one in Colorado, and, finally, a few months back in Iowa. Things had changed in her absence. By then not only did her husband have a new girlfriend, but the value of the rental properties had dropped precipitously. Her estranged husband was, she said, "in deep financial trouble and there was no way to get out of it."

While still in Colorado, Ellie filed for divorce. Now, in a twist on the usual divorce-court tug-of-war for property, Ellie's husband vehemently insisted that as part of the settlement she retain half ownership, which would saddle her with half the debt. "I didn't want any of it," she said. "I didn't want the burden, and there was no way I could support it."

There was another, less tangible explanation for Ellie's opposition to her husband's demands. During her years in Colorado, when she'd managed an art shop in the Rockies, she had breathed the air of freedom. She had acquired a taste for living with fewer things and just a handful of clothes, no more than she could pack into two suitcases. She'd loved having time for herself, cherished her freedom of movement and choice.

"I found out a lot about myself when I moved away from the social structure I was in," Ellie said. "I realized I was just doing all that back in Iowa because I felt I had to. I didn't like to entertain. To have twenty people come to my house—it was just hell. I hated to go to the cocktail parties and stand around and try to act like you're having a good time when you're not. I had trouble with church, having to go in the Midwest. You had to wear your good clothes. I always thought, Why? It would be much better if you could get up and put on anything that you want to, then I might want to go. I didn't know I didn't like these things until I got out of it. I just thought it was life, that's the way life is."

When Ellie refused to don the old straitjacket of the rental properties, her husband retaliated. Since all the business problems, all the bills, were going to be his, she was to get nothing from the settlement, not even alimony. But he did not prevail: Ellie was awarded $400 a month alimony for life.

That was 1987. Ellie had read about a school in San Francisco that trained tour directors. She had an appetite for travel and new experiences, and she was a "people person." Putting most of her worldly possessions in storage for $32.50 a month and packing her trademark two suitcases, she boarded a plane for California. With money borrowed from her son, she enrolled in the school, graduated in a month, and landed a freelance job leading a tour to the Pacific Northwest. At a deli in San Francisco, Ellie had met our friend Sue Rickert, who had a room for rent. Later, when Sue's stepdaughter returned home and reclaimed her room, Ellie moved into her present quarters.

Ellie does have a few of what she called "luxuries." Her phone calls to her children push her total monthly tab as high as $70. She dines out with friends, goes to movies, takes weekend trips to the wine country or to Yosemite. "It's not that I'm cutting back to the bare necessities," she said. "I do things I want to do, but I don't have to pay for things that I don't need or don't want."

The conveniences she's given up, she said, are relatively insignificant. Because she has no car, she has to buy groceries in small amounts and walk them to the house. And sometimes, she said, she has to walk in the rain to and from the grocery store and the bus stop.

Despite her remarkably positive outlook, we wondered if Ellie ever doubted herself, if there was hidden regret in having downscaled to a basement room in San Francisco.

"Well, I'm beginning to realize that things just don't level out and become 'good,' " Ellie said. "You're never 'there.' But

I'm just so much happier now. Of course, my ex-husband thinks I'm crazy. Because he is very traditional in every sense of the word. And what people think about him is the utmost."

"What about your old friends?" Frank asked. Ellie had mentioned a recent trip back to Shell Rock.

Ellie smiled broadly. "When I went back to Iowa last time, it was wonderful. Before, I wanted to go back and be a part of my old life. Now I go back as a different person, secure in myself, just me. And of course they love it because they're in this little circle back there, and I can tell them all these things that I'm doing and what I'm thinking. And you can just feel them thinking, Oh, if I could just be out there and be free. And they think, I'm just tied here; I have all these problems and I have this big house and I have to pay for this and I have to pay for that. They're more secure—if you want to call it security. And they're making much more money than I am. And yet I do much more than most of them do. And I'm free."

As much progress as we thought we'd made, it was still hard for us not to envy Ellie Young on points that touched our lives as well. She has no car to maintain. She has no business debt to worry about, and by all appearances she feels no financial strain. Having always hated to cook for guests, she now does very little cooking, even for herself; her diet consists primarily of fresh fruits and vegetables, cereal, milk, and cheese. And much of the time she can go where she wants to go, do what she wants to do. All of these are freedoms purchased by trading the race with the Joneses for her own singular pace.

But Ellie was wrong in imagining that she had nothing to offer us. Hearing of her freedom from debt only strengthened our resolve to have the same freedom ourselves someday. And she made us think a little harder about possessions of any kind. How many *things*, really, did we need?

John Burroughs, the nineteenth-century naturalist, observed that "the number of things we can really make our own is limited. We cannot drink the ocean be we ever so thirsty. A cup of water from the spring is all we need."

Spending an afternoon with Ellie in her basement room, we felt the truth in Burroughs's observation. What matters day to day—for Ellie and for us—is not the number or status value of possessions, but the amount of pleasurable time a person is able to spend with them. Attentive ownership is one of the real measurements, not of a standard of living, but of a standard of life.

When not working, Ellie Young spends most of her time at home. And what she has "made her own" can be put on a short list: the ottoman, the bed and bedside table, the wicker bookshelves with books. And her white wicker chair, which she bought on sale at Pier One for $95.

"I didn't have a chair for a long time," she said. "It's just a little chair. But when I got it here I just stood and looked at it. I never had been more excited about any purchase. And I'd sit in it and think, Ah, this is so much more comfortable in here now to have a chair. It's amazing how your attitude changes about little things."

The majority of Ellie's worldly goods, in storage back in Iowa, goes all but forgotten. "I thought the other day, I don't know what's there, I can't remember," she told us. "Once in a while I'll think about something that's there. But not often."

Reflecting on the way Ellie relished her things, modest both in number and value, it seemed to us that our Malibu had never looked better. Without public transportation where we lived, we needed a car. But we also needed a spirit like Ellie's to remind us that what we have is sufficient. We didn't need a Honda Accord or even a new Chevy. What we needed most was sustained, appreciative attention to our belongings.

In thinking about our own lives, we were also struck by Ellie's recent encounters with her old friends in Iowa. In times past it's been hard for us to spend much time with people we thought were judging us for our possessions: our Rabbit, our used furniture. Their perceptions were capable of overpowering our own. In her visit to Iowa, Ellie had described herself as "a different person, secure in myself, just me." By her account, the perceptions of the people she visited no longer controlled her, as they had when she lived there, and being herself gave her pleasure. Ellie had sculpted her life to the size that fit her. Let others think what they would.

And the next time we drove the Malibu to the country club as a member's dinner guests, the next time we invited wealthy friends to sit down on our threadbare, secondhand couch, maybe we'd remember this remarkable woman in San Francisco.

If, like Ellie Young, there are those who opt out of life with the Joneses, and if, like hers, a good life with few possessions can be had in the city, there are also those who live far from the bright lights and blandishments of excessive consumption. Yet their rewards of freedom and contentment are strikingly similar to Ellie Young's.

In the woods of central Maine we visited a female couple who work as self-employed painters/carpenters/handywomen and whose privacy is so important to them that they asked to be identified only by the pseudonyms Dale and Terry. Wanda had known them casually for years, having first met them through her mother, who is a friend as well as a beneficiary of their services. In the nine and a half years Marie has owned her two-bedroom, 1920s house in Orono, just a five-minute walk from the University of Maine campus, this skillful team has refinished her oak floors, painted most of the walls, built a bookshelf, constructed outdoor steps, and hung wallpaper in her bedroom.

Dale and Terry make an arresting first impression. Dale is a short, plump, white woman who, though sparing with her words, laughs heartily and seems to take everything in; Terry is a taller, stockier, and more garrulous woman of color. Wearing the sloppy, mannish clothing that their vocation demands, Dale and Terry have a never-met-a-stranger manner, an infectious spirit of merriment and zest. It's not uncommon, they told us, for their clients to invite them over for dinner between fix-it jobs, to give them birthday and Christmas gifts, and even, occasionally, to write them a blank check for their services. That they are ex-nuns who lived in a convent is not surprising; they quickly engage and maintain one's trust.

We followed them thirty wintry miles out from Orono, where they had taken their clothes to a Laundromat, and swung by Marie's house to lead us to their home. Having first warned us about the frost heaves—ridgelike humps in the pavement formed by freezing and thawing—Terry proceeded to make light of them, bouncing down the backroads at high speed in their 1984 Mazda. When we arrived—our innards still churning—at their forty-acre spread, they unloaded their laundry onto a sled and tugged it a quarter of a mile over a packed snow trail, across a wooden bridge they built themselves, and through a birch-and-fir forest to their two-room cabin.

"It's an old hippie pad," Terry said, chuckling. "Believe it or not, two couples lived here." Inside, they introduced us to their three pets and gave us the grand tour, which was over almost as soon as it began. A tool room with two chain saws and an array of hand and power tools adjoined the combination kitchen/living room/bedroom. Old beams salvaged from a barn crisscrossed the ceiling. There was no indoor toilet, no running water, no electricity, and no telephone.

To some degree, this must have been what indoor life was like when the Levering family moved into Alex McMillian's cabin in our cove in February 1908. But the Leverings lived without benefit of the fiberglass insulation Dale and Terry had added here. We sat down beside a picture window that opened onto a clearing, where birds ate suet and seeds at no fewer than five feeders. Late afternoon sunlight dappled in through the fringe of trees. Logs crackled in the woodstove, and Dale served cups of the grain beverage Inka from water heated on top of the stove. We felt as warm and cozy as if we were sitting in our own living room.

Dale and Terry met in a convent years before, two proper Catholic sisters who fell in love and decided that remaining with the order was incompatible with the new directions their lives and loves were taking them. After leaving, they embarked on a secular life of social service on the south side of Chicago. It was the late sixties and early seventies, and, working for the government, they made a combined annual income of $23,000, which felt to them like money to burn.

"Both of us went to the convent at eighteen, nineteen years

old," said Terry, who grew up in a poor family in New Orleans. "We hadn't lived on our own. We bought cameras, tropical fish, went to movies. We hadn't experienced adulthood on our own." They applied for credit cards, used them often, and saved little.

After five years of what Dale called their "acquisitive phase," they grew dissatisfied with their lives, which seemed devoid of spiritual content. Attempts to find a new church home after the convent had failed; they had fallen away from organized religion.

Their disenchantment with a middle-class life was compounded by disillusionment with their jobs. "Seventy-five percent of our budget went to administration," said Terry, who was a case worker for Cook County Public Aid, counseling welfare recipients. "I realized that the people who were going to get off welfare were going to get off on their own anyway; the ones that wouldn't would be in the system for life." The welfare system, she said, "maintained a middle class—us, vendors, doctors."

After an extended vacation trip to Maine, where they were drawn to a widely scattered community of back-to-the-landers from the sixties and seventies, Dale and Terry returned to Chicago, paid off their credit cards, and cut them into pieces. Now they had a clear idea of what they wanted: land of their own and a new life.

"I wanted to live with the ebb and flow of life," Terry said. "The treadmill in Chicago was driving me up a tree. You had to segment your life. Every aspect of your life was slotted. You'll see no clocks here."

For less than a year Dale and Terry saved every second paycheck. Then, with over $5,000 in savings, they moved to

Portland, Maine, a way station en route to their forty acres. There, and later in Bangor, they saved more money while working in a shoe factory and a furniture store. When they wanted to be closer to the stimulation of a college community, they found work as janitors at the University of Maine.

Becoming a janitor wasn't easy. There were twenty-six janitors at the university, all of them men. "I don't think a woman can do this job," the male supervisor told Terry when both women applied.

"Why not?" Terry asked.

"Because this job requires a lot of heavy lifting. I don't think a woman can lift, say, a hundred and fifty pounds."

"I can," Terry replied.

"I weigh a hundred and sixty-five pounds," the supervisor said. "Do you think you can lift me?"

Terry proceeded not only to lift the man, but to carry him across the room. She nodded toward Dale. "She can do it, too."

That sort of spunk lies at the heart of Dale and Terry's life beyond the pale of the Joneses. In 1976 they bought the cabin and forty acres for $12,500 and have lived there so much on their own terms that some people, they said, are "intimidated" by them. "We know people who are afraid to come out here to visit us," Terry said. "We've had people we've worked for—doctors' wives, judges' wives—say they're very threatened by us, by our values." But she hastened to add: "We're not out to judge other people."

"We left proselytizing behind when we left the convent," Dale said.

Outside the picture window the sky turned to pewter and the sickle of a new moon hung over the silhouetted forest. Dale lit a kerosene lantern. In the amber glow it seemed that we had returned to a previous century, that soon the shaggy form of a wolf or a moose would stalk the edge of the clearing.

But what was striking to us, even more than this pristine setting, was how thoroughly these women's lives are organized around what they regard as the basics of good living. To a remarkable degree, Dale and Terry, now in their early fifties, are their own bosses. Without clocks in the house or watches on their wrists, they set their own daily work hours. The day we visited them, they'd just finished a job adding a deck to a house and planned to take two weeks off before starting their next job. This pattern repeats itself year-round, as they work roughly half time. "We schedule jobs eight to nine weeks in advance," Terry said, "to allow pockets of space for rejuvenation. When we do work, we average thirty-two hours a week." Most of the rest of the time they are free to pursue pleasure: to read voraciously—their favorite pastime; to work in their garden; to watch the birds and take walks in the woods; to attend lectures and concerts at the university; to listen to National Public Radio or watch public television on their battery-powered radio and TV.

That is a litany of simple pleasures many wealthier people would envy. "The fewer our wants," Socrates said, "the more we resemble the gods." By keeping their material life simple, Dale and Terry are able to resemble the gods at a bargain price. In 1980, when they started their business, they made $4,000. Now their income averages a mere $7,000 a year.

The latter figure is by design. "We only earn what we need to live," Terry said, "not what the market will bear." They charge $13 an hour for the two of them. With their services much in demand, they could easily command a higher rate, but so far, they have resisted. They pay no federal or state income taxes—and intend to keep it that way.

We had a dinner engagement with friends in Bangor. It was hard to go back into the cold, to leave two women who radiate contentment, like their cat purring beside the woodstove, even though our own contentment could never evolve from sources identical with theirs.

Some of the differences between us are easy to pinpoint. Dale and Terry insisted that they don't worry about saving money for future needs. We do worry about that. And they choose not to carry health insurance. Indeed, they have something of a fatalistic attitude about health care, a mind-set that would seem to hold to the conviction that if they live clean, simple, and joyful lives, illness will not befall them. "I'm going to live to be a hundred and five!" Terry exclaimed. If illness does strike, they will deal with it then. There are public health clinics and public assistance programs to help those living below the poverty line, they pointed out.

Unlike Dale and Terry, we do carry health insurance. While the premiums for self-employed folk seem outlandish— especially since we never "use" the insurance—nonetheless we don't feel comfortable going uninsured. Frightening things happen all too easily on a farm; an orchardist a mile away from us was killed in 1987 by the power takeoff on the back of his tractor. We're not at all prepared to drain all our resources— or someone else's—to cover expenses for serious accidents or illness. From a financial perspective, it seems to us that Dale and Terry's desire to live solely in the present works only as long as they are willing to accept the risks—and the generosity of society.

Other differences between us are subtler. The air was frigid, four degrees above zero, as Terry limned our route with a flashlight beam back to the Malibu. As we exchanged good-bye hugs, she presented us with an offering, a bumper sticker that read "Live Simply That Others May Simply Live."

Her gesture caught us by surprise. Was this an implied judgment of people like us, who spend and consume more than Terry and Dale? Or just a friendly gift, a kind of benediction for our visit? Presumably the wordplay refers to limiting one's use of natural resources—and who can argue with that? As Americans, we can't deny that we are consuming a disproportionate share of the earth's resources. But, alas—if only this dictum were simple to practice.

We drove slowly toward Bangor, braking for the ubiquitous frost heaves. Dale and Terry's life still seemed a testimonial to how little money one needs to carve out one's own niche, to how self-esteem does not necessarily correlate with income, savings, or net worth.

Clearly, they define themselves as being, in some sense, self-sufficient, apart from the world. Yet they are living in America and in the world. When washing their clothes at a Laundromat, they're using water and soap and electricity, resources drawn from a common pool; they're using roads that other people's taxes pay for; they're burning gasoline and kerosene. Should they become seriously ill, they'll gratefully use facilities and supplies other people's money has provided. Inevitably they cannot isolate their own choices—for good or for ill—from those of our society and other nations.

Moreover—in the sort of irony few adherents of simple

living can escape—they work for and take money from those who are not practitioners of their philosophy. Their success in part derives from others' willingness to consume freely. Their lives, like our own, as presently constructed, are sustained by a certain amount of social privilege.

Like Dale and Terry, we don't want to keep up with the Joneses. That is not the aspect of the "American dream"—or the vision of America or the world—that captivates us. But there is surely a middle ground between rejection of our consumer culture and all its values, and excessive consumption. To feed upon that culture, while denying its validity, seems to us an untenable contradiction. To oppose excess, while practicing material restraint and paying taxes for what one uses, seems a balanced course. Precisely what "material restraint" means is for every person to define, guided both by conscience and by the direct rewards of personal freedom.

Ultimately, privatism—what some would call escapism—in its various forms is not the life for us. In our twin professions of writing and farming, we are, inevitably, engaged with society and must acknowledge our dependencies. But we are glad to have visited Dale and Terry. Like Ellie Young, they puncture the pervasive myth—destructive both to individuals and to our culture—that only riches can buy freedom. As other "extremists" have done—Jesus, Thoreau, and Mother Theresa among them—they hold before us the dream of a better, more equitable world, an ethical standard that only cynics can fully reject.

Dale and Terry denied that they ever proselytize. Perhaps they don't. But they did offer us the invaluable gift of challenge. In a sense, the idealism of their thinking and that of their bumper sticker are closely aligned. The widening gyres of keeping up with the Joneses *are* destructive of limited natural resources. Ultimately they may well prove to be destructive not only of resources, but of our ability to live in peace with other societies. Or to live at all. By now the causal link between excessive consumption and environmental degradation is hardly a secret. The scourge of keeping up with our immediate neighbors now has global repercussions.

In the Blue Ridge, we're fortunate to have family and friends who in varying degrees share our perspective. In daily life, being a lone wolf is not as much fun as it appears in two-hour movies.

For almost any American, we suspect, the "wants" never altogether stop flickering in the mind's eye. We're no exception. We would fail even if we could block out most advertising, stop watching TV or listening to the radio, stop reading magazines and newspapers—even if we exhorted ourselves to do the right thing from the pulpits in our brains.

Over time, there's no substitute for developing a feeling of comfort with yourself, your own priorities and values, with your own psychic scales weighing needs and desires. That's where Ellie Young, Dale and Terry, and many other people we know have it right. That's where keeping up with the Joneses is no trick at all.

CHAPTER SIX

Frugality

In the chilly months, our La-Z-Boy recliner and our rocking chair sit side by side in the kitchen, facing the woodstove. Most nights after dinner, glancing from time to time at the fire through the woodstove's window, we read on them by the light of a lamp. Though we paid almost nothing for them, they are the two most seductive chairs we've ever had.

One Saturday afternoon, while poking through the little town of Radford, Virginia, we found the La-Z-Boy in a used-furniture store. It was an off-white recliner that—while otherwise well cared for—had been charred by a cigarette. Wanda sank onto it, then stretched far back, the foot pedestal separating her feet from the floor. The chair enveloped her. On this island of velour pleasure she would gladly tackle *Anna Karenina* in one sitting. The chair cost $25 "as is," declared the owner, who seemed surprised that anyone wanted it and grateful that we would haul it off in our pickup. At home we draped a hand-woven Peruvian wool blanket—a gift from Wanda's father—over most of the chair, hiding the scar, and tussled over who got to use the La-Z-Boy more until we'd found a companion for it.

Frank didn't want another La-Z-Boy; he wanted a rocking chair. One day in October, en route to Charlottesville, we stopped to see a man we know at an antique store north of Roanoke. In the back of our truck were four dining table chairs—low-back, Art Deco chairs from the 1930s that we had bought, along with a dining table, in Los Angeles. We'd never felt comfortable in them but only recently had replaced them with more hospitable chairs purchased at a furniture salvage store. We hoped to find a rocker and engage in the popular Appalachian pastime of horse trading.

Inside the ramshackle store was just the thing Frank was looking for: an oak, mission-style rocker from the turn of the century, with a slatted back and bent arms. We tried it out: it felt sturdy and rocked like the proverbial cradle. After a lot of talk about the weather and other neutral topics—and, at last, a close inspection of our chairs and some hypercritical remarks on their condition, Larry hemmed and hawed and allowed that an even swap might be all right this one time. From a strictly monetary standpoint, though he'd made it sound as though he were doing us a big favor, the odds were that he was getting the better end of the deal. But we enjoyed the bartering game. And without spending any extra money for it, we—especially Frank—have since logged countless hours on the rocker.

"I may not be rich," Frank's thirty-year-old niece, Teresa Van Hoy, once told us, "but I am resourceful." Those words— delivered with Teresa's patented southern drawl—have stuck to our ribs like one of Ben Franklin's proverbs. Like Teresa, who is an elementary school teacher, we've tried to learn ways to stretch our dollars, here in Virginia and in our travels. We've also learned just how much fun it is to be bargain hunters, to buy on sale and in bulk, to haunt thrift stores and resale shops,

yard sales and remnant houses. We go out of our way to find
the sport—even the adventure—in being frugal.

One of our favorite destinations remains the flea market in
Galax, Virginia. For years we've been exploring the cavernous
space, once a church sanctuary, subdivided into dimly lit side
rooms, with chicken-wire walls and doors that could be pad-
locked but never are. All sorts of dusty junk nestles in the
gloom, and you have to dig through disintegrating boxes and
amorphous piles to find treasure, as if from a time capsule. A
plastic hood hair dryer from the 1960s might rest precariously
atop a metal tea cart or typewriter table, surrounded by empty
carafes, stacks of ancient women's magazines, assorted glass-
ware, and an old Allen Drury novel.

Along a rear wall, retirement-age men chew tobacco, puff
cigarettes, and ponder the images on an old black-and-white
TV. When the time of reckoning comes, Hobart, the sixtyish
proprietor, rises to tally the purchases, scratching the tip of his
pencil on a paper bag. There's no license to dicker—Hobart's
assessment is as final as Judgment Day. "Well," he declares,
tugging at the brim of his felt hat and studying the occasional
item that has no price tag, "I'm gonna need fifty cents for that,
I reckon." Whatever the unticketed item, Hobart's verb and
tense remain the same: he's "gonna need" X amount of money.

At times we use the flea market like a dry goods store,
coming in expressly for certain standard items. When, for
instance, we switched from buying milk in plastic throwaway
jugs to mix-your-own powdered milk in cardboard boxes, we
came in search of glass pitchers. We found at least half a dozen,
of which we purchased two—one for $1.50 and the other for
$4.00. The cheaper one was from the 1960s with psychedelic
yellow daisies dancing around its bright blue base. The other

was burnt-orange carnival glass, which of the two makes a sleeker presentation but holds less liquid. Having two pitchers allows us to wash one while pressing the other into service.

Among the other purchases have been occasional chairs, plastic kitchen bowls, and glass milk quart jars for flower vases. For $12 we bought a hand-planed wooden washstand. And God knows how many books have made their way home along the Blue Ridge Parkway from the Galax flea market.

Certain items that we need, like computer-printer ribbons, aren't available just anywhere—certainly not at the flea market! Rather than getting frustrated because we have to drive an hour south to Winston-Salem to replace an indispensable tool of our trade, we've adopted another posture—that of anticipation. We are less likely to run out of computer ribbons now than in Los Angeles because we stockpile them.

In addition to Galax and Winston-Salem, we shop in Mount Airy and Pilot Mountain, North Carolina, as well as in Hillsville, Cana, and Pulaski, Virginia. Although the distances are farther, the drive time is probably no greater to disparate destinations than in Los Angeles. And the custom of this region—in many ways a throwback to the past—makes even routine shopping a pleasure compared with the experience in the faceless malls of California. Here you can establish relationships with merchants, some of whom still extend no-interest charge accounts for which no plastic card is issued. They remember your face, not your number, and many keep accounts by paper.

Of clothes, William Penn wrote: "The more plain and simple they are, the better: neither unshapely, nor fantastical; and for use and decency, and not for pride."

While sharing to some extent the sentiments of the founder of Pennsylvania, we have to admit that we also like clothes that have a little pizzazz; plainness alone seems no cardinal virtue. But we do like to buy good clothes inexpensively. At the Salvation Army store in Mount Airy, Frank regularly buys used jeans, shirts, and sweaters. On our last trip to New York, he packed two of the three brightly colored wool sweaters, purchased for two dollars apiece at the store, and wore them to business meetings. Almost new, to all appearances, when he bought them, these sweaters should last for years. In Pulaski, along with a minor league baseball team, the Pulaski Braves, we've discovered a quality used-clothing store for women that carries contemporary items along with some vintage stuff. Wanda has purchased silk scarves, cotton turtleneck pullovers, and silk-and-wool-blend sweaters for a fraction of the price of the items when new.

Magazine and newspaper subscriptions can be surprisingly costly. And what's the point of subscribing to all those publications if you just aren't getting them read? In the past eighteen months we've cut the number of subscriptions from seven to four—still a high tide of verbiage flooding the house, but one in which at least we can (barely) swim. Friends who made a similar reduction report that they now schedule visits to the periodical room at the Winston-Salem Public Library. Though we only occasionally follow suit, we like the idea.

Now if only we can apply the same read-it-or-don't-buy-it standards to the books we buy! Frank's the guiltier party. "I'll read it one of these days," he protests lamely when Wanda points toward an unread book gathering dust on the shelf.

To atone for his spendthrift ways as a book buyer, Frank gets his hair cut for four dollars at the same barber shop in

Mount Airy where Sam and Garnet Dawson go. He's long since given up on asking for a "medium" cut. The barber, an eighty-four-year-old gentleman who still works long days (and tells salty stories), knows two ways to cut hair: very short and United States Marine. Frank settles for the "very short" cut, reasoning that the Orioles baseball cap he wears away from the house will cover any embarrassment until his hair grows out again to an acceptably shaggy length.

In our travels we've talked with people who trade or reciprocate services to save money. At a place called Eco-Home in Los Angeles, we learned of a network of people on the West Coast who swap services ranging from computer training to plumbing. In Maine, Dale and Terry told us that they do carpentry work in exchange for medical services. Here at the orchard, Sam trades his work grading and selling apples with fellow orchardists every fall. In exchange for complicated mechanical work at which he is no master, Frank has several times worked in a neighbor's packhouse. In addition to saving money, these kinds of swaps help build friendships.

A dear friend once told Wanda that giving a gift away brought bad luck, but Wanda doesn't buy it. Surely it's the spirit of the gift that counts, the sort of spirit embodied by the Amish, who traditionally have not attached the name of the gift giver to wedding gifts. But sometimes that feeling is hard to conjure when faced with gift-giving occasions. Marrying into Frank's large family, Wanda soon got the impression that we— and since this usually fell on her, she—had to come up with a gift every two weeks: holidays, graduations, birthdays, weddings, and now, heaven help her, anniversaries. In order to escape viewing gift giving as an endless (and depressing) exercise in materialism, Wanda adopted the idea of a gift "war" chest, filled with things bought in quantity or on sale and kept tucked away in drawers for future use, things bought in after-Christmas sales for use the following year.

In Wanda's family wrapping paper has always made more than one run, often lasting years. The stuff is surprisingly durable, if you're willing to overlook a few wrinkles (or disguise them with ribbon or recycled Christmas cards). Now Wanda keeps old bows and ribbon in grocery bags and cuts off the tattered ends to make them fresh again. When gifts are opened Christmas morning, we bring out two grocery bags: one for paper to be saved for next year and the other for paper (at last!) to be sent to its final resting place.

When we first moved to Virginia, the idea of recycling gifts seemed an actionable affront that Wanda's mother-in-law engaged in shamelessly. Miriam told a joke about some pine soap that circulated in the family for years with such gusto that Wanda couldn't help but hear it as an endorsement. Her grandchildren—Frank's nieces and nephews—kidded about how many times they'd received copies of *The Good Times Song Book*—and speculated that their grandmother had picked them up overstock at a church book sale. When Wanda gave her in-laws a gift, she watched to see if it would disappear, perhaps destined for someone else's Christmas tree.

With the many occasions back east in which gifts were expected, we began to see the benefit of putting gifts, as Frank liked to joke—borrowing a screenwriter's expression—"into turnaround." After all, as the recipient of more than a few such items ourselves, we figured two could play this game. So when Frank received a wall photograph that we didn't care to hang, Wanda rewrapped it and passed it along to a couple who'd invited us to their wedding. We didn't feel so bad about it:

Wanda had never met the bride or groom, and if he had, Frank couldn't recall when!

The question becomes thornier when giving to close friends and family. But from our experience, almost everyone willingly deescalates the level of giving—as long as you send the first signal. If you give an inexpensive, token gift to someone, it enables him or her to give you something of equal value. Gift giving, after all, is a reciprocal exchange. Wanda gives writer friends subscriptions to the *Utne Reader*. She gave her pregnant sister a subscription to *Parenting* magazine as a birthday present. Her friend Liz Brody likes giving experiential presents, such as tickets to movies, plays, and concerts.

Downscaling gift giving has worked for us. We aren't givers of extravagant gifts, nor are we recipients of extravagant ones. The simple gifts we give and receive seem appropriate for us. Several of our wedding gifts come to mind: a clear plastic napkin holder, a set of beige cloth napkins, a French cookbook. One old Wesleyan friend of Frank's, now a Cleveland artist, presented us with one of her paintings—she'd sent us several slides from which to select our favorite—and she delivered it five years after the big date on a southern vacation trip with her fiancé. On a recent, memorable wedding invitation, a friend and his bride-to-be declined gifts in advance, suggesting that anyone so moved might deliver and share a bottle of wine with the newlyweds when next in town.

Michael Van Hoy, Frank's oldest nephew, told us about a gift exchange in which he'd participated one Christmas in Philadelphia. People brought in gifts they didn't want, couldn't use, or didn't fit, and they had a kind of swap meet and party. Everyone came away happy, Michael said. Things were recycled and ended up with people who wanted them rather than in the great trash heap.

Of all the ways in which it's possible to be frugal, food may be the category most likely to escape notice. Perhaps because most of us buy food in some form almost every day, we tend to think of those transactions as an unalterable fact of life, as absolute necessity. In fact, if we're willing to sacrifice convenience, many food purchases are not necessary at all.

One of the most obvious ways to shrink a hefty food bill is to pack food for the workplace, school, or trip rather than relying on restaurants and cafeterias. Since we no longer go to school and don't work away from home, the one thing we can do is brown-bag it on our frequent day trips, discovering along the way that cheese sandwiches with homegrown tomatoes and lettuce taste just as good as, if not better than, a burger at McDonald's.

Not that dining out is a felony. Once in a while on the road, we'll stop at a fast-food place to eat—the point is, doing it all the time can add up to some real money. The same is true of restaurants around home. In Los Angeles our monthly restaurant tab could make us wince. Nowadays we still like to go out occasionally, but we try to make it a special occasion—an anniversary, a celebration of finishing the cherry harvest. The fact that our restaurant visits are infrequent makes the experience of dining out more special, too.

More than we ever thought possible in California, we've come to relish home cooking. In Los Angeles, when we weren't eating out, more likely than not we'd be eating a Lean Cuisine or Budget Gourmet frozen dinner. We were aware of, but tried to ignore, the long list of preservatives and additives on the box flap, and we knew that given the small size of the pouch or tray servings, we weren't getting much grub for our buck. Still, cooking always took last priority.

These days we take time to cook healthful meals while continuing to observe an urban-style eight o'clock dinner hour. In the summer and early fall there are plenty of fresh vegetables to be had from the garden just below our asparagus patch: tomatoes, beets, collard greens, string beans, summer squash, radishes, lettuce, sweet corn. Year-round, Frank is the salad man. Because he likes salads so much, almost every night he finds himself chopping vegetables and washing lettuce. Every month or so he makes a wreck of the kitchen by concocting a huge pot of onion, tomato, and mushroom, heavily garlicked pasta sauce, which we freeze in pint boxes. With somewhat more finesse, Wanda does the same with big batches of vegetarian lasagna.

When we feel like having something exotic, Wanda whips up a pot of *bigos,* a Polish hunter's stew. She also makes chicken and fish dishes along with turkey burgers and, very occasionally, steaks. For reasons ranging from our consciences to our pocketbooks, we've cut back sharply on meat consumption, often going vegetarian for weeks. Raised a meat-and-potatoes girl, Wanda has surprised herself by developing an appetite for rice heaped with spicy fifteen-bean soup. Lately she's been soaking beans overnight and making large pots that are good for a week's worth of lunches.

Being fruit growers as well as frugivorous (fruit-eating) creatures, we were intrigued to learn that the words *frugal* and *fruit* derive from the same Latin root. This ancient link between fruit and frugality still holds for our customers, who save money by buying fruit at the source, often in bushel-or-more quantities. (At ten dollars a bushel, for example, customers are buying apples for twenty-five cents a pound, an unheard-of price even in the cheapest supermarkets.) This link also holds for us—the only fruits we buy at a store are bananas and, occasionally, oranges. In June, unless the crops have been killed by spring freezes, we have all manner of sweet and sour cherries, as well as red raspberries and blueberries; in July, apricots and summer apples; in August, peaches, nectarines, and Damson and Stanley plums; in the fall, seven main varieties of apples, including the Crispin Mutsu, a grapefruit-size, green-gold apple developed in Japan. During these months, these fresh fruits and berries heavily supplement our diet, and when there's time, we freeze them and make preserves for gifts and home use. Up at the Red House, in addition to doing more freezing and preserve making than we ever seem to get done, Miriam makes her famous fruit compote—a chilled, slightly sweetened mixture of all the fruits and berries that has been known to transport house guests to Valhalla.

As frugal with food as we imagine we are, we're no match for Sam. Few Americans are, at least not voluntarily. Two meals a day—breakfast and lunch—Sam eats nothing but cereal, milk, and applesauce. Only at dinner does he yield to Miriam's more sumptuous fare. In the spirit of Thoreau, who proudly itemized his food costs at Walden Pond, Sam can give you a pretty good idea of how much these first two meals of the day set him and Miriam back.

Twice a year or so, Sam drives his rattling Ford Escort to the Statesville (North Carolina) Milling Company to pick up a hundred-pound sack of raw wheat, bagged directly from the wheat field. At six cents a pound, that's six dollars for the bag, plus maybe another six in gas money for the round trip. Back home, he pours the wheat as needed into a grinder in the woodshed behind the Red House and turns the crank, then cooks the wheat in a double boiler. Three-quarters of a pound of wheat is enough for two meals, he says. Not counting the electricity needed for cooking, at six cents a pound that's less than a nickel spent on wheat for two meals. Add the cost of powdered milk—he uses about a pint a day, which comes to ten cents—and he's up to the lordly sum of fourteen cents. Add the cost of raising the apples for the applesauce, plus a little sugar, and the percentage of the total refrigeration costs for the milk and the applesauce, plus the gas money divided by days of the year, and surely you're looking at no more than thirty cents for two meals. That's fifteen cents for breakfast, ditto for lunch.

What Sam's meals lack in haute cuisine, they make up for in nutrition. And the flavor's not half-bad. When Frank was in his twenties, Sam methodically blended the wheat with ground soybeans, and the results, while richer in amino acids than wheat alone, were a gastronomical dismal swamp. Sam's boglike cereal was notorious around the family for its lip-curling taste, and even its creator and lone champion (Sam never by-passed an opportunity to tout the virtues of the stuff), after years of proving his mental and physical toughness, had to flee to "higher" culinary ground.

Just recently, swayed not by basketball star Michael Jordan and other Wheaties pitchmen, but by Sam's incontrovertible evidence that Wheaties cost $2.52 a pound (compare that with $.06 a pound for raw wheat of at least equal nutritional value, probably better because it's full of bran and fiber), we've been accepting his weekly gifts of "Sam's cereal," hand-delivered to our kitchen counter in microwave-safe containers. What else can we do? These gifts are full of Sam's love for us, harder to express in words than in wheat, full of his hope that we will live as long as he and maybe do the world some good, as he has. Eating his cereal, we love him back. What's more, once microwaved and topped with applesauce, milk, and a sprinkling of brown sugar, Sam's cereal is a tasty breakfast.

But we do draw the line at eating the stuff again for lunch. Surely there's something to be said for a little variety in the menu, a fine point lost on Sam, whose mind often dwells on loftier matters. At lunchtime, our own minds dwell on the transition to Wanda's beans.

One evening Frank sat on the rocking chair reading a magazine when a statistic seemed to jump off the page. The average in-town cost of travel in New York City for businesspeople in 1989 was $312 a day, he announced, whistling through his teeth. That broke down to $163 for a hotel room, $75 for food, and $74 for car rental.

"What do our trips cost us?" he wanted to know. Since moving east, we've managed, on average, two New York trips a year. They are business trips, arranged around meeting editors, with the occasional play slipped in. Frank knew in advance that we had beaten the national average, but the question was by how much. Fifty, a hundred dollars, or more daily? Wanda dashed upstairs to check our tax files.

There she found records of our two trips, one in January and the other in November. She discounted the first trip with its artificially deflated cost: that time we apartment-sat for a friend. The second—four full days in New York, including garaging our car; taxi, bus, and subway fares; lodging; meals; and miscellaneous expenses—came to a total of $576 for the two of us. The price worked out to $72 a person a day, or over four times cheaper than the businesspeople surveyed. And this cost was typical, if not somewhat high, for our trips.

For starters, we're living cheaper in New York by buying bagels for breakfast and sandwiches for lunch and bringing them back to our room, avoiding high-priced restaurants—and by walking or taking the subway as often as possible instead of a taxi. But the biggest saving is in lodging that is far less expensive than that of the average businessperson. And of course two can sleep cheaper than one. We stay at the Leo House, a homey, unassuming Catholic hospice run by the Sisters of St. Agnes on West 23rd Street, which welcomes guests of all faiths, barring only unmarried members of the opposite sex sharing the same room. Because we have different last names, we were required to present a copy of our marriage certificate when we first checked in. Even the computer seemed skeptical about our legitimacy as a two-name couple and has mistakenly identified us ever since as Mr. and Mrs. Frank Urbanski.

After the manner of an old-style girls' dormitory, guests can entertain outside visitors in the first- and second-story lounges but are not permitted to bring them to their rooms. Our clean, simple room, with twin beds, toilet, sink, and a sliver of a closet, costs $55 a night; the bathtub and shower are down the hall. Wall-mounted telephones in each room take incoming calls but will not place outgoing calls. It's a service that might not suit everyone, but it works for us.

In part because the city is so frenetic and we find it easy to be sucked into that mode, we try to pad time around each appointment or event to create a cushion of unhurry when we travel there. We leave time to make calls and pick up callback messages at the switchboard. We take a few minutes so that if one of the two pay phones in the lobby is in use when we need it, we can wait without growing anxious, or if someone else in line for a phone appears in greater need than we, we can surrender the telephone. When we lived in Los Angeles we often ran late for dates, but when in New York we make it a point to arrive everywhere early, thus reducing the stress and heightening the pleasure of a new place.

The Leo House is not the Plaza or the Waldorf, but we feel comfortable there. And though its address impresses no one, it makes trips to New York within our reach, financially and emotionally.

We do know whereof we speak. We have tasted the Plaza. Actually it wasn't the Plaza, but we supposed it wasn't too far off. After staying with friends in Louisiana, we decided to spring for a fancy hotel in New Orleans's French Quarter. It was Wanda's first visit to the famous city, and in her fantasy she saw streets crawling with horse-drawn carriages, heard Cajun fiddlers, and savored the sharp, wafting smells of Creole cuisine—things that could be found only in the heart of the French Quarter.

We spent much of the afternoon checking out the hotels for our splurge, scouting out the perfect room. Once we signed in, there was the bellboy and at dinner the waiter to tip and the perpetual obligation to look presentable, even when strolling through the lobby. After dinner and a brief walk through the French Quarter, we returned to our room, determined to get our money's worth. But by now we were exhausted. Instead of feeling refreshed by luxury, we'd pressured ourselves from the start to have the "perfect" experience. The results made us feel stale, anxious to leave.

The next day we drove through Texas and on into the wee hours west of San Antonio, feeling liberated in our return to the open road. Frank steered the Malibu into a roadside rest area and we stretched out on the car bench seats for a deep sleep.

When we described this juxtaposition between the luxury of our hotel and vehicular camping to our friend Ellen Hoffs—herself a traveler who favors the simple experience—she observed with a laugh that we'd crossed over the line. "When I've spent eighty dollars on a hotel, I'll try to find a cheaper place the next day, too. But never would I stay in a rest area. That I know I won't do."

"It's uplifting in its way," Wanda responded. "And when Frank starts to drive at seven in the morning, I continue to lie in bed!"

Why it's uplifting is a tantalizing question. Have we become so enamored of frugality that we enjoy sleeping in the car more than a luxurious hotel? Apparently so, for we haven't slept in a fancy hotel since, but we have, three times, in the Malibu. That night in west Texas our senses were fully alive before we fell asleep: stars glittered through the windows, and the wind smelled of desert plants. For the first time in her life, Wanda heard the eerie keening of coyotes talking to each other. And though it wasn't a long night's sleep, even Motel 6 couldn't beat the rates.

Truth is, as the night in west Texas would suggest, over the past few years we've come to expect that frugal travel, at least for us, will be more spontaneous, more adventurous. It's an active, not passive, experience, a vivid alternative to the guided tour. Travel can be a way of getting outside yourself, of preventing cultural myopia from setting in. Contrary to the myth that spending tons of money enhances travel, in fact, such lavishness can insulate you from other people and from the natural world. The way we like to travel, we've discovered, is a pretty good metaphor for the way we like to live.

In the fall of 1987, after a year and a half at the orchard without a vacation, we joked to each other that the only foreign vacation we could afford would be in Eastern Europe. The joke soon became reality.

When we journeyed to Poland that December for the Christmas and New Year's season to visit with Wanda's first and second cousins (whom she hadn't seen in ten years and whom Frank had never met), we shunned hotel accommodations in favor of sleeping on couches in tight apartments and touring the country through natives' eyes. The price for getting close enough to a foreign culture to see the reality of day-to-day life was waiting in line behind five persons to brush our teeth and use the toilet or driving around western Poland in a crowded Polski Fiat.

We flew into Berlin the weekend before Christmas and, after touring West Berlin by day, took an afternoon train to Poznan, home of Grzegorz Urbanski, Wanda's first cousin, a physician, husband, and father of two young children. The West Berlin train station was packed with Polish laborers, who worked and lived temporarily in both East and West Germany and were returning home for the holidays loaded down with all manner of consumer goods: enormous color televisions, VCRs, and bags full of gifts. It was pure chaos trying to press our bodies and luggage into the train. After the short ride into East Berlin, we changed trains in a bewildering maze of tracks and platforms. Luckily we met an educated, English-speaking Polish woman named Biata, traveling the same route, who steered us to the right train.

Once there, she squeezed us into a compartment crammed with jolly Polish workers who were passing around a bottle of vodka. Delighted to have two Americans aboard, they toasted our health and offered us sips. Knowing no English, they were patient with Wanda's Polish, unlike the educated Poles who, out of some combination of politeness and desire for self-improvement, would invariably switch to English. More frequently, Biata, an assistant director at a theater in Hamburg, served as translator. In this cheek-by-jowl fashion, enjoying no more comfort than an ordinary Pole, we rode for six hours until arriving at Poznan.

By not cushioning ourselves in the luxuries of our culture, by electing nonstatus, low-cost travel (a two-hundred-mile train ticket cost us the equivalent of two dollars), we avoided some sanitized version of the Polish experience. At the same time we were able to take advantage of opportunities created in the United States. We spent two days with Kasia Gintowt-Bajon in Warsaw—the woman who drove with Frank across the United States in May of 1987—and her husband, Filip, a prominent film director in Poland, whose newly released film, *Magnet*, we saw in a theater in Warsaw. We attended a New Year's Eve party in a festively appointed Krakow *piwnica* (wine cellar); met a schoolboy friend of Wanda's father, an actual prince who lived in a virtual museum to his noble family; and, for the *Los Angeles Times*, Wanda interviewed Tadeusz Konwicki, one of Poland's foremost writers, in his Warsaw apartment.

During our stay in Krakow, our host's cousin, a cabdriver, took us on two day-long round trips: one to Zakopane, where the unseasonably warm weather had melted the famous ski slopes, and the other to Auschwitz. His charge for the trips were $20 and $15, respectively.

Pawel, our Krakow host, reluctantly accompanied us on the excursion to the death camp. For Pawel, who was a young boy when Poland was invaded in 1939, Auschwitz was the source of recurring nightmares that were grounded in the reality of close family tragedy. His Polish Catholic aunt was among its earliest victims. "If they had had their way, they would have killed all us Poles," he told us, bracing himself before entering the gates. "That's what they intended."

Indeed, at Auschwitz we learned—something little known in the United States—that the camp was used exclusively for ethnic Poles until late 1942; that more than a million of the approximately four million killed there were non-Jews. No matter what the ethnicity or religion of its victims, however, the most poignant reminder of the Auschwitz tragedy for us were the remnants of snuffed-out life: the aging mountains of boots, hair, and antique eyeglasses.

The trip was emotionally and physically exhausting, at times harrowing, but nonetheless spectacular. Frank saw for the first time communist Eastern Europe in its last days before collapse. He met peers in age and education whose own daily struggles for food, drink, gasoline, and clothing put his own disappointments into perspective. For us both, it was the kind of travel we like best—reality, not fantasy travel.

Beyond the glaring material deprivations of the Polish people was the range of human experience—so often lacking in our consumer culture: the intensity of focus on history, politics, the arts, family, and spiritual life. While it would be presumptuous to argue that Polish want is superior to American over-abundance, it struck us nonetheless how often these people manage to create joyous lives given their circumstances, and that we had much to learn from them.

Malcolm L. "Mac" Hunter, Jr., proves Rudyard Kipling's maxim "He travels the fastest who travels alone." Kipling might have added, "And without excess baggage." A thirty-nine-year-old professor of wildlife at the University of Maine, Mac has trotted the globe for much of his adult life, pursuing such far-flung goals as working to preserve biological diversity and to promote wildlife conservation and the sustainable use of natural resources. He has conducted conservation research in eighteen foreign countries, among them India, Iran, Zaire, Poland, Finland, New Zealand, and Greece. When we visited his primitive log cabin home on the Penobscot River in tiny Milford, Maine, Mac had just returned from a recent three-week trip to Nepal and was unpacking the backpack—closer in size to a large knapsack—that contained the sum total of his belongings. He usually checks the backpack through on the plane and takes his camera equipment and research papers with him in a small carry-on case.

"I always wear khaki-colored clothing because it doesn't show dirt," he said, sheepishly trotting out a grungy pair of pants to illustrate the point. He pulled out a Peruvian wool tie. "I'd received a cable telling me, 'Please be sure to bring a tie,' " he said, laughing. "They know how I usually dress." A water canteen, sandals, shirts, underwear, jacket, and socks rounded out his belongings. Mac showed off an emergency/utility kit containing a flashlight, matches, first-aid kit, sewing kit, candles, compass, paper clips, elastic bands, pencils, a one-dollar bill, a quarter, a dime, a small lock, a pair of sunglasses, duct tape, masking tape, and regular tape. "I carry this everywhere. When I'm driving to campus, it goes on the front seat of my car."

When Wanda first met Mac in 1974, he had just won a Rhodes scholarship from the University of Maine to study zoology at Oxford—the first Rhodes scholar selected from the university in forty years. Despite the honor, Mac possessed a somewhat limited knowledge of travel, as he is the first to admit. He remembers transporting ten wooden crates to England that fall, most of which contained his library. "Fifty percent of those books, I never opened," he admitted. "Now I'm tempted to travel with practically no clothing, but you need more. You get invited out to the ambassador's house or something, and I've been in the position of having to go and buy clothes."

A trick to carrying a minimal wardrobe is knowing how to launder under any circumstances. "Put soap on the clothes and while you're taking a shower, jump up and down. Wash them, wring 'em out, and hang them up to dry."

Two weeks after we visited Mac in Maine, we took our trip to Mississippi, Louisiana, and points west—a journey that lasted more than a month. In contrast with many previous trips, this time, directly influenced by Mac, we decided to travel as lightly as possible. So we limited ourselves to one medium-size suitcase apiece for clothes, plus a briefcase for reading and writing materials. The results set the standard for subsequent trips of any length: one suitcase apiece, period. It makes travel far less cumbersome; rather than having piles of things to choose from that become obstacles to easy movement, we take just a few things to use over and over. Less luggage gives us a stream-lined feeling that carries over into the spirit of the place and of being frugal. Travel light, we tell ourselves, or don't travel at all.

In the years we've been together, our thinking about money has not evolved painlessly. When Wanda moved in with Frank in 1980, he was living in a run-down duplex in Venice Beach, for which the rent was $225 a month. It was the kind of place you could call a hole, and it quite literally had one—in the bathroom floor, large enough for a terrier to climb through into the earthen crawl space beneath. (We nailed a piece of unpainted plywood over it.) Frank had lived on borrowed money for part of 1979 and, although he was driving a cab by the time Wanda moved in with him, was still borrowing from friends and family in the conviction that his screenplays were bound to hit the jackpot. Time was on his side, he reasoned. He was not so much extravagant with himself as he was extravagant with his dream.

When Wanda entered the scene, she quickly fell into the role of money prude, parting with cash reluctantly, stressing the need to generate income. She allowed that although Frank's screenplays might hit it big one day, he should cover his expenses till that moment arrived. Recognizing her own need for steady employment, she embarked on a job search that led her to the *Los Angeles Herald-Examiner*.

Still unwed, we recorded our every expense in a ledger book: each bag of groceries, every gas bill, even quarts of milk, which we would eventually divide right down the middle. But when we decided to pool resources in a common pot, those accounts were abandoned. As months passed our battles over the buck grew less frequent and less heated. Frank grew scrappier, more aggressive about pursuing screenwriting and other work. He solicited newspaper assignments and took steady freelance work for a corporate newsletter. In time, having the additional pressure of repaying $6,400 in loans, he came to regret having ever borrowed money in the first place and wondered how he could have done it, having always loathed the feeling, growing up, of being chronically in debt at the orchard.

As much as lavish spending, borrowed money can be the bane of frugality. At least in his profession, the trouble with borrowing, Frank realized, was that it created the illusion of prosperity, that money wasn't all that important because there was plenty of it to be had. It was reality deferred. And so, Frank spent money he didn't have—until the accounts came due.

"I can see you're not new-car people," the man said, taking in the Malibu—now splashed with roadside mud and wintry slush—on his rural Mount Vernon, Maine, driveway. He spoke approvingly, motioning with an over-the-shoulder glance toward his 1982 Datsun. Dressed in a red plaid shirt, jeans, suede moccasins, and thick wool socks, red-bearded Russell Libby looked the very picture of the rugged outdoors Maine man. The looks weren't deceiving. Russell and Mary Anne Libby had intentionally stretched their salad days into years, and the payoff was a piece of earth and a self-designed house where they could raise a family and eventually, they hope, enough food to supply all their home use.

The Maine Protestant and the Ohio Catholic paired up in

1980, married in 1982, and embarked on an ambitious life plan that has already borne fruit. During the first four years of their marriage, the couple lived off Mary Anne's paycheck as a medical librarian and were able to deposit Russell's salary from the Maine Department of Agriculture (where he is now director of special projects) directly into the bank. By living *below* their means, they had saved enough by 1986 to purchase outright the thirty-one-acre, $42,000 former farm on which they subsequently built their dream house.

"We borrowed nothing for the property," Russell said, sitting in the great room of their wide-open house. Its most distinctive feature, a stone-built Russian hearth, partially divides and separates the dining room from the living areas. "We felt very strongly about not getting into debt." There was a ramshackle house on the property, which they initially considered renovating, but abandoned the idea after estimating the cost of making it habitable to be $50,000.

Financing the construction of their new, 2,300-square-foot house proved somewhat trickier. They cashed in Mary Anne's pension, which came to almost $40,000, added their savings, and bit the bullet and took out a $12,000 loan. A five-year-loan, Russell explained a tad defensively. "It's something you could pay off with a minimum-wage job if you had to."

In June of 1986 forty volunteers showed up from all over New England to break ground on the house and participate in an old-fashioned house raising. The crew included neighbors, family members, and old college pals of Russell's, along with "some people we didn't even know—brothers of friends, a couple of doctors. We put up the whole frame in one day, except for the north end." The framing was of hemlock timbers from a local mill, which were secured with pegs. Russell and

Mary Anne envisioned the place as being chemical-free and self-sufficient, although in the end they made some compromises, including the use of plywood (which they'd opposed at first because of its "toxic" glue component) and hooking up the house with the power line (initially they'd wanted to install their own generator).

Russell took off Fridays that summer to work alongside their full-time carpenters, and the Libbys moved into the house in September. By investing sweat equity and recruiting the volunteer labor, Russell said, the house ended up costing just over $30 a square foot, instead of the $80 they would have spent by contracting it out. "By the time we're done, we'll have $70,000 to $75,000 in it," he said. "It adds up to a lot of money, but consider the mortgage on the entire place is $12,000."

For the Libbys, thriftiness is not just a means to pay off their mortgage, but a lifelong commitment. This year, for instance, "I might make $30,000 for the first time," Russell said. "We live at a $20,000 income threshold and save. Even though we have a loan out, we're still putting a little money in the bank every month."

One important reason for keeping their spending low is to enable Mary Anne to stay home and raise their two daughters, Annie, five, and Maisie, almost three. As we ate the lunch she'd made of acorn-squash casserole and salad, Mary Anne said, "I'd rather be dirt poor and able to be at home with the kids [than be comfortable and have to ship them off to day care]." Though far from "dirt poor," Mary Anne practices thrift by buying used toys for the children and used clothing and books for the entire family.

But what has stayed with us most is how the Libbys put

such a low ceiling on the amount of money they were willing to borrow to finance their dream house. Our visit with them fortified our own resolve to pay as we go. Long before leaving California, Frank "got religion" on the point of not borrowing—not for ourselves, not for the orchard. Like his grandparents, Ralph and Clara Levering, who neither borrowed nor lent money, Frank had come to believe that if he didn't have the money, he could get by without the thing he wanted. It was an antique sentiment, and, inevitably, there would be exceptions to the rule. But it was good to learn that others shared his viewpoint.

After remodeling our kitchen with money we had on hand, rather than borrowing to finance additional home improvements, we agreed to hold off further renovation work. For the time being we've adopted the attitude seen on bumper stickers of old cars: "Don't laugh, it's paid for."

In Los Angeles Frank once half-seriously suggested to Wanda that we accept every credit card offer that arrived in the mail, after the fashion of a movie producer friend who supported himself for several years in this way, while getting his film off the ground. In Los Angeles we had three credit cards. Frank's attitude had changed 180 degrees by the time we met up with Gary Zapatka, a software specialist with Apple Computer in Cupertino, California, who works with Wanda's sister, Jane. Gary gets a kick out of mutilating the occasional credit cards that come to him through the mail. "I cut them up and use them as guitar picks."

Not long after meeting Gary, we returned home and, as quickly as we could, paid off all our accounts and reduced our cache of credit cards to one. We keep this one for identification, for rental cars, and for airplane tickets and make sure to pay the bill in full before the exorbitant interest rates kick in. Though Wanda reluctantly parted with the company that first issued her a credit card in 1981 (a sentimental, if dubious, symbol of independence), she agreed that our one card should be with a company out of Indianapolis that donates a percentage of its profits to charitable causes, such as Habitat for Humanity.

From our arrival in April 1986 until April of 1988, frugality gained the upper hand at Levering Orchard. In contrast with earlier years in the eighties, we bought no new equipment, instead making do with what we had. By doing much of the mowing, picking, hauling, grading, and selling ourselves, we slashed labor costs to the bone. We cut costs by selling more "tree-run" peaches, nectarines, and apples—merchandising the fruit directly to consumers rather than grading and packing to sell wholesale.

Then came a fruit "set" on the cherry trees—the number of pollinated blossoms that become infant fruit—that was wondrous to behold. After the small cherry crop in 1987, when most of the fruit buds had been killed by cold weather, the trees rebounded in 1988 with a prodigious number of buds. In April the weather turned sunny and warm, ideal for pollination. By early May green cherries the size of peas hung massed on the tall trees in quantities no one here—not Sam or Miriam, not Garnet—had ever seen the likes of before. In 1986, the previous record crop, we'd had enough customers to let no cherries go unpicked. This time how would we ever get enough customers to pick even half the cherries? Having been frugal for two years, we were rewarded with a now legendary extravagance on the part of Mother Nature. But how to harvest the bounty?

It was a season, as Garnet observed, that "we might not ever see again." Many customers told us that they sent their friends to the orchard because only seeing was believing: no words could describe the tiers of leafy boughs, bent over with blood red cherries bunched together like grapes. From the first week in June until the last week in July, every day but Sunday, the crowds came, the weather stayed miraculously dry—and the cherries left the trees. On the Fourth of July—when Frank foolishly let two weary ladder-setting helpers have the day off—743 people signed in at the entrance gate to pick cherries.

We never got the crop picked; short of hiring a large, costly picking crew, there was simply no way we could. But because of phenomenal word of mouth, our first year of advertising and newspaper stories about the conjunction of the record crop with Levering Orchard's eightieth anniversary, we picked an estimated 85 to 90 percent. At the end of July, bone-tired and mentally numb as we have never been before or since, what cherries were left had shriveled to raisins on the trees. We left them for the birds.

In August, after a short breather, we harvested the other stone fruits; in September and October, the fall apples. By year's end the orchard debt we had faced in April 1986 had been slashed in half. In very real terms frugality was paying off—in the way we felt not only about ourselves, but in the business that, at times from California, we had all but given up for dead. Perhaps the real money was elsewhere. But the life we wanted was here.

CHAPTER SEVEN

The Renovation

Miriam appeared in our kitchen at six that April morning before the carpenters arrived. She had come to make a last-ditch effort to dissuade us from tearing down the wall that separated the kitchen from the small, spare room that over the years had been used first for dining and later as a spare bedroom.

"I'm urging you to build out, not tear down. It's not too late," she said, as if speaking a truth that, once grasped, we'd be unable to contest.

We had done the figuring and made the mistake of telling her it would cost roughly the same to add on as to tear out and remodel. To her way of thinking, the choice was obvious. Why not gain additional square footage for the same money? More was better. Why not leave the downstairs as it was with two guest bedrooms? That was always handy when a crowd appeared.

We thought of the time Wanda's father and sister were here visiting along with Frank's friend from college, his wife, and his toddler son. Housing all five called for three guest rooms, and since we only had two, Jane ended up stretched out on a sleeping bag in Wanda's porch-office.

For a moment we wondered if Miriam weren't right. After all, she had spent forty-six years in this house, thousands of hours in the kitchen, many of them fantasizing about ways she would do the place over if she could. It was touching that she cared enough to climb out of bed so early that morning and warn us against the big mistake she was sure we were making.

Still, her last-minute plea failed to alter our plans. We had new and different ideas for the kitchen, for the house, and for our lives. Our situation did not remotely resemble Sam and Miriam's—nor could we imagine that it ever would. If we had children, we certainly wouldn't have six. Nor did we have an extended family with nieces and nephews traipsing in to spend summers with us. Frank's nieces and nephews were all but grown now, and Wanda's only sibling hadn't started her family yet.

We didn't want to take care of any more square footage than we already had. Even after three years in Virginia, our living space seemed more than adequate for two people—certainly by Los Angeles–apartment standards. And we knew that the extra space would carry the hidden price tag over the years of extra work—in mopping and window washing, in dusting and maintenance.

Exactly fifty years after the house had been built in 1939 for $5,400, we plunged, with more excitement than trepidation, into its murky recesses to give it its first major overhaul. That Wanda would be the architect of our new nest, of what we hoped to transform over time into our dream home, was a challenge she'd been awaiting all her life—since girlhood when she used to sketch house plans from her apartment-bunkbed perch while other girls were doodling horses, daffodils, and cupid's arrows.

Remodeling Frank's boyhood home amounted to an act of reclamation, like saving a pet from a pound. We were putting into action our growing preference for reuse over expendability. And we were doing it on a piece of family history.

We met a couple at a wedding in Cleveland that year whose business it was to oversee the kind of project we were undertaking (along with more formidable ones). Their field was inner-city residential restoration. "Take an old house and make it livable," they told us. "It may cost you the same money as building from scratch, but it costs society far less." As we toasted our mutual friends, the newlyweds, they explained: "The infrastructure for that old house, for that whole neighborhood, is already in place. The earth has been moved. The sidewalks have been paved, and sewer lines are in place. Why extend the city and start carving up virgin land?"

They articulated an ethic that we were developing as our own: of reclamation and resource recovery, of mending and caring for things rather than throwing them out and replacing them. It is a philosophy that applies not only to houses, but to cameras, shoes, and leftover food and—we suspect there is a connection—to people.

Two carpenters walked into our lives one April evening after work and stayed for hours, talking excitedly about the prospective job of transforming our kitchen into a large expanse that swept from the north end of the house to the south. Paul Everts, a tall, sturdily built man with curly blond hair and blue eyes behind tinted, wire-rim glasses, had come highly recommended by friends for whom he'd worked. He brought along with him Victor Hawks, a featherweight carpenter originally from Carroll County with a high-pitched, hair-trigger laugh.

They had met, we soon learned, at a local Christian businessmen's association and were straight as T squares. They didn't smoke, drink, or take the Lord's name in vain. They were happily married with wives and young children at home. They didn't work Sundays or observe the "pagan" holiday, Halloween. Best of all for Wanda, who planned to write in her porch-office during this renovation period, they didn't feel it was a necessary tool of the trade to play loud music while hammering and sawing.

One of the friends who had recommended Paul told us that he had made his own inquiries about us. Of Wanda he wanted to know, "How come she didn't take the name Levering?" And he elicited her help in practicing to pronounce "Urbanska."

We had just returned from a trip west and had expected to get the ball rolling on tracking down and interviewing good carpenters—a process we figured might take months. We thought hours would be devoted to mulling over and refining the rough plans Wanda had sketched up.

Instead, working on a late-night bag of soft-batter, chocolate-chip cookies with these two men, we were faced with making an immediate decision. Paul was fixing to leave the area. Having lived in Carroll County for several years, he believed better opportunities awaited him in a more populous part of the state. He would be here only another month—or, at best, two. If we wanted him, we had to grab him now. Our kitchen would be his last job here.

We didn't like the sound of that. If ours was Paul's last job here, what would he care if the sanding were uneven or the cabinets crooked? He wouldn't be around to take the flak if things fell apart. He wouldn't need our seal of approval for future references. And if he was eager to get moving on his new life, wouldn't he likely cut corners to get things done expeditiously? Even worse, might he tear us down and leave us holding the proverbial bag, this time in the chaos of deconstruction?

All these doubts seemed legitimate, but standing there before us, soberly studying Wanda's plan, Paul Everts didn't remotely resemble the kind of a guy who would do that to you. He quizzed us about materials and put a rough, don't-quote-me-on-it price of ten thousand dollars on the whole job, including putting in new flooring, subflooring, and wallboard in the downstairs bathroom, along with a tub surround and other needed work. Paul and Victor would work on an hourly basis— ten dollars each—so they were not, they made clear, bound to that preliminary estimate.

We blinked when Paul threw out the ten-thousand-dollar figure, as that was precisely what we had to work with, no more, no less. If it went over, our budget would be depleted and the work halted. We couldn't quibble with their rates. Good carpenters were high, even in a part of the country where some adults still made the minimum wage. And those prices sounded reasonable against what we'd pay in a city. What worried us was the conventional wisdom about remodeling—which held that if you're given an estimate, double it. And here we not only didn't have an estimate, we had a guess—and only a hunch for security that these guys might be as good as or better than their word.

Seeing our hesitation, Paul turned on what for him was the

hard sell. "At that price, I'm a bargain," he said with conviction.

We talked it over and called him the next day. "We'll do it," we said.

When we moved into the brick house in April of 1986, major house renovations, though out of reach for the moment, were very much on our minds. You couldn't quibble with the amount of space we were getting. In addition to the living room, kitchen, and two baths, the house had four bedrooms upstairs and two downstairs. We designated two upstairs bedrooms as side-by-side offices. The largest bedroom became ours. This left a small upstairs bedroom, last occupied by Frank during his summer vacations from college, which Wanda dubbed "Frank-boy's room" (after John-boy Walton). It was underused, its only function serving as a giant catch-all closet.

Despite the number of rooms, the house added up to just two thousand square feet of living space, minus the basement. As was the style in 1939 when the house was built, most of the rooms were small, boxy, and closetless. Wanda was determined to remake the house in our image.

Between the time we moved in, in April 1986, and the start of the kitchen renovation in April 1989, we tackled several small projects. The first was our bedroom. We covered the bare walls with fresh paint and pink-and-gray wallpaper. A local seamstress custom-made curtains for the three windows for twenty-five dollars, and we bought an area carpet at a remnant shop in Mount Airy for less than it would have cost to refinish the floors. From there we moved on to the basement, where with the help of a carpenter friend we converted a giant playroom into an office both for orchard paperwork and for writing. We spread gallons of white paint over the first floor: the guest room, the hallway, the stairwell, and the living room ceiling. And for the first time ever, the eight dark wooden doors and frames—a visual disturbance in the narrow front entry hall—were painted white. We sanded most of the downstairs oak floors and laid down several coats of polyurethane. Our last job before the kitchen was spackling and painting lilac Frank's small upstairs office, formerly his parents' bedroom.

The kitchen renovation represented a more serious claim on our time, money, and energy than any of our earlier projects. It was also an important emotional turning point in our relationship with the house, as if by putting our creative imprint on the place we were somehow laying permanent claim to it. And under our plan, Polonius would have nothing on us: we were neither borrowers nor lenders. Further, the fact that as two writers living outside a major communications center we were doing well enough to underwrite an entire kitchen renovation was a real source of pride.

On the last Friday in April, Paul and Victor arrived for their first day of work. They had instructed us in advance to empty the kitchen cabinets and to move every sponge, cleanser can, dust mop, and stick of furniture from the kitchen into the living room. In fact, we were in a last-minute scramble to carry out their orders when Miriam showed up to offer her eleventh-hour appeal.

We set up a makeshift kitchen in the living room, opening out the leaves of the dining room table and, for protection, covering it with a flannel-backed plastic tablecloth. As if for an extended picnic, Wanda set out what she guessed would be enough dishes, glasses, and mugs to last the duration of the remodel, which Paul had estimated would not be longer than three weeks. She added a few often-used spices, such as pepper and garlic powder, and stood the silverware upright in mugs to save table space. We moved the refrigerator next to the table and scattered dining room chairs around the house.

Since we were without a functioning stove or oven, Frank unearthed a hot plate from the bowels of the basement. But we soon discovered it took close to fifty minutes to bring a full pot of water to boil, so we transferred our allegiance to "refrigerator food"—sandwiches, fruit, and frozen meals that could be heated in the toaster oven. Our usual pasta dinners were reserved for those rare nights when we could wait an hour to boil noodles. After some debate we purchased our first microwave oven and became overnight converts, zapping our desk "companions"— cups of coffee, hot chocolate, hot cider, and surprisingly good hot orange juice.

Lacking a functioning kitchen sink, we tried to use dishes judiciously. We washed things out in the small downstairs lavatory sink, stretching out a dish towel over the toilet lid to air-dry them. Dishwashing in the bathroom wasn't a particularly appetizing venture—especially after the plaster walls and wallboard began coming down and bits of dislodged material were scattered everywhere. We made frequent use of flimsy paper plates held stiff by wicker liners. Though we were roughing it indoors, we didn't mind it much, given the magical transformation that was starting to take place.

Once we gave our carpenters the go-ahead, Wanda threw herself into the project while Frank worked in the orchard, preparing for the 1989 harvest season. The idea was to keep the kitchen as simple and homey as possible while upgrading its efficiency and eye appeal. And we wanted a kitchen that was as maintenance free as possible. We tried to bear in mind not only what we needed and wanted today, but what we—or the next occupants—might want forty or fifty years down the line. Wanda made phone calls and entered product information into an old reporters' notebook. She scoured back issues of magazines for photographs of the look she wanted and stapled them into a three-ring notebook. An artful use of wooden ceiling beams (which in our case could cover major ceiling cracks) caught her eye, as did a clever microwave shelf that held the appliance off the counter while blending in with the lines of the kitchen cabinets.

Wanda sketched in greater detail the plan she'd roughed out earlier. Since the sink's position was fixed (we left it where it was in order not to alter the plumbing lines), we placed the stove down the counter from the sink and the refrigerator directly opposite the stove. Basically the kitchen consisted of two parallel counters that extended north-south along the side of the house. At the north side, perpendicular to the counters, we planned a window seat that would open up for tool storage. On each side of the window seat were bookshelves, always at a premium in our house. In the giant new room there would be nine windows, with light streaming in from the north, south, and west. On the south side of the room was space for the dining table and chairs. On the east side would be our main source of heat, a wood-burning stove, along with a shallow broom closet and pantry.

"To know what to leave out and what to put in; just where and just how, ah, that is to have been educated in knowledge of simplicity," Frank Lloyd Wright wrote in *The Natural House*. Following Wright's observation, we wanted to avoid mindless purchases and decorative frills. We nixed adding a garbage disposal, for instance, because we kept a compost pail for scraps under our sink. Initially Wanda wanted to keep rather than replace the curvilinear 1939 sink—because she liked its vintage look and because she thought that every good room, like a wedding ensemble, should include something old along with something new. The sink's intransigent stains could be dispensed with by the fresh enamel of a local porcelain refinisher. In this case, however, Miriam argued convincingly that it would be a false economy to keep the old, one-basin sink, as deeper double basins were frequently desirable.

The dishwasher question was trickier to resolve. If we wanted one, now was the time to write it into the script, as built-in dishwashers were far more desirable than roll-around portables. But we weren't sure we wanted one. Having survived nine years of domestic life without one, we'd found dishwashing was as often a pleasurable exercise for us as a pesky nuisance—though we couldn't deny the not infrequent sin of procrastination, where piles of dirty dishes accumulated in and around the sink. Still, was it really necessary to bring a loud, noisy, obtrusive appliance into our lives? If not here, where would we draw the simple-living line?

Ellen Hoffs, a friend from Los Angeles who'd visited the previous year with her husband, happened to call at a critical moment of debate. When Wanda laid out the pros and cons of having a dishwasher, Ellen offered her wisdom about its advantages when entertaining. "Dishwashers are very good to have when company is over," she said. We realized then that others might not view our piles of dishes as indulgently as we did, and since we seemed unlikely to reform (and since overnight guests were an important ingredient of our social life in the country), we decided to bite the bullet and buy a Maytag. We were happy to learn, some months after our purchase, that dishwashers actually use less hot water (and therefore less electricity) than does washing by hand with a continuously running tap.

The decision about the flooring was easier, though no less challenging. The floors of the two conjoined rooms were different: the old guest room, like the rest of the house, was oak, but the kitchen floor was pine, chosen for its reputed water resistance. The oak had weathered the years better than the pine, which had soaked in grease stains from the stove and from glue dribbling into the cracks where linoleum had been laid in the 1940s. No amount of sanding would remove these greenish black stains marching down the floor in north-south rows.

Instead of covering the whole thing with a unifying piece of vinyl flooring (new wood was out of our budget), we decided to stick with what we had, warts and all. We pickled the oak floor light and pickled the lighter pine dark. Although, in the end, the stains were only partially obscured by the pickling, the eye unites the two and gets the impression of a seasoned floor, leaving us satisfied. Nonetheless one visitor who saw the kitchen several months after its completion blurted out, "*When* are you going to get to the floor?"

Our hearts were not set on custom-built cabinets—not until Wanda checked out the prefab units and, except for the most expensive ones, found them all to be at least partially constructed of particleboard. Although many had attractive fronts, we did not think board would wear well, that it would warp if it came into contact with water or might break if a nail was driven into it with too much force. It seemed pointless to tear out our functional (albeit unsightly) wood cabinets and replace them with something destined not to last.

Wanda interviewed several custom cabinetmakers, but either their prices were too high or they wouldn't build what we wanted. Then, ten days into the remodel, Joe Dalton stepped through our permanently ajar door. An amiable, graying man who always dressed in a tan uniform even though he was working for himself, he had driven over from Woolwine, an apple-growing community about forty miles to the east of us. Tape in hand, he took down the dimensions and pencil-marked the wall where the appliances and cabinets would stand.

"Could the cabinets measure thirty-eight inches high rather than the standard thirty-six?" Wanda asked timidly, having been chastened for such heresy by one previous candidate. All our lives we tall folk have stooped over kitchen counters built for the average-size, five-foot-four-inch American woman. At five ten and six one, we simply didn't fit.

"I don't see any reason why not," Joe answered merrily, seeming to relish the challenge.

Emboldened, Wanda asked if it would be possible to build the cabinets all the way to the ceiling, to avoid either adding dead, dust-collecting space above the cabinets or boxing in usable space.

"Whatever the lady wants," Joe said, meaning it. What's more, he would have the cabinets ready by next week.

Joe Dalton proved true to his word. He completed the unfinished, three-quarter-inch birch plywood cabinets with plain fronts and installed them by early the next week, having taken eight days from the time we first met him until he nailed the units to the walls. The bill he presented was two-thirds that of even the cheapest prefab cabinets. Wanda was so delighted that she wrote Joe a gift certificate for a free bucket of pick-your-own cherries.

For all our economies and lucky breaks, we splurged on two fronts. One was the kitchen counter, for which we chose tile instead of the standard Formica. Although the price difference was significant—three times as much—and though we were advised to put on the factory-cut countertop for now and replace it with tile at some later date, we ordered exactly the counter we wanted: large, chunky, off-white tiles from Florida. They added another half inch to our counter height and considerably more to the aesthetics of the new room. And they obviated the need for trivets; you could set a hot pot anywhere.

Our other major extravagance was the stone hearth that we added to the space where previously there had been only a chimney-flue opening above narrow broom closets. Stone-masonry work was one of Paul Everts's specialties, and though we hesitated to commission it, in the end we gave him the green light, reasoning that it was better to do any work now that we might want done later. For several days in early evenings after work, Frank led Wanda on rock-hunting expeditions through our woods and orchards. Though quartz and metamorphic schist rocks glittering with mica were abundant, finding the right specimen—the rock to live with for a lifetime—proved exacting. We wanted stones that were light in weight and color, attractive to the eye, and as flat as possible. We trudged through patches of forest and dug through the rock piles scattered throughout the orchards, where over the years fields had been cleared and rocks heaped. Once home, we scrubbed years of dirt off the rocks, using an old toothbrush to reach into the cracks.

It's a primitive, homey hearth, on an eleven-inch, stone-masonry platform. Per Wanda's suggestion, Paul laid a large flat stone to jut out from the wall as a natural mantel. The hearth is composed solely of native rocks, except for one—a rounded, sea-washed stone that Wanda and her mother collected from a public beach in Connecticut the summer they drove the Malibu down from Maine.

With amusement, Paul recounted that one day Garnet Dawson came in from the orchard to size up the progress. Shaking his head in dismay, Garnet told him, "I'd leave those rocks out in the woods where they belong. Wouldn't you?"

Paul's reply was vintage Appalachian. "Some would," he observed.

Our biggest jolt came—though not without warning—when Paul announced that he was leaving after three weeks, before the job was finished. It was upsetting, of course, but we had to make the best of it. With only Victor working on the job, progress slowed considerably.

May turned to June, when we expected not only the usual bustle of cherry-picking season, but extended visits from Marie and an actress friend from California. We were still eating on paper plates, with no functioning kitchen, sink, or stove. We felt no small embarrassment when a visiting United States congressman from southwestern Virginia and his administrative assistant arrived at his old pal Sam's door at lunchtime. Culinarily crippled without Miriam—who was visiting her sister in North Carolina—to serve as hostess, Sam brought the distinguished guests to our house, where the congressman was forced to share the couch with a set of wrenches and balance his lunch plate on his lap.

Paul had put in long hours, occasionally staying till midnight to finish a job; but left to his own devices, Victor adopted another approach, more in line with the reputation enjoyed by free-lance carpenters. He started taking on other projects, juggling jobs and showing up for only one or two hours a day, sometimes not at all.

We started getting desperate to clear the debris from our house and yard and put our lives back to normal. The downstairs commode had been sitting in our front lawn for weeks. Wanda called in a local fix-it service, which sent over three men one day. In a hurry, they built a small pantry and hooked up the sink and dishwasher, along with tackling myriad other jobs. For three days running, after work at the packhouse, Wanda polyurethaned the kitchen cabinets. At last the end was in sight. When the final tile was laid in July, eleven weeks had passed. Although the carpenters had grossly underestimated the time, at least one part of the initial promise held true: the money. Incredibly, after all this work, all these men, and lo these many weeks, with custom cabinets, tiles and masonry, two new major appliances, a ceiling fan, and bathroom repair, the tab came in *under* budget. We had spent just under $9,500.

The renovation forced us to take stock of what we had and to do some serious deck shuffling. Having no place in the new kitchen, we had to move the copier machine, a former occupant of the small downstairs guest room, to Wanda's upstairs porch office. The mirrored armoire, a gift from Sam and Miriam when we moved in, found its new home in the remaining downstairs guest room. Frank suggested moving Cholla and Winnie's bowls to the basement landing, a move Wanda resisted initially on the grounds that she got a kick out of watching the cats eat. In the end she had to concede that the mess of scattered cat food, like so many brick shavings, was better left to the imagination—and the cellar landing—than to our refinished kitchen floor. Twin beds that had come with the house were returned to the senior Leverings. And the list went on.

Rearranging the inside of our house helped us create a warm new environment. Though we had remodeled just one quarter of the house, the desire to streamline and make it more livable spilled over onto the entire spread. We began to draw up lists of future projects: redoing the upstairs bathroom, turning Frank-boy's room into a respectable guest room, and embarking on a thorough purging of the basement and attic—two areas that remained cluttered with detritus from Sam and Miriam's regime.

Changing the status quo of the house helped us lay claim as a couple to what had hitherto been Frank's parents' home. Hovering over us for several years after we'd moved to the orchard was the idea, held by some family members, that our commitment to the place was shallow, that one day we might just pack up and leave. But the dramatic and costly changes we had made seemed to lay to rest that idea once and for all.

Still, there was ambivalence from several of Frank's siblings, who, protective of their youthful memories, weren't sure they liked us mucking around with their childhood home. One vigorously protested painting over any natural woodwork. Another came to gaze wistfully at the spot where she was born, now a kitchen counter.

Sam and Miriam had been wonderful—not only about surrendering the house to us, but turning over its emotional custody as well (Miriam's advice about the placement of the kitchen notwithstanding). By and large Miriam applauded the changes and became so entranced with the transformation that she frequently dropped in to watch the workmen plaster, paint, and mortar. And Sam, never one to take any interest in decor, was too oblivious of the goings-on to offer any objection.

The more the place became ours, the more attentive we became to it and to the things inside it. We were living more consciously, more fully, in the physical world of our house. Ironically, while simple livers are often linked with antimaterialism, we found that things themselves had become more real, more intrinsically meaningful, to us.

Smaller things commanded out attention, like the shower curtain in the downstairs bathroom. No one could deny that it was hanging on by three hooks and its fingernails, the rest of the holes having ripped through the plastic. It was only a matter of time before the whole shebang would give way. It was the kind of thing that in the past we would have let go of until we threw our hands in the air, purchased a replacement, and tossed the old curtain in the garbage. Although neither of us would accept responsibility for yanking on the curtain with force sufficient to rip it from its rings, this time, instead of pointing fingers, we rounded up a paper punch and salvaged the curtain with new holes.

Mending and caring became our new catchwords. We began taking shoes to the shoemaker for new soles and heels, despite the fact that the money expended would have gone a long way toward buying a new pair. But that wasn't the point. The point was that we already owned the shoes; and except for the soles, they were perfectly decent. An ethic of conservation about the things in our home was taking root.

Once committed to taking better care of our belongings, most of us are forced to do some paring down. Few can better testify to the salubrious, therapeutic, and even spiritual side effects of streamlining one's possessions than Sue Garrett Rickert, a tall, bespectacled woman of fifty. Frank has known Sue, a family friend, since childhood. Now living in San Francisco, where she's a wife and mother of three, she spends much of her spare time doing hospital volunteer work.

More than once throughout her life, Sue has shorn herself of impedimenta—the way others embark upon fasts—to refocus priorities while achieving a state of detachment. Sue, who was raised Episcopalian, says her spiritual life took a profound turn when she acted upon a dream. At the time, she was a young elementary school teacher in Lynchburg, Virginia. During that period, the civil rights movement was rumbling throughout the South.

In Sue's dream she "saw an ad in the newspaper, in the classified advertising section," she said, recalling that watershed dream of almost three decades ago. "It was offering to give away twelve to fourteen dresses. At the end, my name was given and my phone number. The next morning, I woke up and jotted down the dream. I called the newspaper and gave them the ad word for word. I got one call the next day from a woman saying, 'You are the answer to prayer. We're on welfare, and my husband has broken his back. We live out in the country and have no source of income. We will come right over.' The mother and three teenaged girls drove over in this old, beaten-up truck, on Saturday night—the night before Easter—and came in and tried on everything I had put out: dresses, purses, shoes. They took everything."

After giving away her clothing, Sue felt so lighthearted that she decided to expand her offering to household items. She took out a second ad and emptied her apartment.

"Now I was totally free," she said. "I felt I could go any-where I wanted to go and do anything I wanted to do. I was totally free in spirit."

And so she did. She took a leave of absence from school and set out alone to travel for six months in Switzerland. Her European trip led to a two-year stint with the Peace Corps in Tanzania, where she taught in one of two girls' schools in that country.

"Giving away my clothes—that small step of following the leading I had," said Sue, "had a huge effect which I did not know then. I did not know what a transforming life experience that would be, so crucial to all the things that were to occur afterward."

When they learned about her giveaways, Sue's family, who lived in nearby Roanoke, began to worry. Their concern mounted when Sue announced her decision to enter the Peace Corps. She remembers her mother reading her the riot act: " 'Susan, you are twenty-four. This is the time you should be catching a man. If you wait two years and get out of the main-stream of things, you'll never catch a man.' " Sue laughed. "Mom was wrong; I caught two!"

The first of her two husbands was a fellow Peace Corps volunteer in Tanzania. As we talked, Sue pulled out photo-graphs of this most romantic part of her past. "This is a picture of the dining room," she said. "They had no china or utensils for eating. They ate with their hands. Everybody carried every-thing on their heads there. . . . The amazing thing to me was how easy it was, how much more satisfying it was and unclut-tered. When I was there I thought, This is as near to paradise as I'll ever be. I'm so free and unencumbered with things and litter, the kind that distract our minds. . . . I was surprised that I didn't have culture shock when I went into that environment. When I first saw the village, it seemed more natural to me than it did when I came back to the United States."

Today Sue lives in a comfortable two-story house in San Francisco's Saint Francis Woods district with her second husband, Tom Rickert, and her three children. Tom's two college-age kids come in for vacations and holidays. The house—which was awarded to her in the divorce settlement from her first marriage—is spacious with a full furnished basement and plenty of attic room.

Coincidentally, when we saw her, Sue had just completed the latest of her cathartic purges. Still following the leading of her dreams, Sue said, "Before Christmas I woke up two or three times to the Shaker tune ' 'Tis a gift to be simple, 'tis a gift to be free. . . '

"I'm always conscious of the happiness I had living [in Tanzania] without anything material for two years. I'm haunted by how happy I was. I'm also trapped in a cultural milieu where it's understood that in order to function you must have some of these things. I'm trying to get down to: What do we really need? How many chairs? How many tables? What is the bottom line of how we can function?"

The week before we saw her, Sue had ordered a huge dumpster to be dropped by her house. "Within the space of three days, I filled the entire dumpster myself." She threw away "a lot of trash, old magazines, old newspapers, toys that were broken, games with pieces missing that I knew we would never play. I gave three carloads of the children's and my clothes to Goodwill, things we had outgrown."

Editing down one's holdings can be especially difficult when others, namely children, are involved.

"I did it while the children were in school almost surreptitiously, because I felt it was a private act. They did see the dumpster filling up, but they didn't say much because it wasn't their stuff. Their bicycles and stuffed animals are still here. This was my stuff, up in the attic and down in the storeroom and in old drawers. I'm not through yet, but I'm beginning to feel the same buoyancy and lightness of spirit as when I put the ad in the newspaper so many years ago."

"It must be hard to aspire to simple living when you have children," Wanda said.

"Yeah. They're always reminding me that we don't have cable TV, that our TV is broken, that we won't have a computer soon because Sara will take it away [to college], that we don't have an electric typewriter, that we don't have Nintendo."

"How do you respond to that?" asked Wanda.

"That it's more important to me that you have a good education, that if I have extra money, it goes into your education."

Like Sue, we found that getting rid of clutter instead of holding on to it on the off chance that it might someday be needed was almost always liberating. During the period of the renovation and afterward, Wanda made generous donations to the Salvation Army. Boxes of seldom used pots and pans, dishes and plates, were discarded. Grocery bags bursting with clothes, curtains, and knickknacks, were carted off.

Though we are both inveterate pack rats, parting with these things proved relatively easy. The real test lay in letting go of the things to which we were attached. The 1948 Chevy that

Frank had driven to Mount Airy High School in the late sixties and 1970, which was an antique even then, with its giant lumbering doors and seats wide as twin beds and sun visor on the hood, had taken up a stall in the car shed without seeing any road action for close to two decades. Though no one here knew enough mechanics to put in the new engine and transmission it needed, no one wanted to let go of the car either. One day we'll get it running again, Sam would say. Soon it would be a valuable antique.

So there it sat, a rusting shell of a car, occupying one of three spaces in the car shed, vines growing up the wheels and under the hood—more eyesore than antique. One day, perhaps under the spell of a Sue Rickert–like dream, Frank woke up and said, "Let's give it away." Losing it did not mean parting with good memories. Wanda and Miriam gave the nod. Sam was the last holdout for keeping it, but seeing the tide had turned against him, he reluctantly agreed to let it go. So it was given to Perry Haynes, a young orchardist, close friend, and ace mechanic. Delighted with the gift, Perry promised that once he got the old Chevy running, we could take it out anytime for a romantic spin on the Blue Ridge Parkway.

Like Perry, we have also been recipients of gifts and know the pleasures of being on either end of the receiving line. When they visited one fall, Frank's uncle Alton and aunt Elizabeth Smith Lindsey carted a family heirloom as a housewarming gift in their silver Chevy Nova for 650 miles. It was an antique, three-drawer, walnut dresser with a heavy marble top made by Eastlake, one of the first assembly-line furniture manufacturers in America. A gem from the mid-nineteenth century, with intricate, hand-carved ornamentation over the manufactured base, the chest was passed down from his and Miriam's mother,

Lois Whitmarsh Lindsey, to UncAl (as he playfully refers to himself). Inside the top drawer, UncAl thumbtacked a short history of the piece for the sake of posterity.

When we offered thanks for this treasure and for their having gone to the trouble of delivering it, characteristically, Al and Elizabeth insisted we were doing *them* a favor. This self-effacing generosity surprised Wanda more than Frank, who had grown accustomed to their ways after spending the summer with them in 1974.

"We had too much in the house in the first place," said Aunt Elizabeth. "It looked like a furniture store. The more you have, the more you have to take care of."

It strikes us how often people look back with longing on certain times in their lives: the crowded Spartan life of college dorms; boot camp for those who've gone through the military; summer camp with no more than a bedroll and canteen; trips to nether regions lugging backpacks; the salad days of one's profession before becoming encumbered by all the trappings of prestige and success. Although lost youth is most often identified as the source of this elusive pleasure, the simplicity of the life itself is usually overlooked.

We cannot hope to take our meals at a mess hall, nor do we wish to live once again in a twelve-by-ten room and bed down on squeaky cots with lumpy mattresses; but it's always worth bearing in mind how the reduction of possessions, the streamlining of the clutter in one's personal domain, can enhance one's life.

. . .

Not long after the renovation of the kitchen was completed, Victor Hawks came over to put a few finishing touches on the job. He surveyed the other rooms in the house, overwhelmed by the magnitude of what remained undone, of bringing the whole place up to snuff. Back in the kitchen, leaning on a counter he had recently tiled, he turned to Wanda as Frank stood nearby.

"When you get rich," he asked, "are you going to build you a new house?"

"I don't think we'll ever build a new house—not unless the bank takes this one away from us," Wanda joked. "I like this house fine—better all the time."

"Oh, I would if I was you," he countered. "I wouldn't hesitate for a second."

"Besides," Wanda continued, "it would be a shame to cast aside a good home. It would feel like tossing out an old friend."

Victor looked her square in the eye and laughed as he said, "Wanda, you wouldn't even mind working at a junk shop, would you?"

Wanda looked him back, not sure if his words were spoken in ridicule or admiration. Either way she had to admit he was right about her. She smiled broadly. "Where do I sign up, Victor?"

CHAPTER EIGHT

In Our Hands

ORCHARD GAP
CREST OF THE BLUE RIDGE
ELEVATION 2675

We started at the crest of the range, where the Orchard Gap Road that Sam's father surveyed in 1917 meets the Blue Ridge Parkway. All were present from our cove: Sam and Miriam, dressed for unseasonable April heat in sneakers and slacks and T-shirts; Virginia Price, in a cotton jumper; and us, toting quantities of green garbage bags and, in the back of the pickup truck, nine empty wooden apple crates. After months of talk we had at last set aside that Sunday afternoon to clean up the roadside from the Orchard Gap Deli to our mailboxes two miles down the looping mountain road.

On that sparkling day, with fifty-mile views of the Virginia and North Carolina piedmont below, we set out down the mountain, like a scout troop out for an afternoon expedition. We made our way slowly: two grandmothers well into their seventies, a stooped man in his eighties, and two thirtysomethings hunching over the roadside, picking up pop bottles, beer and soda cans, polystyrene hamburger clamshells, six-pack beverage yokes, disposable diapers, plastic oil quarts, cigarette lighters, brick-pack juice boxes, and tampon applicators. Over the course of the afternoon we found an Astroturf doormat decorated by a yellow plastic daisy, a pill box, a coat hanger, weathered flip-flops, and the fleshtoned arm of a plastic baby doll. Most of the litter flung out of car windows onto the road shoulders was fast-food trash: oblong, single-serving catsup pouches, plastic forks, paper plates, plastic cups, and paper bags from Hardee's, Druther's, and McDonald's filled with the leavings of many a meal on the go.

As the garbage bags slung hobo style over our shoulders grew full and heavy, Wanda and Virginia set to sorting the debris at the back of the truck, a familiar task not unlike grading peaches, nectarines, and apples down at the packhouse. Clear glass went into one box; brown and green into others; aluminum cans were separated from bimetal cans, which were discarded along with everything else into the trash bags. As the two sorters finished separating one load of garbage, they would pull the truck ahead of where the three trash scavengers were working, so they could drop off their latest loads.

Passersby in cars and pickups gawked, sometimes honking what we took to be their approval. Even when handling broken glass or trash laden with dirt and worms and ants, our spirits never flagged. For us it was an Easter egg hunt in which walking a too long stretch without scooping up a prize proved a perverse disappointment. The joy of retrieval was tied directly to the availability of the bounty. Later, upon reflection, we realized that our reward consisted of having purged the landscape of trash—at least for a time.

At the end of the afternoon, after our day's pickings were sorted and cleared, we surveyed the results: nine bushel crates filled with recyclables. Two boxes each of aluminum cans, green glass, and brown glass and three of clear glass would be driven off to Mount Airy Iron & Metal Co. and sold for $4.35. Eleven garbage bags would be earmarked for the county dump or—today's euphemism—the sanitary landfill in Hillsville.

A year earlier almost to the day, we were yelling at each other. As we drove home from California, a fight erupted over a small polystyrene cup.

On our road trip we had brought red travel mugs for coffee. Wide at the base and narrow at the rim, the mugs would hold their center of gravity when the car took bumps and curves on the road. The idea was to present these mugs for our coffee whenever we pulled into a fast-food restaurant or convenience mart and thus avoid having to use those environmentally abusive polystyrene cups.

Like a truck driver with no intention of quitting to observe the conventional hours of sleep, Frank had steered the Malibu from Reno through the high desert of central Nevada into the wee hours. Bleary-eyed, he'd stopped in a small Nevada town to refuel both himself and the Malibu.

Stretched out on the backseat, Wanda opened her eyes long enough in the moonlight to spot the surreal whiteness of an outlaw foam cup in Frank's grasp. When he settled behind the wheel, she challenged him. How could he have forgotten the travel mugs resting idly in the back?

Frank was running on empty, pushing to get home for spring duties at the orchard. The last thing on his mind was carrying a plastic mug into the convenience center at two in the morning and having to deal with some puzzled clerk. Frank snapped defensively. His voice rose, loud enough to wake the sleeping town. Who was doing the driving and who was getting the free ride? He felt like flinging the hot coffee at his wife.

Wanda sank into a furious silence as the car roared onward. She felt like making its driver eat the polystyrene that, when littered along the roadsides, birds mistake for grain. She'd like to see it pass through *his* digestive tract.

The next morning, when we could talk calmly, something came clearer to us. To live with fewer feelings of guilt and negligence, we needed to make extra time to behave more thoughtfully. We were still too easily and regularly seduced by that courtier, convenience.

No doubt about it, minimizing one's damage to the environment is a direct by-product of simpler living. Washing dishes rather than buying throwaways and tossing them; shopping discriminatingly and buying fewer items—when possible, in bulk—rather than purchasing hastily and discarding promptly are manifestations of simpler, more conscientious living. Bundling errands into one town trip; hanging clothes out to line-dry when possible, and taking the time to winterize or summerize a home are all thoughtful actions. So is taking care not to heat or cool unnecessarily.

Without being regular activists, we have long been environmentally inclined. In 1973, while a high school junior in Maine, Wanda wrote a paper advocating passage of a returnable beverage bottle law. Maine, in fact, went on to enact one of the earliest such laws in the nation. And in 1977, when still in college, Wanda watched President Carter's famous fireside chat in which, dressed in a simple tan cardigan, he called for the creation of a national energy policy. The man made sense.

Finally she had found a politician who could and would become a personal hero.

Strongly influenced by his uncle, Dr. Alton Lindsey, a professor of plant ecology at Purdue with whom he spent a summer at Mt. Rainier in Washington, Frank joined the Wilderness Society in the tenth grade. Uncle Al—who'd been on Admiral Richard E. Byrd's second expedition to Antarctica in the 1930s—was a role model for Frank as he grew up, a rugged outdoorsman, conservationist, and ecologist who spoke with scientific knowledge of environmental devastation years before the subject became fashionable.

Our lives in the eighties, however, ran along the lines of the middle-class Americans we were, with crammed schedules, a preference for convenience, and formidable accumulations of garbage. And it was hard not to feel paralyzed in the face of apocalyptic threats to the global environment. What difference could we make? Were our memberships in the Sierra Club or our financial contributions to other environmental organizations really going to help stop global warming and species depletion, stabilize human population, or close the widening hole in the ozone layer? At heart we were deeply confused about our individual roles. More than we cared to admit, we'd let our confusion stymie us. Even seemingly small questions were hard to answer and endless: Were paper bags, which were biodegradable, better than plastic bags, which took up less space in the landfill? Was it worthwhile to drive extra miles to purchase a product with less packaging? Too often, good and bad deeds for the environment seemed hopelessly intertwined. Who could answer these questions, and where did you draw the line?

But lacking clear-cut answers did not abrogate the need to

take action. Inspired in part by those whom we met on our western trip, people who raised their lives to meet their principles, we resolved to accelerate change in our lives. One must take as a given that we're all caught in the web of contradictions that accompanies contemporary life. But, we've come to feel, within that web, it's important to take even the smallest steps—if for no other reason than to be able to live with ourselves.

In San Francisco we met a couple, Suzanne Moore and Robert Holland, who spurred us into almost immediate action. Suzanne and Robert live right in town, on the edge of Golden Gate Park, and had spent the previous year finding ways to reduce and recycle their garbage. In their rented brownstone, in a small, outdated, but cheerful kitchen, they've made room for receptacles in which to recycle paper, glass, plastics, aluminum, and bimetal cans.

"My little sister was the one who helped me find a recycling station here in San Francisco, close by," said Suzanne. "It's amazing—nearly everything is recyclable. The only thing that isn't recyclable is Styrofoam right now. The plastics are recyclable, all the glass, aluminum, and paper. Our downstairs neighbor and Robert and I are composting in the backyard. We're amazed at how little trash we actually have. And there's a feeling of well-being about that." As a result of their efforts, their weekly garbage drop-off went from two bags to a third of a bag.

For bath and shampoo, Suzanne and Robert use Dr. Bronner's soap, which is free of harsh chemicals and enables them to reuse the "gray water" for watering plants in their small backyard—especially important with California's longtime drought. "We recycle our water. We collect the bath water in buckets to flush the john," said Suzanne.

The drafty, uninsulated town house is inefficient to heat, so except during the bitterest cold snaps, they make do without, piling on more sweaters and socks to rattle around indoors and heaping extra blankets onto their bed at night.

Living in the city enables them to use public transportation. However, both Suzanne and Robert put miles on their legs each year, she walking to her nursing job at the University of California at San Francisco and he to his studies to become an X-ray technician at the University of San Francisco. Her bicycle and his motorcycle serve as efficient backups. She has one, seldom-used vehicle—a Volkswagen minibus from the seventies—which she uses primarily to haul recycling materials and, every three to four weeks, for the occasional weekend getaway.

Aside from their abundant happiness, the visual image from their home that has stayed longest with Wanda is milk in a glass quart. "This is the first time I've seen a commercial glass bottle of milk in twenty-five years," Wanda exclaimed, "since I was a kid in Illinois!"

Wanda took that bottle as a symbol, a harbinger of change, a physical demonstration that the clock could be turned back, that sensible packaging and practices from the past might return. If we could transform our home and lives into something of a model, might those visiting us feel as uplifted as Wanda did at Suzanne and Robert's?

The trip had shaken us out of old habits. No longer could we let ourselves off the hook about recycling, for instance, by rationalizing that Carroll County, Virginia, was not San Francisco, that these progressive ideas hadn't yet found their way here. While in some American communities there was already curbside pickup of recyclable materials, in ours it was still considered forward-thinking to dispose of things in the sanitary landfill. Not long before, rural residents had burned garbage in metal cans or open pits in their yards or buried it in the backyard.

When we got home from our trip, instead of waiting for the introduction of a countywide recycling program, we cleared off our basement landing and rolled up our sleeves. We stacked bushel apple crates three high and three wide, so that we could place empties over full crates and stack, making the need for trips to the center Wanda had located nearby less frequent.

For her first trip to the Mount Airy Iron & Metal Co., located along the railroad tracks not far from Frank's alma mater, Mount Airy High School, Wanda unscrewed the lids, soaked the labels off the jars and bottles, and washed the insides with hot soapy water.

David Pearce, the tall, middle-aged owner, directed Wanda's loaded pickup onto a set of car scales. The vehicle was weighed before and after unloading the recyclables. Pearce picked through her aluminum cans and tossed out some alloys that had found their way into the mix. He poured the aluminum cans into a machine that crushed them and shot them in rapid succession through the air into the bed of a tractor-trailer.

"Next time sort glass by color," he said. "And don't bother soaking off the paper or removing the lids." He handed Wanda a key-chain magnet to check the cans for metal. As of this writing, we have returned seven times and collected a total of $32.48 from our combined sales, including the $4.35 of our afternoon mountainside cleanup.

It was a thrill to be doing our own independent recycling, even if David Pearce appeared puzzled by the figure Wanda cut in his junkyard of broken glass, scrap metal, and discarded industrial parts and kitchen appliances. At one point he commented that she didn't look like someone whose "next meal is coming from what you bring in here." He could only figure that she thought it her "patriotic duty" to recycle.

Without learning until later the term for what happened next in our household, we fell into it. It was "precycling," or evaluating the recyclability of an item before acquiring it. For instance, if there were a choice between a plastic and glass peanut-butter jar, we would choose the latter, since we have no way to recycle plastic. If the cost were moderately (but not astronomically) higher for a product we could recycle, we'd pay it, chalking it up as our contribution to the cause.

Like most vital things, our desire to recycle grew beyond its original boundaries. Before long we started scooping up aluminum cans and glass bottles from curbsides or grocery store parking lots and depositing them in our car trunk or truck bed.

Our regular mountain jogs assumed a new dimension: resource recovery. The jogging road, which undulates toward the Willow Hill Moravian Church where Frank's paternal grandparents are buried, makes for a strenuous jog through our neighbors' apple and peach orchards. On weekends young boys on the road kick up trails of dust on their dirt bikes, and on weekend nights older boys drink beer and toss their cans out their car windows. Once we set up our recycling station, Wanda found herself picking up these outcast aluminum cans and carrying them home. Occasionally she has collected as many as eight or ten on a single run. Sometimes she totes brown beer bottles, large wine bottles, or pop cans. The paper litter she leaves alone, fully aware of the irony that it will decompose more quickly along the roadside than it would in a landfill.

Our excitement about recycling proved contagious. Virginia Price was an enthusiastic convert. After carrying several loads of glass down to our basement landing, where she had to transfer them into apple crates, Virginia suggested that we set up a second recycling center—at the barn, which stands closer to her house and is also in better striking distance of Sam and Miriam's. With its warped and weathered boards just barely hanging on, the trilevel Pennsylvania Dutch barn, built by Frank's grandfather, is now used primarily for storing ladders, firewood, buckets, and other orchard miscellanea. There we stacked the apple crates for the second recycling station.

Virginia pushed our recycling efforts one step further by locating a place that accepted plastic beverage bottles in Greensboro, an eighty-mile drive that she took frequently to visit her older sister, Peggy.

Then she became our resident bag lady.

Each of us has a place—arbitrary and often unexpected though it may be—where we draw the line. For Virginia those ubiquitous white plastic bags to which our local grocery stores had recently made a complete transition from paper bags were that line. One day she decided that she'd wadded up and thrown away her last plastic bag. An expert knitter, Virginia purchased several large spools of heavy synthetic yarn—probably used for upholstery manufacture—from a local remnant shop and duplicated the pattern of the plastic grocery bag with handles. Each roll of yarn made anywhere from six to twelve bags, which she gave to friends and family, to anyone who wanted one. The gift shop at the retirement home in which Virginia's sister Peggy lived called for the recipe. So did many of Virginia's friends. She wrote out instructions and ran them off on our copier machine. She included her phone number and address in case her converts had questions.

The instructions run to two pages. Being nonknitters, we thought they read like Tibetan:

Knit Grocery Bags

Use size 13 or 15 needles
Cast on 60 stitches
Knit 40 rows
Row 41—bind off 5 stitches
Knit 15 stitches and place on holder
Bind off 20 stitches
Knit last 20 stitches . . .

And so forth. . . .

Bold as she is, Virginia can also be timid, and the trickiest part for her was using her new knitted bag in public for the first time. When her courage was screwed to the sticking place one afternoon, she bought a few groceries and at the checkout thrust out her bag and commanded, "Put them in here."

The startled but polite clerk pulled out a plastic bag. "Don't you want me to line your bag?" she asked.

With two thousand square feet and no central heating (the original coal furnace is defunct), we shuttle between microclimates within the house. With no air-conditioning, in the summer our basement office is the coolest room anywhere and a magnet to us both. On a hot July day, of course, no room in the house is truly cool—but there is something satisfying about not insulating ourselves from the weather outside. What isn't pleasing is stepping into air-conditioned spaces with the inevitable rush of cold air and then facing the shock of a return to the natural climate. Knowing that air conditioners use large quantities of electricity and ozone-depleting Freon upholds our convictions. And in the most sweltering of summer days, Wanda puts her hair up, and we wear breezy cotton clothing. We throw the windows open to let in the breeze and move our two box-size room fans around the house to circulate the air.

In the winter we heat primarily with two woodstoves that burn logs from cut-down apple, peach, and cherry trees. Our kitchen/dining area and living room are served by one woodstove, and an open vent in the ceiling channels hot air into our bedroom directly overhead. The woodstove in the basement office ably heats that space, sometimes so ably that the door has to be opened to the basement to let in some cool air. Electric floor heaters—which are turned on and off as needed—serve the other rooms in the house. We use them as little as comfort allows, positioning ourselves where sunlight pours through windows, layering with warm sweaters and letting our bodies adjust to room temperatures.

We are cutting down on such taken-for-granted habits as jumping in the car for day trips or weekend rambles. Thinking through the desire for trips has been especially tough on Frank, for whom—like his parents—hitting the road has long been one of life's greatest pleasures. Sometimes the values we associate with simpler living come into conflict with each other. Is it better to burn the gas and drive twelve miles into Mount Airy to attend the silent Quaker meeting that nurtures our spiritual life in a group setting or to meditate at home?

Answers don't come easily. The fact is, staying home more, carpooling with other residents of the cove, and conserving trips have at times felt constrictive. One has to overcome the long-ingrained habit of immediate gratification. But the rewards are real: the less cash we spend on gas, the more money we have for other things. The less we travel, the more we see what's here on the mountain, all around us.

An environmental audit of our home would reveal a number of curious pecadilloes. One might notice the stacks of used envelopes and letters that sit near our telephone. Most of them are junk-mail envelopes. Some are the white backside of the letters inside. These envelopes are perfect for shopping lists and notes to each other and ourselves. Even squeezing one extra use out of a throwaway item somehow lessens the sting. This goes for foam cups (whenever they find their way into our sphere), plastic wine or other glasses, and even tin foil and cellophane wrap, which we hand-wash and reuse until it breaks or frays. Freezer bags are washed and reused repeatedly. Except for the most soiled specimens, even our paper napkins are reused— stuffed into a cup to serve as surrogate paper towels. (For Christmas Wanda has asked sister Jane for a set of twelve cloth napkins that we can wash and reuse.) Rags serve for floor cleanup and dusting chores.

In our bathrooms, an open bag collects cardboard toilet paper rings, which we use along with kindling in the wood-stoves.

A clean-home purist might be astonished to happen upon the occasional spiderweb in our home, which reveals two aspects of our housekeeping philosophy. First, unless it gets to dustball stage, why not put it off another day or week or month? And second, it would take a true infestation (of something like termites) to drive us to the exterminator. Other insects we can live with—or swat.

In a number of ways, we concede, what's acceptable to us is probably unacceptable to many fellow Americans. But it's easy to see that applying the standard of unmarred perfection to every aspect of our lives—from our skins to the skins of our vehicles, from carpet to the siding on a house—can not only consume much of one's waking life, but can eat away part of the soul.

When living more simply, one finds the time to borrow and lend possessions. We learned this first on the orchard with costly equipment that you have no choice but to borrow or rent from neighbors, and now we apply it to the rest of our lives. We use Virginia's food processor often, and she borrows our tools. We borrow Sam and Miriam's lawn mower; they borrow pots, pans, and use of our oven when cooking for crowds. And we all raid one another's cupboards.

We no longer regard it as lowbrow (but as sensible) to ask for a doggie bag to take home leftovers when at a restaurant. In fact, once you get away from the idea that everything should be perfectly clean, unmarred, unblemished, and new to be acceptable, it becomes fascinating to see the changes. A spotted blouse suddenly becomes usable again. You can leave the house with a pimple on your nose and no makeup on your face. An older car that has a dent in the side is more practical—it needs no burglar alarm system. In fact, perfection in the consumer culture and in personal appearance now seems to us a tainted ideal—an island of self-indulgence on a planet crying out for help from all of us.

There's a contradiction here, of course, not unlike the contradictions confronting anyone who thinks of him- or herself as environmentally sensitive yet uses electricity or gasoline or anything else that degrades the environment. As orchardists we sell fruit in a marketplace that demands a measure of perfection—not a pockmarked peach or apple with worms inside, but one worm free and with a visually appealing exterior. Perhaps in time more consumers will accept locally grown "organic" fruit. (One of the problems in discussing "organic" fruit is that there are no national standards on what organic fruit is.) In our wet eastern climate, that means much "organic" fruit, if fungicides are not used, will also be rotten by the time it ripens; the cost of growing a high percentage of rotten fruit would necessarily be shared by the consumer. Perhaps we could create our own market for cosmetically flawed apples and other fruit, though the transition, in which we would lose many if not most of our old customers, and be stuck with acres of unsold fruit, might very well bankrupt Levering Orchard.

Whatever the direction we take in the future, apple growers nationally are under fire these days. The 1989 controversy over Alar, the chemical agent by which some growers enhanced the color and firmness of certain varieties, led not only to its withdrawal from the market, but also to a new public image for many orchardists. No longer were apple growers producing the fruit that proverbially keeps the doctor away. Many consumers felt they were using the vilest of substances—chemicals—to jeopardize public health. Consumers no longer held apple growers above suspicion. Armed with blanket statements about all pesticides, some omniscient souls pronounced only "organically grown" apples and other fruits and vegetables safe to eat.

Though Sam had used Alar only one year some twenty years ago on a trial basis (it was not particularly effective here), since 1989 we have repeatedly answered questions about Alar and other chemicals. Many of our customers want to know how our fruit is grown and what effect eating sprayed apples, peaches, cherries, apricots, nectarines, and plums will have on their health. As we've answered these questions, and as the orchard has become ours as well as Sam and Miriam's, we've also been giving more attention to the effects of our practices on our immediate environment.

Fruit grower's jargon for how we cope with the insects and fungi that rot and disfigure fruit in eastern America is "integrated pest-control management," or IPM. The idea, essentially, is to let natural predators do the work of defending the fruit and leaves as much as possible. For example, ladybugs and predaceous mites, which some entirely chemically dependent growers kill in the course of their sprays, eat red mites, which, when left unchecked, will virtually strip an apple tree of its leaves, leaving the fruit small and the tree weakened. By not using chemicals that kill these predators, we don't need the miticides that are still widely in use. The same principle applies to several other so-called pests.

Unfortunately, in a wet climate it isn't possible—particularly with stone fruits like cherries and peaches—to grow fruit that won't rot in large quantities without spraying. But there are ways to spray as little as possible, stretching the time between applications to the absolute maximum. In years past most fruit growers simply sprayed on a fixed schedule based on stages in the development of blossoms and fruit. A better method is to keep a close track of the weather and of the fungi, such as apple scab and brown rot that flourish in rainy periods. Timing and watchfulness are critical. By keeping a close vigil for the spring emergence of the destructive coddling moths, we spray only when really needed, not the many times that are still called for by some experts. Make no mistake, in highly concentrated form and during the time of their potency, insecticides and fungicides—commonly lumped together as "pesticides"—are toxic chemicals. When handling them, we have to be careful not to inhale or swallow any of the liquid or dust. But unlike the infamous DDT, which remains poisonous for years, the compounds of the organic phosphates, which are the only spray materials we use, break down under weathering in a matter of weeks. Guthion, for example, a mainstay against coddling moths, becomes calcium phosphate (often used as a food additive) within three weeks or so after application.

Ideally, of course, we would prefer to use no chemicals at all, not only because of the period of toxicity, but because of the thousands of dollars we could save every year. But the blanket notion that all agricultural chemical usage threatens human health and farm and surrounding ecosystems is far from accurate. Here at the orchard we are practically swimming in bird, insect, and other forms of life. And not only are we forbidden to apply toxic chemicals at any time close to fruit harvest, but we are also annually tested by the state of Virginia for toxic residue on our fruit. In all the years that samples have been taken, the laboratory in Richmond has twice found legally harmless traces of one toxic metal—lead. Since lead has not been used at the orchard in spray materials for more than fifty years, we were more than curious the first time as to where the sample apples had been picked. It turned out that they came from a tree right along the Orchard Gap Road—these apples had inhaled the fumes of leaded gasoline!

Like other farmers, orchardists must also concern themselves with soil fertility. Before Sam's parents arrived, this land had been planted in corn every year for many years without regard to soil erosion, and some of the topsoil had washed away down the mountain. The first thing Sam's father, Ralph Levering, did when he bought the property in 1908 was to build stone walls along the contours of the hillside; these caught much of the washed soil. Nowadays, given the thick mat of weeds and grass that we mow twice every summer, there is virtually no water runoff or soil erosion. The black dirt, enriched every year by the mowings, stays home rather than clogging the small creeks that wind along the timbered edges of the orchard.

Our soil, however, remains naturally low in boron and nitrogen, both of which are essential for tree vigor. We add borox in spring sprays, where it's taken up by the fruit tree leaves. We add nitrogen to the soil by spreading it by hand under each fruit tree in the form of calcium nitrate, about five pounds to each mature tree. At this amount the trees take up the nitrogen, and aided by the ground cover, we avoid troubled waters. Nitrogen that seeps into groundwater remains an environmental threat in many agricultural areas.

Some farmers and gardeners who think of themselves as organic allege the superiority of "natural" over synthetic fertilizers. One can, in fact, make a reasonable case that in the best of all possible worlds, less environmental harm is done by avoiding the manufacture of fertilizers. And it's essential to promote soil fertility through natural processes, a fact too often forgotten in the widespread use of synthetic fertilizers. But to tout the superior fertility of "natural" fertilizers is a dubious business. The borox we use is indeed natural—only nature produced it. But in fact there is no chemical difference between the nitrate of soda that derives from the concentrated nitrogen in bird droppings in Chilean caves and the brand of calcium nitrate we use, manufactured in Norway by the Haber process, in which an electrical discharge fixes the nitrogen. Certainly our fruit trees—almost all of them a showcase of green vigor in the height of summer—make no distinction as they stretch toward the sun.

The truest form of enviromental simplicity is abstinence: leaving nature alone. We can't do it with our fruit trees. But we can practice environmental abstinence in the forests that surround the four coves where we grow fruit.

Every year since we moved here from California, timber cutters have knocked on our door with a wolfish gleam in their eyes. They'd been prowling in our forests—either on previous occasions before we moved or, in two instances, without our permission shortly before they reached our door. Each timber cutter, friendly but not shy with his opinions, howls the same high-pitched tune: You'd better cut your trees, they say; if you don't they're going to be past their prime and you'll lose them.

Perhaps we're just peculiar; perhaps, like Sam's father, who started this tradition of not cutting in the forests, we think the trees are doing just fine on their own; or perhaps, as Theodore Roosevelt once wrote, "nothing is more practical in the long run than the preservation of beauty."

But as time goes on, we'll happily "lose" them—the huge ninety-year-old poplars, the maple and ash trees, the various kinds of oaks. They're the biggest trees on private land in

Carroll County, or so the county forester tells us. And short of unforeseen circumstances, we'll let them all grow old and fall. The black earth will gladly take them back. It will also replace them—a job it does very nicely when left to its own devices.

Ours is a logic that defies financial reason. Neighbors who regularly cut their timber and who know about our orchard debt shake their heads at yet another eccentricity from the Leverings (and now a woman named Urbanska). Why, hell. If they don't want to cut 'em all, they could just thin 'em out a little. Wouldn't hurt those woods one bit.

But we persist in the status quo. In fact, with even the most careful of loggers, "thinning them out" means logging roads, soil erosion, fewer trees for years to come, and a haggard look to these undisturbed groves—and maybe that is the bona fide reason we send the timber cutters back to their pickups. But it's probably not the reason that strikes at the heart of the matter.

Sure, it's nice to have trees. "The forests are the lungs of our land," Franklin Roosevelt once said, "purifying our air and giving fresh strength to our people." And it's nice that they're beautiful in every season—inhaled daily, beauty does a lot more for the soul than money in the bank. But it's something more, we think.

Compromised like every environmentalist we've met, we yearn to live closer to our ideals. With these forests we leave behind our profane world and say, "This is sacred. This is where, without compromise, we give back to the environment a small measure of what we have taken." They may not be the most spectacular trees in the world. Their preservation may not make much difference against the riptide of environmental degradation. But at least for our lifetimes, these forests are in our custody. Toward that just and lasting peace that must come between economics and ecology, this is one step we can take to defend an ecosystem on privately owned land. This is our hallowed ground. And keeping it that way is our way of forging a link to the ideal.

CHAPTER NINE

Volunteering

Befitting our Quaker guests, we sat down to a simple lunch: egg-salad sandwiches and tossed salad. Having visited relatives in Florida, E. P. "Red" and Madeleine Stephenson were working their way up the East Coast en route to Pendle Hill, the Quaker "think tank" near Philadelphia, where members of the Society of Friends retreat to meditate, to mingle with kindred spirits, to take classes and write pamphlets and books. It was late March, and Red and Madeleine would be staying at Pendle Hill as Friends in Residence through May.

Frank had met the Stephensons the year before and had dined with them at their home in a rural intentional community north of San Francisco. These were not communal hippies living in some time warp in the California hills, but retirees, still vigorous in their early seventies. Tall and freckled, with clean-cut reddish hair, Red had looked as middle American in his California home as he did now. Ditto for Madeleine, a short, spunky, gray-haired woman with a gleam in her eyes.

We had invited Sam to join us for lunch.

"I remember thee from Philadelphia!" Madeleine said, reminding Frank's father of a conference they had attended together forty years ago.

"Why, yes!" Sam replied, his favorite phrase when he is feeling sociable. He turned to Red at his elbow. "And where is thy home?"

Red told him with considerable animation, explaining that he and Madeleine and a group of like-minded, simple-living friends owned most of their property in common.

"And where art thou from originally?" Sam went on, apparently assuming that no one Red's age could originally be from California.

"North Carolina."

Getting hardly a word in edgewise, we sat listening for an hour as the three Quakers, speaking the same language, merrily caught up on each other's lives. It was not just the "thees" and the "thys" and the "art thous"—traditional Quaker-speak since the seventeenth century, locution that Frank's father reserves for Friends of his own vintage and for Miriam. It was also the language of the Quaker ethic of volunteer service, an ethic that Red, Madeleine, and Sam have long embodied.

The Stephensons met on a ship bound for Europe in 1946, each committed to helping rebuild areas ravaged by World War II. For eighteen months Red built houses and worked on a transport team in Poland—a country targeted by the Quakers because it was more devastated by the war than any other. Working under the auspices of the Anglo-American Quaker Relief Mission, he delivered food, clothing, and building supplies. Food was scarce and had to be distributed selectively, to those who most needed help. Red vividly remembers the anguish of denying rations to hungry women who maintained they were pregnant but who were not yet showing it. Another agony was requiring young children to eat their portions on the premises, lest they run home and share them with parents and older siblings.

In a program sponsored by British Quakers, Madeleine delivered food and medical supplies in southern France and West Germany. Each earned only living expenses for their efforts. Those efforts are well documented, as the sweethearts wrote each other incessantly and now have in their personal archives hundreds of letters and reports from that period. In 1947 they returned to the United States, where they married and moved to California. Both have been active ever since in the American Friends Service Committee (AFSC), a Quaker organization founded in 1917 to help victims of World War I. In 1947, together with its counterpart, the British Friends Service Council, the AFSC won the Nobel Peace Prize.

That honor acknowledged a tradition of impartial service to human need, based on the theologically egalitarian notion that there is "that of God in every person." Tracing the history of Quaker relief efforts in the first half of the twentieth century, Gunnar Jahn, chairman of the Nobel Committee in 1947, noted in his address: "The Quakers gained confidence in all quarters through their work. Governments and individuals knew that they had no other aim than to aid. They did not intrude on people in order to convert them to their faith, and they made no difference between friend and foe."

Not distinguishing between friend and foe has often led Quakers into alien territory. In 1920 and 1921, after the communists had seized power, Quakers delivering food helped save the lives of hundreds of thousands of starving people in southern Russia. Similarly, after World War I the AFSC undertook a massive food relief program for sick and undernourished children in Germany. Twenty years later, in 1938, AFSC leader Rufus Jones journeyed to Berlin with two other Quakers, where he met with members of the Nazi Gestapo, offered relief packages, and urged lenience toward Jews.

Growing up, Frank was well versed in the parallel stories in his own family. His uncle Griffith, Sam's older brother, was a Philadelphia insurance executive when he took a two-year leave of absence from 1947 to 1949 to direct the Friends Ambulance Unit in China during that nation's civil war. Working without pay with roughly fifty volunteers in central China, Griffith Levering delivered medical supplies and oversaw inoculations for the dreaded south Asian disease kala-azar for partisans on both sides as well as civilians caught in the crossfire. It wasn't surprising, therefore, that in 1962, as spokesman for a Quaker delegation of six that met with the president for thirty minutes in the Oval Office, Sam Levering urged John F. Kennedy to help relieve famine in Red China by sending shipments of surplus American wheat.

"You mean feed your enemy when he's got his hands on your throat?" Sam remembers Kennedy responding.

"Why, yes," Sam answered him. "That's how you make friends of enemies. That is exactly what Jesus taught us to do."

"There are six of you talking to me," the president said. "How many people do you have talking to congressmen on the Hill this morning?"

Sam replied that they had seventy-four.

"That's fine," the president responded. "Send some more."

Listening to Sam and the Stephensons talk about past triumphs, we were getting that old, hollow feeling. Once again it was hard for us, especially Frank, not to feel that we weren't making enough room in our lives to help others or to work on world problems. All their adult lives, Sam and Miriam have volunteered much of their time in organizations working to promote peace and justice. Though twice we had given Wanda's cousin in Poland what for us were large sums of money, and though we contributed regularly to worthy organizations, we had made no sacrifice comparable to that of the Stephensons, donating eighteen months of their lives to helping victims of war. Giving only dollars seemed paltry by comparison.

On some questions we remained ambivalent. But on that day in which the Stephensons passed through our lives, we knew that we would like to follow their path in getting involved in some form of public service. Despite our physical isolation in Orchard Gap from world hot spots and decision makers, it was clear that major global problems—of war, of starvation and overpopulation, of environmental degradation and destruction—reached us even here, deep in the Blue Ridge. It was time, we knew, to live beyond mere self-interest, to act on the real stake we had in our community and our world.

It wasn't just the urgency of world problems. It was also the internal urgency of knowing that we were connected to "the main," in John Donne's words, and that acting on that connection could help fill the vacuum we felt by devoting so much time to our own concerns. Clearly some deeper satisfaction, deriving from more than token gifts of themselves to the world, was written on the faces of our three guests. In Sam and Miriam we had seen that satisfaction for many years. And it was no coincidence that three of the people to whom we were most drawn in Carroll County were former Peace Corps and Vista volunteers. One of them, a white native of Harlan County, Kentucky, had worked in the sixties helping register black voters in Mississippi. These people had given something back. Now active in local affairs, they were calm, empathetic, generous with their time, positive yet realistic thinkers.

During our twenties and early thirties, with occasional, transitory exceptions, we had not gotten involved. We'd convinced ourselves that we would "make it" first, then have enough time and money to address problems outside our immediate spheres. In the effort to simplify our lives, though, we were beginning to see this line of thinking as a fallacy, albeit a common one. There was never and never would be "enough" time or money. The challenge was to make room in our present lives for volunteer work.

"Sacrificial giving," Millard Fuller told us in Georgia, "is not all that big in America. But we're strong on giving a portion."

To make room for that portion, most adult volunteers who are also working for a living clear their schedules for an evening, a Saturday, a weekend, and occasionally a week or two of volunteer work. With some of the roughly 120,000 American Quakers, it is still not uncommon to push volunteerism even farther—to take a leave of absence from work, as Griffith Levering did, to set sail on a European mission like the Stephensons. But one expects that some semblance of normal life will resume upon one's return.

With Sam Levering, however, there neither is nor has been a "normal life" for almost fifty years. Sam's idea of giving a "portion" is half his time or more, every year, to unpaid service. That he is carrying out this notion well into his eighties—not only driving to his destinations, but making the trips in an unreliable old car—is a source of anxiety to his family. But not to Sam. For Sam, it is not a question of fitting his volunteer work into his schedule; rather, it's a question of organizing the rest of his life around his volunteer work. Since his mid-thirties Sam has enjoyed the remarkable luxury for an unwealthy man of spending roughly half his time as a volunteer.

In his essay "Quakerism and the Simple Life," Rufus Jones wrote: "Ask almost any young man what he wants to become and he will answer, 'I don't know yet.' He is waiting for somebody, or some occasion, to help him discover himself, to reveal to him what his own life means to him. Strange paradox, that I do not even know what I myself want and that I need outside help to discover the ideal of my own life."

In 1930, when Sam was twenty-two and a graduate student in pomology at Cornell, he heard a sermon on campus in Sage Chapel. As Millard Fuller told us, quoting an unidentified sage, "When the student is ready, the teacher will appear." For Millard, that teacher was Clarence Jordan at Koinonia Farm, the Christian community in Georgia. For earnest young Sam Levering, it was Rufus Jones, then a philosophy professor at Haverford College.

In the hands of parents bent on instructing their children, some old family stories, like biblical tales, take on mythic dimensions, oversimplifying the reality of self-revelation and life choices. Yet, like the story of Paul's conversion on the road to Damascus, Sam's story in its very simplicity—in its blinding flash of light that changes things forever—has always, for Frank, been unquestionably real, so real that he has often yearned for a comparable experience, a revelation "of what his own life means to him."

As Sam tells the story, he was sitting in the choir that Sunday morning when Jones spread Sam's life before him. "There are four great issues before our time," Jones told his listeners. The issues were the relationship between each individual and God; how to recover from the Depression; racial equality around the world; and war and peace. "To make the maximum contribution," Sam quotes Jones, "one needs to specialize in one of these four critical areas. If I were a young person, I would want to become an expert. I would want to know enough to really be helpful. That will take time. It might very well take ten years in which one would be learning before being able to make a real difference."

In order to do such work, suggested Jones, a founding father of the American Friends Service Committee, one could divide one's life into two halves. In one half a person would live simply and provide for necessities with a job. In the other half one would be free to make a significant contribution to solving global problems.

Following Jones's prescription, young Sam had determined "the ideal" of his life. But in which area should he specialize? In the summer of 1930, after running cross-country for Cornell in the Oxford-Cambridge meet in England, Sam had traveled on the Continent and heard Adolf Hitler speak at a Nazi rally in Munich. The experience had chilled him, convinced him that war was coming again in Europe. In his sermons Rufus Jones had said that "war is becoming so destructive that man and war cannot live on the same planet." Sam decided to devote himself to "the peace field," as he likes to call it. In time he would return to Virginia to take over his father's orchard while simultaneously working to end war throughout the world.

Sam met Miriam Lindsey at a student public speaking contest. A Cornell undergraduate majoring in history and government, Miriam chose as her topic "The Farmer and World Peace." She did not win the contest, but she won Sam's heart.

The daughter of a Methodist minister in Pittsburgh and a member of the state champion debating team in high school, Miriam shared Sam's interests in peace but—he claims—romanticized American farmers! Sam and Miriam married in Sage Chapel on her graduation day in 1934 and moved to Washington, D.C., where Sam spent five years working for the Farm Credit Administration before moving back to the orchard in 1939.

The rest is family history. From 1943 on, Sam says—once the orchard business was in gear—he began to lead his double life. Sam was a co-founder in 1943 of the Friends Committee on National Legislation, a Quaker lobby headquartered on Capitol Hill, which continues today to voice Quaker concerns in the halls of Congress. In its statement of purpose, the FCNL shuns pressure-group lobbying and "the manipulation of power," pledging instead "to work by means of quiet influence through personal contact and persuasion." As chairman of the executive committee of the FCNL from 1956 to 1972, Sam played a pivotal role in the development of the organization as a respected lobby for peace and social justice.

Garnet Dawson, Sam's longtime foreman, once offered a vivid image of the boss in his younger days. "Sam, he'd be out in the orchard wearing overalls," Garnet said, "and the next thing you knew, you'd see him pull off his overalls and underneath he'd be wearing a suit. Then he'd jump in the car and head on down the road."

Always the most ardent supporter of Sam's activism, Miriam, in time, joined him out on the stump. Family friends remember Miriam in the late forties packing her brood of young children into the Chevy carry-all and sallying forth to make speeches on behalf of World Federalism and the United Nations. As Frank grew up in the fifties and sixties, the sixth and last of the clan, Miriam seemed every bit as committed to world peace as his father.

Beginning in 1972, all the years of idealistic effort culminated for Sam and Miriam in their effort to promote an international, United Nations–sponsored Law of the Sea treaty and its ratification both in the United States and throughout the world. At stake was nearly three-fourths of the earth's surface. Who owned all that water, the right to fish in it and navigate through it? Who owned the vast untapped mineral wealth on the ocean floor? Who was to be held accountable for ocean pollution?

This was the real test of Sam and Miriam's joint decision to specialize in what for them had become the necessary link between peace and international law. Although in 1946 Sam had co-founded the World Federalists of North Carolina—the host organization for the founding convention of the United World Federalists in 1947, which enjoyed the leadership of North Carolina Senator Terry Sanford and the late Norman Cousins and fleeting support from none other than Ronald Reagan—by 1972 he had abandoned the World Federalist dream of a world government as hopelessly utopian in the real world of national sovereignty. Nor, clearly, was pacifism always the road to peace. As Rufus Jones had suggested, specializing in one problem area was an experience of endless study and growth. With the Law of the Sea negotiations, the senior Leverings saw an opportunity to draft what amounted to a constitution for the governance of the oceans.

Sam and Miriam worked in a top-floor office at the FCNL (for a time sleeping on a makeshift couch there and cooking in the employee kitchen). Their work was funded at a subsistence level by private contributions. Except during harvest times, when Sam had to be home full-time, every Friday evening for eleven years, he and Miriam would drive to Orchard Gap in their 1965 Dodge Dart, spend the weekend putting out fires on the home front, then return the 340 miles to Washington, D.C., on Sunday night. Remarkably, this grueling binary existence continued for eleven years—with interludes in New York, Geneva, Caracas, and Montego Bay, Jamaica, where the international conferences were held. At ages when many Americans were retired or on the verge of retirement, the Leverings were working as hard as or harder than their prime-of-life children.

It was an extraordinary period for Sam and Miriam, a testament to what informed private citizens with modest living demands can accomplish. To broaden their base of support beyond Quakerdom, Sam launched and became executive director of the United States Committee for the Oceans and was also appointed to the United States Public Advisory Committee on the Law of the Sea. In those capacities he worked closely with, among others, Jimmy Carter's ambassador to the Law of the Sea, Elliot Richardson. Between Law of the Sea conferences, Sam lobbied and testified frequently on Capitol Hill and worked to prevent passage of domestic legislation harmful to the negotiations.

As founder and executive director of the Ocean Education Project (OEP), Miriam directed an ever-changing cast of volunteers and several paid staffers. OEP's regular mission was public education on the Law of the Sea negotiations. Together with the United Methodist Law of the Sea Project, OEP organized more than sixty brainstorming seminars in Geneva, New York, and Washington, D.C., where conference delegates and experts from academia, industry, and the UN Secretariat met to discuss issues involving oil, fish, deep-seabed mining, and the continental margin. At these informal sessions, a number of ideas arose that helped break deadlocks at the conferences. Additionally, the two organizations published a conference paper, "Neptune," that served as a nonpartisan source of conference information for delegates.

Despite the Reagan administration's refusal to sign the treaty, Sam and Miriam's labors, along with those of countless others, were not in vain. In December 1982, at Montego Bay, Jamaica, 130 nations did sign a treaty that set limits to national jurisdiction, established navigational rights, provided for additional scientific research and environmental protection, and set forth guidelines for international management of the oceans as "the common heritage of mankind." It was, wrote *The New York Times*, "the greatest achievement in the development of the rule of law since the founding of the United Nations."

In a photograph they treasure, a radiant Sam and Miriam pose with four fellow organization members and Elliot Richardson under a tree at Montego Bay. It is their ascent of Everest, their marathon runner's triumph at the finish line. Though the United States has not yet signed that treaty, and the ratification process continues (sixty ratifications are needed for the treaty to come into force), Sam and Miriam closed up their Washington office in 1983 and returned to the orchard to live full-time.

With war and the use of nuclear weapons still a threat to the earth they have inhabited for a combined 161 years, Sam and Miriam's work is not done. These days they can regularly be seen on the highways of eastern America, traveling to board meetings, conferences, hearings, and lectures, Miriam's Ford Festiva and Sam's Escort their small boats in treacherous waters.

· · ·

Late one winter evening, well past everyone's bedtime, we were talking with Frank's parents and a mutual friend, sitting near the woodstove in Sam and Miriam's cozy living room. Patricia Devoe is a new friend, a fifty-two-year-old minister who had recently assumed the pastorate of the Methodist church in Hillsville. "Preacher Pat," as her folksy congregants call her, was asking Sam and Miriam how they became so committed to their ideals.

"Well," Sam said, "George Fox, the founder of Quakerism, put it succinctly. He said, 'We must become changed men before we go out to change others.' "

Miriam exhaled sharply. "I don't believe that," she said. "I think you change as you do something. If you wait until you are the person of your dreams, it may be too late. Moses had his body in the water before the Red Sea parted. You take the self that you have and you put it in the water."

The room was silent for a few moments, almost like a Quaker meeting, as if the five of us were groping for that "inner light" Friends prize. Sam and Miriam, it seemed, had sharply divergent views. But for us, we later reflected, the larger truth was with Miriam—not only in our desire to become volunteers, but in our entire lives as they continued to change. As the Catholic theologian Henri Nouwen once put it, "You don't think your way into a new kind of living; you live your way into a new kind of thinking." For us, that new kind of living would come sooner than we could have guessed.

· · ·

We first heard the news one weekday in July 1989. Just across the state line in North Carolina, on a Christmas tree farm at the foot of a hill we can see from our house, was the site of a proposed medical-waste incineration facility. A few days later we attended a public meeting and learned that the company planning to build the for-profit incinerators had grander visions than merely burning medical waste from North Carolina. Slipped into its application for a state air permit—the thing that most angered local residents—was a company request for permission to burn "brokered loads" of industrial and household waste from "the Northeast corridor of the United States." The company intended to expand its operation to a market predicted to grow at a rate of 300 to 500 percent within five years, with additional incinerators built to accommodate the growth and no apparent limit on the units added.

We were aghast. Would our fresh mountain breezes become laced with acid mist? Would the toxic-ash residue of the incinerators end up in local landfills, leach into the groundwater, and poison our soil? Would our pastoral, dairy-farming, fruit-growing section become the final resting ground for industrial by-products from New York and New Jersey? The answers seemed both obvious and horrifying. How could this nightmare happen so close to home?

In fact, we learned that first night, it could happen with chilling ease. As long as the company met North Carolina's lax air-quality standards, the state was obligated to issue a permit. With virtually no zoning laws, Surry County had little legal say in the matter. The absentee landowner of the 250-acre site had already agreed to sell his land to the start-up company, founded by three men who lived in a neighboring county to

the west, none of whom had any experience operating incinerators. Insiders estimated that any local firm that could get a
commercial-waste incinerator in place could turn around and
sell the package to a national waste conglomerate for a cool two
million. What's more, the location off a major interstate, in a
sparsely populated area just two miles from the state line (where
many people who would breathe the emissions had no political
clout in the state with jurisdiction), seemed ominously ideal for
environmental exploitation.

One dairy farmer at the first meeting said what we were all
thinking: "If it was so safe to burn this stuff, why would they
want to truck it all the way down here?"

It was peach season at the orchard, but even as we picked
and sold peaches, all we could think about was the prospect of
looking out our window and seeing incinerator smokestacks
spewing toxic emissions seven days a week, twenty hours a day.
The hot August days hung heavy and strange with a sense of
imminent apocalypse. Expelling toxic dioxins and metals into
the air, the incinerators would mar the beauty and threaten the
health of our community. Who knew their effect on our fruit
and that of our fellow orchardists? And of the substances permitted to be burned, experts said that at least twenty-one would
be carcinogenic. But of even greater concern to us was who
would monitor each load carefully enough to screen out the no-
no's that might be slipped into the mix. The answer seemed
obvious. With a skeletal staff, we feared no one would.

Like countless others before us, we rolled up our sleeves
in self-defense. A high school know-it-all, working at the orchard that summer, pronounced us "NIMBYs" (for Not in My
Back Yard). The charge was true enough, but we refused to

accept its pejorative connotation. If we didn't fight to protect the environment of our community, who would? Certainly not those who stood to make a quick buck off such a project; certainly not those in urban areas who sought to ship their garbage out of sight and out of mind.

At the public meeting we'd attended, a group called Citizens Against Pollution was founded. We joined what was initially a small, furious, frightened band of rural folk, many of them farmers, and went about trying to slay what looked like Goliath. Working as a peach saleswoman by day, Wanda took to the telephone by night, catching up on the latest developments from other organizers, putting out the word to residents in Virginia. For two months, on into the apple season, Wanda threw herself into the cause, with Frank helping when he could.

A Carroll County chapter of Citizens Against Pollution formed, and Wanda was drafted as chairperson. She testified before the county governing body, the Carroll County Board of Supervisors, urging the supervisors to pass a resolution against the proposed incinerator facility, which they did. She spoke at local meetings and handed out form letters to sign, petitions and sheets with names, addresses, and phone numbers of public officials to call. She wrote our Virginia representatives, asking them to bring pressure to bear on their North Carolina counterparts, urging them to consider our county's opposition to this facility. Newspaper editors in both states ran Wanda's letters. In the end, thousands of letters poured into state agencies in Raleigh, evoking bureaucratic amazement at the sheer volume emanating from this rural pocket. We pulled Keith Love, a Los Angeles journalist friend, into the act. Keith contacted an editor at the *Greensboro News and Record* and proposed an article on the anti-incinerator campaign, which resulted in a long news story.

After all the attempts to influence officials in Raleigh, a simple thing happened. Throughout the campaign the incinerator company remained intractable, its principals refusing even to talk with the opposition. But the owner of the land himself caved in to public pressure. After months of personal appeals, in October he sent a registered letter to the three businessmen, terminating their option to buy his land. And although they threatened legal action to force a sale, nothing has come of it so far.

It was an exhilarating victory. More than that, the experience of uniting with other people in a common cause, of being a factor in a happy outcome, gave us our first real taste of social action. The experience had broadened into some measure of personal revelation. Working with others for the public good was now in our blood. We were eager to volunteer our talents again.

In the anti-incinerator campaign, we worked closely with the then chairman of the Carroll County Board of Supervisors, J. Eddie Vaughan, organizing opposition in the county. It was a lesson in the workings of local politics, at least in our county, where everybody knows everybody else. In December 1989, Eddie Vaughan, a staunch Republican, called Frank to ask if he would accept an appointment to the eight-member Carroll County Planning Commission as the new representative of the Fancy Gap Magisterial District (his and our home district).

The county badly needed "public-minded" people, he said. Though the job paid only gas money, it was an opportunity for Frank to play an active role in helping to shape the future of the county. Frank accepted.

Carroll County has changed markedly in Frank's lifetime from an agrarian society with a distinctly Appalachian flavor to a social polyglot of natives and "outsiders," many of the latter being retirees or second-homers in developments capitalizing on the scenic beauty of the Blue Ridge. Many of the older mountain people, fiercely independent, esteem private property next to God and view government regulations of any sort with deep hostility. To some natives the word *zoning*, or the idea of regulating land development in any way, remains synonymous with communism.

For Frank, serving on the commission—with its monthly meetings and regular clashes among members—has provided a window into the torturously slow process of public decision making. As we write, the commission is beginning to draft a comprehensive plan for land use in the county, and issues like zoning and farm and rural heritage preservation are at the forefront of intense and often heated discussion. Frank has already found the experience to be an illustration of how one lives one's way into a new way of thinking. Once an armchair critic of local decision making and benighted attitudes, he's now been forced into the more tolerant and creative role of trying to be a part of the solution.

With new ways of thinking come new priorities, new urgencies we never anticipated. When we left California, the focus of finding ways to simplify was almost exclusively on ourselves, the quality of our own lives. In Virginia we've developed a stake in our community. Here, having developed a visceral appreciation for volunteer service, we are asking ourselves how to make more room in our lives for that work.

We do not, however, care to bite off more than we can chew. The problem of overextending ourselves as volunteers—though hardly an imminent one—can be serious, with haunting examples right here in the cove. Sam himself admits that by spending so much of his time on higher concerns, he neglected his business, which in turn racked up a burdensome debt. Equally disquieting, though, was that when growing up, Frank and the other siblings often resented playing second fiddle to their parents' idealistic concerns.

We did not want to become so swept up by a cause that volunteerism became a surrogate brand of workaholism and intruded on our other goals.

Being a useful volunteer does not necessarily entail saving the world. It does mean making the best use of your opportunities and talents in your own context—in short, finding a need and filling it.

"No day, no hour, comes, but brings in its train work to be performed for some useful end—the suffering to be comforted, the wandering led home, the sinner reclaimed," wrote the social reformer Dorothea Dix, who in the 1840s led a one-woman crusade to improve the attitudes toward and living conditions of the mentally ill.

Like Sam and Miriam, Sue Rickert, our friend in San Francisco, has made a life of volunteering. When young Sue was teaching English in Tanzania as a Peace Corps volunteer from 1964 to 1966, she "got in the habit of giving my time and making a gift of my profession. I was doing it for the love of it, the excitement of it."

But service in the Peace Corps does not a lifetime make. Sue married fellow volunteer Steve Jacobs, an affluent young man from San Francisco, and moved with him out of Africa into a house high on a hill overlooking pastel houses and the blue Pacific. While Steve developed shopping centers and made life financially stable and materially comfortable for Sue and their three children, Sue threw herself into what Wendy Kaminer, author of *Women Volunteering*, calls the long, honorable tradition—especially among well-educated, middle- to upper-class women—of "public housewivery," or unpaid social service.

Sue chaired an organization based in Haight-Ashbury that sheltered runaways and helped to reunite them with family members. She sponsored refugees, helping them find work and places to live, offering herself and her home. A young Vietnamese couple with a small child moved in with Sue and her family for a year. "It was not much from us, just a place to stay and moral support," she said. "But it meant so much to them." Today, she told us proudly, the husband is a computer programmer, his wife a unit manager at a bank, and they own their own home.

In the summer of 1980 we, too, were the beneficiaries of Sue's largesse. With our car loaded down with Wanda's belongings, we were making our roundabout way from Wanda's Manhattan apartment on East Forty-first Street to our new home together in Venice Beach, California. Staying with Sue and Steve for almost a week, we never could have guessed that before the decade ended they would be divorced and Sue would be living in the same house with her children and her second husband, Tom Rickert.

With Sue's new life has come diminished prosperity. Despite the change of circumstances, she continues to find ways to volunteer and—if she resumes teaching—is determined not to eclipse that part of herself with professional obligations. "It may sound strange," she said, "but I enjoy doing what I want to do for free. It's voluntary rather than obligatory, even though your commitment to it can be just as strong. It's more fun to do it for the love of it than to get paid for it."

Every Tuesday Sue reports to San Francisco General Hospital and makes herself available to nurses, doctors, and social workers for massage therapy. Sue also brings her healing hands to her work as a lay minister at the hospital. San Francisco General is one of the few hospitals in the country with lay chaplains, and she's one of about twenty there.

Her ministry is unusual. "I'd rather do a nonverbal visit," Sue said. "When people are in the hospital they are often so sick they don't want to talk. A lot of them are starved for touch. So I asked the head chaplain if I could do massage. I trained for six months as a massage therapist and went back and said, 'I want you to know that there is a chaplain who is also a massage therapist.'"

On a typical day Sue usually starts with "a chair massage to seven nurses at Ob-Gyn. We're having a huge crack epidemic in San Francisco, with women giving birth to crack-addicted babies. So I've chosen the nurses who are working with the addicted mothers. They're with the mothers before, during, and after the labor; they're stressed to the limit. They will take me to patients who are about to give birth or are in the middle of labor. I am a presence for them."

For a woman with three children to put through college,

working entirely for love may no longer be an affordable option. For many prosperous retirees, however, volunteer service does offer the happy prospect of love's labor gained.

Over the past few years we've come to know many such retirees—we talk with hundreds of them every year at the orchard, where they constitute a significant number of our customers. What strikes us most about these well-to-do retirees is just how many of them seem to be starved for a sense of purpose. Ironically, coming from retirees, this refrain often takes the following form: their lives of leisure are too booked up, too full of distracting activities; there's no time left for the challenges they crave.

After he retired, Dr. Stefan P. Wilk, a former radiologist and professor at the University of California Los Angeles Medical School, and his wife, Wanda Harasimowicz Wilk, spent much of their time at L.A.'s Lakeview Country Club playing golf and bridge, eating and drinking, passing time with friends. After a few months they could stand the life of leisure no longer. "I felt I was wasting my time," said Wanda Wilk. All but abandoning these pastimes, they flung themselves into two causes—the advancement of medicine in Poland and the collection of Polish music—which now consume as much as forty hours a week for each of them, sometimes more.

"Medical knowledge and music don't concern themselves with politics, beliefs, national boundaries," said Stefan, by way of explaining their focus. "They are deaf to foreign accent, blind to skin color. These are universal languages. Music and health always unite people."

The Wilks say that becoming full-time volunteers with twin

missions was the best decision they could have made: they've never felt better. "I'm seventy-one," Wanda said, "but I don't feel my age."

We sat with the Wilks in their Studio City home overlooking the San Fernando Valley, the late afternoon sun flashing on the dark glass towers below at Universal Studios. By Thoreau's hairshirt standards, the Wilks' life is hardly simple. Stefan drives a sleek, late-model Cadillac and their house is worth a king's ransom in Los Angeles.

It has often been argued, as it is by Duane Elgin in his book *Voluntary Simplicity*, that "living closer to the level of material simplicity" helps one achieve an "awareness of world reality," breaks down the insulation of wealth, and helps create the empathy for others that is the soul of volunteerism. No doubt this is often true. Talking with the Wilks, though, we immediately became aware that prosperity in itself need be no barrier to active concern for the less privileged. The Wilks are a prime example of how affluent retirees can simplify their lives by focusing their energies as volunteers.

At seventy-four Stefan is a trim, handsome man with a chiseled jawline, a thick shock of gray hair, and hands that carve the air as he speaks in chivalrous, sometimes irreverent tones. Orphaned in rural eastern Poland at age seven, he emigrated to the United States in 1952, a thirty-five-year-old physician—"just another displaced person," he said. That same year he met and married Wanda, a Polish-American born in Hamtramck, Michigan.

"When I came here, I didn't speak English," joked Stefan in a still-noticeable Polish accent. "I said the best way to learn a foreign language is to go to sleep with a dictionary. Consequently, I married a dictionary!"

Having traveled to Poland frequently in recent years and witnessed what by American standards were appalling deficiencies in medical resources and information, the Wilks started the Children's Medical Care Foundation (CMCF) in 1981 with a $100,000 founding donation. Stefan is now president of the foundation, which includes, among its trustees and officers, the chancellor of UCLA and the dean of the UCLA School of Medicine.

"We don't know how many lives of children we've saved because in Poland they have only seven or eight kidney dialysis machines for the entire country," said Stefan. These overworked units, he explained, had been able to accommodate only two to three out of every ten children who needed them. Today, thanks to CMCF's work, an ambulatory dialysis method has been introduced that is taking some of the burden off those few machines.

"In 1984 they did the first kidney transplant in a child because of our program," said Stefan with pride. "As of a month ago, they'd done eighty. The other major thing, we've gone into neonatology. We found that the worst infant mortality rate in Europe, next to Albania, is in Poland."

In practical terms, what CMCF does is send American doctors to Poland to train Polish doctors, bring Polish doctors to study at UCLA, and sponsor joint research projects. "We limit our medical help to children," Stefan said. "In World War II, 2.2 million Polish children perished, innocent children, because of neglect, hunger, abandonment, gas chambers, and everything else. We have to focus somewhere. So we concentrate on children."

Stefan's days are full: fund-raising and overseeing a range of foundation activities, including organizing an annual charity ball. Often the Wilks play host for weeks, sometimes months, to Polish physicians studying in the United States.

When not cooking for or chauffeuring her houseguests, Wanda Wilk spends most of her volunteer hours as director of the Polish Music Reference Center (PMRC) on the University of Southern California campus. The reference center—housed in an impeccable, densely shelved room decorated in red and white for the Polish flag—was Wanda's brainchild. In writing her thesis for her master's degree at USC, the former music teacher was appalled at being unable to find even one book on the history of Polish music printed in the United States. "Poland has much talent," she declared, "and outside of Chopin, it's largely unknown in this country."

Fired by her desire to correct this glaring omission, Wanda has guided the center to its present status as "the largest collection on Polish music outside of Poland. . . . Students are writing us from all over the world," says the buoyantly energetic Wanda. "Where can I find this music? Where can I get this recording? It will all just keep growing."

Following in the tradition of Edmund Urbanski, who faithfully sent packages of food and clothing to his family in Poland during the postwar years and, in 1961, arranged to sponsor his older sister, Janina, here, we have several times played host to Wanda's Polish cousins at the orchard. In 1988 we found work picking cherries for the sister and new spouse of Wanda's second cousin's husband. We wanted them to have a little spare cash with which to tour America and something to take back to Poland to improve their lives.

Wanting to help the Poles has been a consistent impulse of

Wanda's ever since she first toured Poland with her father in 1977, the summer of her junior year in college. The Poles she met were, by American standards, the ultimate simple livers (though not by choice). Most lived in dormitorylike spaces and queued up for scarce food. They traveled on mass transportation and celebrated books and art and music and family. They studied English and other foreign languages in their spare time. And though there was much generosity, intelligence, and abundant pride in their heritage, the Poles rightfully felt they were still living under foreign occupation.

The concomitant sense of impotence, Wanda sensed, was exacerbated by the fact that Poland never had the chance to recover from the devastation of World War II. Even as late as the late seventies, the Poles were subject to the complex that Nobel laureate Czeslaw Milosz so aptly coined in 1953—the "captive mind"—of performing "mental acrobatics" in order to abide by an ugly political reality. In purely human terms, Wanda's first trip to Poland brought home to her how rare was the American life-style of abundance in the global community and how great were the needs of other peoples. If Quaker activists pricked Frank's conscience, Wanda's ideals were stirred by the work of the Wilks. And although we'd entertained Poles, no humanitarian objective had been attached to our hospitality. Perhaps someday one would be.

In Stefan and Wanda Wilk, as in every other freely giving person we'd encountered, the energy of volunteerism could move mountains. Back on our mountain, we knew from experience with the incinerator battle that people working together toward a common objective could accomplish what individuals could not. What would happen if every able-bodied man, woman, and child on earth released as much white-hot energy as did the Stephensons, the Fullers, Sue Rickert, and the Wilks? The earth would move beneath our feet. Mt. Everest itself would tumble into the sea.

"They're like kids," Wanda once said when Sam and Miriam burst in on us late one evening, returning from a trip to Washington, D.C. "Your parents are just like a couple of school kids when they come back from the road."

They're on top of the world, in fact. Almost always. Bragging about their latest exploits. Talking excitedly about the people they've met. Laughing and carrying on.

We'd gladly settle for that second childhood ourselves.

CHAPTER TEN

The Ties that Bind

On October 1, 1983, we were married in Castine, Maine, in a small, stone Episcopal church overlooking Penobscot Bay. The site was Wanda's choice. Raised Episcopalian, she had loved tiny Castine, with its frame houses marching down to the salt water, since her high school days in Orono. Settled in 1613, Castine boasts two charming old inns near the water's edge and is the home of the Maine Maritime Academy and home harbor to its large training ship, the *State o' Maine*.

On the night before the wedding, Frank's parents hosted a dinner at the Pentagoet Inn for guests who had gathered from as far away as California. After dessert came the roasts and the toasts, followed by conversations late into the night. As Wanda visited with friends and family, Frank stole away at one in the morning to camp alone on a rocky beach. Sleeping little if at all, he listened to tinkling buoys and watched the stars yield to the red ball of the sun, lifting out of Penobscot Bay.

Our wedding day passed in a solipsistic rush. Escorted into the church by her handsome, elderly father, the bride wore an antique lace jacket over an apricot silk camisole and an off-white, silk, tea-length skirt from the thirties. The groom had purchased a new dark navy suit. Later we joked that we had "walked the plank" with the Reverend David Plank, the affable, open-minded Episcopal rector. The ceremony was a religious hybrid that must have seemed peculiar to some guests. In addition to the abridged Episcopalian vows, we observed minutes of silent meditation traditional in Quaker weddings, and family and friends read passages from Anne Morrow Lindbergh's *Gift from the Sea*, the Bhagavad Gita, and the writings of Quaker mystic James Nayler.

Wanda's mother, an avowed skeptic about the institution of marriage, nevertheless staged a lively reception high aboard the *State o' Maine*. Renting the entire top deck for fifty dollars and hiring uniformed cadets from the Maine Maritime Academy to pour champagne and a band to play Scotch-Irish fiddle tunes, Marie provided us and our guests with a stunning setting. For less than a thousand dollars, Marie—with the help of her daughter Jane, who made the wedding spice cake from an Emily Dickinson recipe, and an Orono couple who catered the event (complete with Maine lobsters!) for love, not money—put on the wedding reception.

Ducking down the gangplank through squalls of rice, we drove southwest toward Boston into the sunset, astonished that we were now actually husband and wife. In those hours of self-absorption, we believed that we had only married each other. In fact, as time was to demonstrate, we had also married each other's families. This simple truth, self-evident to many graybeards of the institution, had not been readily apparent to us in California. As long as a continent loomed between us and the majority of our families, we saw relatives infrequently and then (usually) only at exalted occasions.

But after we moved to Virginia, neither of us could doubt that on that day in Castine we had entered into a wider marriage of family traditions and values. Like many before us, we had tried to remake ourselves in California, to cocoon ourselves, in a bond that belonged to us and not to our families back east. In Virginia, with Frank's parents and cousin literally within shouting distance and siblings in every direction, with Wanda's father and stepmother in Silver Spring, Maryland, her mother in Maine, and her aunt and cousins in Georgia, North Carolina, and Washington, D.C., we were back in "the bosom of the family," as Miriam liked to say.

Over dinner recently, a woman in her early thirties, with whom we were just getting acquainted, turned to Frank and said: "So what's it like living so close to your parents?" Before Frank could reply, she went on: "I don't see how you do it. I can't even imagine living in the same *city* with my parents— much less next door!"

For a few moments, with his questioner, Wanda, and two others waiting for his answer, Frank was at a loss. In a polite, five-way, dinner-table conversation, surely this woman whom he hardly knew wasn't soliciting a discourse on the range of his feelings about the subject. Yet she was studying him intently, apparently genuinely curious.

"Well," Frank ventured, "it's like any rich experience— it's not all roses. I'm sure my parents feel the same way about living close to me. But I feel very lucky to have this chance to know them at this time in their lives. And,"—he paused— "they seem a heck of a lot wiser now than they did when I was growing up."

Frank had meant it sincerely—his parents *had* changed; his father especially had mellowed with age—but everyone broke into laughter at what they took to be his joke, so he laughed along. When the subject shifted abruptly, as subjects generally do among strangers, Frank was off the hook—which was not altogether where he wanted to be. In fact, his new acquaintance had raised a compelling question. In abbreviated form he had given her the straight goods.

Perhaps we're getting older, getting "wiser" with age, as Frank had said of his parents. Perhaps we've also realized that there is never enough time for family unless you make the time. And to make the time, you can't be obsessed with work, or money, or even your marriage in the narrowest sense. Not just because we moved east, but because we have chosen to circum- scribe our work to make time for, among other things, family, we have come to know each other's families—and our own— as never before.

For Frank, whose parents never seemed truly old before he returned to Virginia, seeing his mother and father make the passage into old age has been an experience that defies synopsis. They have never seemed more paradoxical, more courageous (as Sam was on the eve of his quadruple heart bypass operation at age seventy-eight), yet more fearful of physical vulnerability; more emotionally needy, yet more obstinately independent; more generous with their memories and their time for family, yet often driven as if by a dwindling hourglass.

No longer their towheaded last child, their chafing adoles- cent, or their wayward son in Hollywood, Frank has learned in his thirties to turn down much of his own volume and accept his parents as the struggling mortals they are. For Frank, though, the reward for all the hours spent with Sam and Miriam will always be in having known them intimately as an adult, known them in thousands of images and words that will be memories long after they have gone.

Frank's socially adept dinner-table questioner next turned to Wanda and gave her the chance to respond: "What's it like living so close to your in-laws?"

There had been no big eruptions, no major battles, with Sam and Miriam, but Wanda's mind quickly focused on the thing that had bothered her most early on and, still sometimes, to the present day: their not knocking when coming into our home. We couldn't argue in peace, or make love in the daytime, or take a nap during work hours without being "caught in the act" . . . or potentially being caught.

But from their point of view, why should they knock? They had lived in this house for forty-seven years without knocking. No person had ever been a stranger to them, so why should they be strangers in their old house? Besides, it wasn't strangers, or even neighbors, they were dropping in on—it was just family.

Having "just family" so close at hand as to strike at any moment made Wanda squeamish. Having lived most of her life in cities and towns, she didn't think it appropriate for anyone—except Frank—to walk into her house uninvited. Entering without consent was an invasion of the privacy she'd always enjoyed. Why couldn't she expect the same courtesies here?

Frank had no real quarrel with the custom of the cove, but he empathized with the woman who hadn't grown up here, who'd been willing to move to his old turf. Still, if Wanda wanted his parents to knock, fine. *She* must tell them so.

Their not knocking continued to grate on Wanda's nerves,

yet she couldn't bring herself to confront them about it. A friend in Los Angeles suggested she install locks on the door (there had never been any) and keep them locked. This way they'd have to knock. But she couldn't do it.

One of our first visitors was Wanda's godmother from Texas, a close friend of Marie's since their college days in Oklahoma and a loyal family friend during trying times in Kentucky. Irene Haskett sized up the tension and took Wanda aside, advising her to "go slowly" at the orchard. "Try not to tread on anyone's feelings," she'd said. "These are older people. They don't bend the way younger ones do."

Wanda had to agree. She realized it was not only a family here on the mountain, but a culture, with much to admire, a certain amount to dispute, and much from which to draw and to learn. Besides, Sam and Miriam had been here first. She would have to be flexible, make the adjustment.

Rather than risk hurting their feelings by asking them to knock, Wanda decided to make her point by knocking on their door and waiting for an invitation to enter. Perhaps the senior Leverings would grasp her point and follow suit.

"Why are you knocking?" asked Miriam, apparently puzzled. She smiled. "*You* don't have to knock."

"Oh," Wanda said. "Well, I think it's always better to knock." She hoped she was making her point obliquely.

"You don't have to knock, dear," Miriam said, dismissing the matter and waving Wanda in.

The next time Miriam came calling at our house, she burst through the door, calling out her customary "Yoo-hoo!" from the entryway. Likewise cousin Virginia Price. Sam continues to invade on remarkably catlike feet, declaring his amiable presence when he is hard upon us, usually in our offices, peering over our shoulders at our computer screens.

Wanda has since come around to the entrenched custom of entering the other houses in the cove without bothering to knock. Her adaptation to her no-knock neighbors is one small measure of how she's gotten to know the family by immersing herself in its customs. Experiencing this and many other informalities in the Levering family, she's come to see how, growing up here, Frank developed a preference for informality in behaviors ranging from dress to the friendly way he greets customers who appear at our doorstep after hours. In such small interactions as well as by spending time with her in-laws, Wanda has gotten to know her spouse far better than she ever did in the Levering-free zone of California.

We like to think that even as differences come more sharply into focus in a hotbed of family values, a marriage can quicken as it probes and honors its many dimensions and differences. Moving to the center of Frank's Quaker and southern heritage has offered Wanda a front-row seat in the theater of his psyche.

Long before we arrived here to live, we worried about the imbalance our new address would create: the far heavier dose of Frank's family. In the abstract it was fine to be passing so much time with his parents and cousin, not to mention all the siblings, in-laws, nephews, and nieces, uncles, aunts, and cousins who flock to the orchard in the summertime. But all that family becomes an issue if not counterbalanced by time both of us have spent with Wanda's scattered clan.

Under the circumstances, it is of course impossible to balance the equation, nor do we aspire to balance it formulaically. But among the fringe benefits of our twin professions and our simplified life-style has been the repeated ability to "work in" members of Wanda's family as we have traveled on various writing projects, as well as the ability—because we are not nine-to-fivers working fifty weeks a year—to visit them when we choose.

In the course of many of our travels, we make it a point to pass through Silver Spring, Maryland, where we visit Wanda's father and stepmother, invariably spending the night. In marked contrast with Sam and Miriam's informality, Frank (still) refers to his father-in-law as "Dr. Urbanski," which seems to suit him. Monastically quiet by day, the Urbanski apartment comes alive in the evening, when lamps cast an amber glow on the Latin American Indian artifacts Edmund Urbanski has collected over a lifetime and Wanda's father feverishly burns the night oil with engrossing stories of his travels and research as a Latin Americanist. On request he will produce from a glass case the grapefruit-size shrunken head of a Peruvian Indian and offer details of how the job was done. Or he will tell of the days of his early manhood in Poland, when he was a shipyard journalist in Gdansk writing, among other things, anti-Nazi articles, of how his name was put on a Nazi death list, and of how in 1939 he escaped to Mexico on a sugar boat under an assumed name.

That Wanda's father came not only from the old country but was born in the first decade of this century has made Frank more tolerant of Wanda's need to observe more formal rituals that initially had seemed restrictive to him—such as the sit-down meals at appointed hours that Wanda prefers (his own family generally took dinner trays to the TV set). Wanda's impatience with group conversation in which six people speak at once and interrupt at will likewise has its roots in her father's love of focused, salon-style discourse.

While visiting Mainers who have simplified their lives, we stayed nine nights with Marie in Orono. It was one of many visits we've made to Maine since moving east.

Marie comes to visit, usually during the summer, and gamely helps out at harvesttime signing in cherry pickers and working the cash register at the packhouse. Edmund came down to the orchard for several consecutive summers after we first moved east, but more recently, as he's entered his eighties, he has been reluctant to test his wobbly legs on our hilly terrain.

When we drove down to Georgia to meet Millard and Linda Fuller, we spent a weekend with Wanda's aunt, Marie's younger sister, Margaret Olesen Corbin, and her husband, Charles Corbin, who live in Macon. Just when Frank was convinced that his fast-talking wife was strictly a child of immigrants—first-generation Polish-American on her father's side and third-generation Danish-American on her mother's father's side (and a damn Yankee to boot)—he spent a few days with Aunt Margaret and Uncle Charles. In Aunt Margaret's slow, elegant speech and refined manners, Frank heard the southern quarter of his wife's roots.

Wanda's maternal grandmother, Esther Mitchell Olesen, grew up the daughter of the mayor of Oxford, North Carolina, a small tobacco town in the eastern part of the state, about 115 miles, as the crow flies, from Mount Airy. Esther married Charles Olesen, a Danish-American petroleum engineer from Salem, Massachusetts, and raised her three daughters in Pennsylvania, Texas, and Oklahoma—always yearning for the gen-

teel South of her youth. In her later years, living with the
Corbins in Macon, Wanda's granny perhaps recaptured something of that lost world in the gentlemanly manner of her son-
in-law, a Macon native, in her youngest daughter, in the
Corbins' three solicitous sons, and in the formal appointments
of the house shaded by tall pine trees on Hillandale Circle.

When Frank first met Wanda in Cambridge in the spring
of 1977, she was planning a summer trip to Poland, where
her father was lecturing in Spanish at the University of Warsaw. Prior to Wanda, Frank's previous exposure to Polish-
Americans had been confined largely to several formidable
players on the Wesleyan football team. One bright and cheerful
young man named Kochanowski, who was a rock-solid 210
pounds, had regularly butted helmets with Frank in the in-
trasquad scrimmages.

Wanda's keen interest in her Polish roots was both novel
and intriguing to Frank. Like most Americans, he possessed
only the most cursory knowledge of Poland's history and culture, all filtered through the biases of the American media. And
whoever heard of anyone Wanda's age wanting to spend an
entire summer hanging around her elderly father and aunt in
their native land?

We exchanged letters that summer. As Frank wrote of
cherries and peaches, farmers and heat waves, Wanda described
exotic places like Toruń and Warsaw, Krakow and Poznan.
When we returned to Cambridge in the fall, she elaborated,
sprinkling in unpronounceable Polish phrases. Long before we
were a couple, Frank associated this exuberant young woman
with royal castles and secret police and cousins with exotic names
like Grzegorz and Witold.

For Frank, our journey to Poland in December of 1987 was as much an inner journey into his wife's "deep past" as it was a succession of places and people. Staying a week with cousin Grzegorz Urbanski and his family in Poznan, we made daily pilgrimages to family landmarks, beginning with the boyhood home of Edmund and Jozef Urbanski, Wanda and Grzegorz's fathers respectively—brothers who grew up in Ostrów Wielkopolski, when the country was still partitioned and that section was under German rule.

Traveling by car, train, and foot in a multitude of towns and cities, we tracked down old apartment buildings where family members had once lived, schools and universities they'd attended, buildings where they had worked, and cemeteries where some were buried. From Grzegorz and his mother and sister, we heard dozens of stories: how Wanda's grandfather had established his business selling Singer sewing machines in Ostrów; how Grzegorz's father had fought the Germans in 1939, then escaped from a prisoner-of-war camp; how the war had uprooted the family and how some—but not Wanda's grandparents—had managed to survive.

In Warsaw were more relatives, more stories, more of the tapestry of family history. As Wanda has done by living in Virginia, Frank did for a period of brief intensity in Poland: entered into the web of family history and myth that is at the core of identity.

In 1990 we attended (Frank for the first time, Wanda for the sixth) the forty-eighth annual meeting of the Polish Institute of Arts and Sciences in America, held that year at Georgetown University.

Attendance at these meetings—which for Edmund since

retirement has been one of the high points of the year—has drawn Wanda closer to a father she had not lived with since age nine. Preoccupied with his scholarly work before and after the divorce, Edmund saw Wanda during the summers, as she and Jane grew up with Wanda's mother in Kentucky and Maine. Since moving east, Wanda has made a priority of continuing the mission she started in her 1977 trip to Poland of getting to know her father. Her frequent short stays in Silver Spring and Edmund's occasional longer visits to the orchard have balanced the picture of the man, helping to forge a bond neither she nor her father could have imagined a few years earlier.

This intensified interaction with our families has by no means been all sweetness and light. Our efforts to connect with our families—and through them with each other—have created some heavy weather as we've tried to come to grips with what we don't like in ourselves, each other, and our kin. At times it is tempting to offer an argument diametrically opposed to that offered here: to say that it would make our lives less complicated to see less of our families; that life would be easier without being reminded so frequently of family flaws, many of them mirrored in our own psyches.

At this time in our lives, though, the physical and emotional closeness with family, even though it carries with it old wounds and painful truths, is precisely what we hold dear. That our parents have not always been models, that we have not always been thoughtful, that hurtful sibling rivalries persist even into adulthood, are realities that we now prefer to face. We are, therefore, motivated not to simplify by eschewing family, but to simplify so as to have family in our lives.

. . .

For many people, friends are as much family as blood relatives—sometimes more so. In Los Angeles we knew more people who had little to do with their biological families than those who had close family ties. Perhaps we too were in that category, substituting friends for family on holidays as well as throughout the year.

Because of what happened in California—saving little time for each other while too often blurring the line between friendship and business—in Virginia we have become more cautious about engaging in friendships. In the movie business, and to a lesser extent in the world of journalism, one lives in the world of possibility, where friendship might lead to employment and, therefore, "friends" come cheaply. But often, after striking up sudden friendships, we found ourselves burdened by their maintenance: the birthday parties, the dinner parties, the weddings, baby showers, and, not least of these, the need to lend a sympathetic ear upon demand. Too often because we wanted to be accommodating, we juggled these friendships while neglecting our own needs and downplaying our own values.

Letting go of these quasi-friendships was liberating. Anne Morrow Lindbergh resolved in *Gift from the Sea* to shed "hypocrisy in human relationships. What a rest that will be! The most exhausting thing in life, I have discovered, is being insincere." Indeed, a handful of our closest friends—the ones who have stood the tests of time and distance, the ones with whom we are able to be honest—remain in California.

But by moving here, we have laid to rest the myth that meaningful and stimulating friendships are the inevitable casualty of leaving the city. The truth is, were it not for our resolution to discourage friendships we don't want to pursue in Virginia, we are at least as much at risk of overextending ourselves socially here as we were in Los Angeles. And that is not because there is danger here of blurring friendship with business. In fact, of our close friends in Virginia only one shares the writing profession. Among our friends are a man who runs a print shop, several high school teachers, a husband-wife physician team, an ophthalmologist, and a banker. For us, at least, such diversity of close friendship was impossible in Los Angeles.

For all their variety, one constant that we've found among friends everywhere is the yearning for a sense of community, for belonging to something larger than oneself. It's a yearning for a community where you are valued but also challenged to stretch beyond where you are now, to keep learning, to work and play more creatively.

Many of us get a taste of this experience in academic communities, as we did at Harvard and Wesleyan. Indeed, the simplicity of collegiate life—the focus on coursework and working toward a degree, the prime importance of friendships—can haunt one for years afterward. A nostalgic thirst for better times is hard to slake with pale adult substitutes such as the company for which one works or the often jaded company one keeps.

When Frank visited Red and Madeleine Stephenson, it wasn't surprising, then, that a part of him was drawn to their communal way of life.

When the Stephensons returned the visit a year later, they saw three discrete households in our cove, each with its own possessions, each more often than not engaged in its own activities, each with recently plowed earth for gardens. When Frank spent half a day at the Manzanita Association (at the

Stephensons' request, we have changed the name of their community but not their names) in rural northern California, he saw houses owned collectively, saw people working together for common goals, and walked across the compost-rich bottomland where the huge community garden was being tilled for spring planting.

In Frank's brief visit to Manzanita, and in the Stephensons' even briefer visit to the orchard, it was impossible to learn all the intricate details of how the association works. Still, the radiance of this retired couple was enough to give his skepticism about communal living considerable pause. After all, if one is trying to live simply in our society, isn't it, as Madeleine said over brunch in their house high on a coastal mountain, "easier to live simply in a community where other people are doing the same"?

Nineteen adults and seven children are Manzanita members; each family is housed separately on the hilly, 440-acre tract amid manzanita and oak forests and green fields. Two families, Red said, are now "visiting" the community in preparation for membership. About half the current members are Quakers— a fact suggested by the sign Frank passed as he drove into the community up the steep gravel road from the state highway:

> Slow please
>
> Save your car
> the road
> our kids
>
> 10 1/2 MPH is plenty!
>
> Thank thee!

But Manzanita has no Quaker meeting house and is not a religious association per se. Two of the newest members are Jewish.

The Stephensons were living in Berkeley—where Red was the executive director of Planned Parenthood for Alameda and San Francisco counties—when they and a group of friends began talking about buying land and living together in the country. From 1970 to 1973, while searching for property, the group discussed how they would govern themselves and what sort of ownership structure would be best.

"We thought we'd like to be a housing co-op," Madeleine said. "But after we got all that set up, we discovered that by doing that we'd be subject to subdivision regulations, so we went back to the drawing board."

There were also discussions about whether the group should pool capital and income and live together under one roof. To the Stephensons' satisfaction, it was decided that group members would contribute to a common fund but not pool all resources. Families would live in separate houses but share regular group activities such as cutting wood, gardening, canning produce, and conducting business meetings.

In the fall of 1973 eight families purchased the 440 acres from a farmer who remains their neighbor. They formed a legal partnership, the Manzanita Association, in which no one owns a particular piece of property, and no member can sell his or her share, but each member has an interest in the un-divided whole. If a member decides to leave, he or she must sell his or her interest to the association. To meet association expenses, a schedule was arranged in which younger members pay less than older members.

"When we came to build our house," Red said, "we put up all of the money. The partnership owns the house, but because we put up all the money, we didn't pay the partnership anything and they didn't pay us anything. Our house belongs to Manzanita. The partnership built the house. We loaned enough money to the partnership to build our house."

Because the community wants to set limits on growth, and because it puts a premium on simplicity, the Manzanita Association reserves approval of all housing plans. "The houses here are all pretty minimal," Madeleine explained. At 1,100 square feet, the Stephensons' house feels—if not exactly minimal—at least, as Madeleine put it, "a house for two people whose kids have grown." In addition to a comfortable living room, it has a dining room, a kitchen with a breakfast nook, a bedroom, and a mud room that doubles as Red's office and guest bedroom. Picture windows with a southern exposure provide a passive solar source of heat, and like all the houses at Manzanita, additional heat is provided by woodstoves and the water heater is equipped with solar panels. When the house was built in the mid-seventies, Red did all the kitchen and bathroom tilework and laid the vinyl squares on the floor, while Madeleine sanded the cabinets, puttied, and put trim on the windows.

After brunch, with no apparent qualms, Red ushered Frank into the unlocked house of his nearest neighbors, a retired couple who were gone for the day. The house, which Red's neighbors spent two years building themselves (with some help from Manzanita members), was like none Frank had ever seen. As you enter the main room the eye is drawn to two broad madrona tree trunks, burnished a dark red and twisted with age, which, along with their severed branches, extend from floor to ceiling. The ceiling is a latticework of fir beams. Above three feet or so of mortared stones rising from the floor, oak poles cut from the community forest taper elegantly toward the beams. Elsewhere in the house, wooden limb props, about an inch wide by three and a half inches long, salvaged from an orchard going out of business, have been used as wall paneling. The kitchen counter is made of salvaged maple flooring; the cabinets in the house from salvaged redwood. A real forest had nothing on this house.

Frank made the short walk with Red to the community center, which has the dark, woodsy look and smell of a summer camp and serves as a gathering place and library. A guitar hangs on the wall; an ample supply of books is neatly shelved. Here the bimonthly business meetings are held, as well as holiday celebrations, dances, pot luck suppers, and impromptu gatherings. All community decisions are made by the Quaker-inspired process of consensus—with none finalized until all members are in agreement.

From there the two men descended into a flat, open area to a well-equipped wood shop, where a young man was making new doors for the Stephensons' house. Woodworking was his work contribution to the community, he said. He'd recently moved here from New York City.

Had he simplified his life?

He scratched his beard. "We're all living with contradictions and paradoxes," he mused. "For me, just being an American means that we're consuming a disproportionate share of the world's resources. I'm trying to find a balance here. To live fairly comfortably while using less resources."

"I'd say the definition of simple living would vary from

person to person in the community," Red said. "We have some community members who won't use a tractor—but they will use a rotary tiller! How far you go is the question."

How far does he go?

"I'm not energetic enough now to do hand digging," he said. "I use the tiller."

Red also uses a tractor. Like the young woodworker, each member of the community is expected to make a work contribution, and Red drives a John Deere tractor with a scraper blade to smooth out the fresh gravel applied every year and to clean out the ditches. With a master's degree in music, Madeleine teaches piano. Theoretically each Manzanita member works sixteen hours a month for the community. According to Madeleine, Red puts in many more hours than that. With no enforcement procedures for laggards, the system functions on trust.

As he led Frank toward the orchard and garden, Red cited the ways he and other members of the community have simplified their lives. "Our houses cost less to build because of their size. Our food costs less because we grow so much of it here. Our utility bills are less because of the woodstoves and solar heat. Therefore, our young people aren't forced to go out and earn as much money. They have more time for their families, in part because families work together here. And," Red continued, "we don't have lawns. We do it nature's way." Nature has provided them with a scruffy mixture of rocks and, for vegetation, semidesert plants, trees, and shrubs. In the community, nature's lawn is crisscrossed by wood-chip and dirt paths.

Frank, who is something of a lawn-mowing refusenik, thought that sounded pretty good. But there was more. Red continued in an almost jubilant tone, "You can leave your keys in the car. In fact, we ask people to leave keys in the car, in case of fire or other emergency. And if Madeleine wakes up in the middle of the night and can't go back to sleep, she can walk all around the place and I have no fear."

We stopped to look at the dwarf fruit trees, fenced in against deer. "It's possible that you could live cheaper in town than we do," Red said. "It's fairly expensive to maintain roads. But I don't know if you could live better."

These examples were attractive, but all were possible—and to some extent already in place—on our mountain. What engaged Frank most was the notion of living with twenty-some neighbors who shared the enterprise. Perhaps it was possible in a communal setting to have the best of both worlds: real latitude for individual expression, yet a sense of belonging.

Of course, we could never be sure unless we lived at Manzanita or some place like it. But Frank's visit there brought home a feeling we've long held: the ideals of rugged individualism and self-reliance are grossly romanticized in American culture. The central fact of life is interdependence. In nature and in society, no one escapes it. As a microcosm of what a better society could be, Manzanita is clearly a community that celebrates this interdependence—among people, between culture and nature. It gently asks its members to live up to the ideals of simple living.

We are not parents. Someday we hope to be. But among friends and in our travels, we are often drawn to parents who devote time to their children. Without deifying their kids, as so often happens among our peers today, these parents put emphasis on making better people, on striking a balance between the needs of parents and the needs of children.

Our friend Linda Terry Lastinger, a physician in nearby Galax, is the mother of three children: Brooks is twelve, Lauren nine, and Adrienne seven. Linda and her husband, Len—both trained at Duke Medical School—have a practice known throughout our community for its excellence. But the Lastingers—who do not own a big house or drive a fancy car—have decided to make a priority of their progeny. Tuesdays and Fridays Linda works alongside Len at the clinic. The rest of the week she's at home. On school days she drives the kids to school, then picks them up later in the day; she's at home with them late afternoons and evenings. It's a balancing act of needs that seems to work, both for Linda and the kids. The home-cooked, sit-down family dinner is a ritual at the Lastinger home. The children are exuberant but not prima donnas. They're easy to be with and talk to. Adults can talk without constant interruptions from the peanut gallery. As frequent guests at their home, we know only what we see: family members enjoying one another's company.

At the suggestion of a mutual friend, we had driven an hour and a half west from New Orleans to meet Ed Hammerli—another parent doing his own balancing act. Along with his wife, Angela, and their two sons, Stan and Walt, aged fourteen and twelve respectively, Ed lives in a high-ceilinged, renovated old house in downtown Thibodaux, Louisiana. Driving through the bayou country, we had arrived at sunset, dined with Ed and Angela, their sons, and a motley crew of dinner guests, and spent the surprisingly chilly spring night under a down comforter.

The next morning, after the boys went off to school and

Angela left for work (she teaches dance at nearby Nichols State University), we sat with Ed in the large, sunny room off the hall where he conducts his small business, Compare de la Pens.

That is, Ed told us, "Br'er Rabbit" in Cajun. When Ed was a child in St. Joseph, Missouri, his favorite stories were the Uncle Remus tales. A few years ago he was reading a version of these stories to his boys that used Cajun names for the animal characters. Like Br'er Rabbit to the Tar Baby, Compare de la Pens stuck as the name for Ed's business.

Ed makes picture frames. As we talked with him, the walls around us—the framed prints that Ed sells and the display of frame samples and colors he shows to customers—continued to distract us. In a good week, Ed, who is self-taught and has been framing professionally since 1976, will fashion as many as fifteen frames, mostly from prefinished woods like black walnut. He is known around Thibodaux, he said, not for originality, but for "quality and reliability, guaranteed. If anything goes wrong, I fix it free of charge if it's my fault."

Though it is satisfying work and Ed befriends many of his customers, framing does not make him rich. There are four other picture frame shops in Thibodaux—and in a town of not quite sixteen thousand, that may be several too many. The previous year Ed reported $5,000 income after deductions. As we talked with him much of the morning, it became clear that Ed and Angela have decided that it is more important for Ed to be able to work at home and spend time with their sons than it is for him to be out making more money. With Angela's $28,000 salary and whatever Ed can pull in, they figure they have enough money—and have the kinds of sons they want, too.

"I guess I do more than half of the parenting," Ed allowed.

"Angela's not around the kids as much as I am." But he added quickly: "When she is around she's a more strict parent than I am."

Ed Hammerli (the last name is Swiss) is a blond, muscular man in his mid-forties with a gritty, deep voice and a steady eye. If Ed were an actor, he might well be cast in a war movie as a career soldier, and that casting would not be entirely off the mark. In 1966, right out of college, Ed chose to enlist in the army rather than be drafted and—luckily, he said—was sent to Germany rather than Vietnam.

"Do you feel pressure to make more money?" Wanda asked. "There is an established tradition for women to do what you're doing. As a man, how do you deal with it?"

Ed shifted uncomfortably on his seat and shot his eyes to the floor. "I just try to be up-front and laugh about it," he replied. "And say, 'Hey, I don't make much money here.' Occasionally I get that pang, that people are judged by how much money they make. But I think people judge me differently. And I know a lot of people who judge people on that basis have a certain respect for me. Because I'm doing what I want to do."

"How do your sons feel about it?" Frank asked.

"I'm not sure if they're even aware of that kind of thing yet. They have never been embarrassed about my not making much money." Ed laughed. "Lord knows they've got enough clothes."

They also have a rare treasure, one they won't fully appreciate until adulthood: plenty of their father. "I'm here when they come home from school," Ed said. "That's important. I see lots of parents who both work and the kids come home without supervision. If I weren't here, they would be on the street or by themselves. I would rather have them here in a relaxed atmosphere. I can see what they're doing, and they're not getting into a lot of trouble. They know I'm very concerned about them. Still, they're able to be on their own here, too."

Lately the boys have been bringing friends with them to skateboard in the backyard. "I'm here and they come in and use my tools for the skateboards," Ed said. "They know I'm here and they can come in and I'll help them any way they need."

With Angela arriving home late—she often attends meetings and teaches dance classes in the evening—Ed does most of the suppertime cooking. "I don't know if you'd call it cooking," he said, laughing. "I open cans."

He also helps about an hour a night with the boys' homework. And he is the "head man" of the youth soccer league in Thibodaux, spending many volunteer hours a week during soccer season as coordinator and coach. "People call me constantly during the day about soccer problems," he said. "I spend a lot of the workday with soccer. And not many people can do that, because they don't have jobs that allow them to do that."

Because he wanted his boys to play soccer, Ed originally organized the league and now coaches two teams of fourteen boys each.

Ed reminds us of Robert Lasser, a friend in Washington State, a married man with a wife and three bright school-age daughters who has spent the last two years building himself and his family a house while living in an apartment. Robert also does community volunteer work, lots of parenting, and has a hot dinner on the table when his veterinarian wife, Shelly, gets home from work. Miriam knows the family and once commented to us that she wished Robert would get a "real job" in order to save money for his daughters' college educations.

We begged to differ—perhaps having a happy, stay-at-home parent would, in the long run, be more helpful to the emotional health and intellectual development of the girls than having their father work to give them access to the "finer" schools, but little or no access to himself. And though we both had the advantage of Ivy League educations, we have wondered more than once if we couldn't have learned as much at less prestigious public institutions. Looking back on our own lives, we remembered that having regular attention from our dads was in both cases not in the cards.

But even in this era of the supposed "soft" male, we haven't met many men like Ed or Robert. We've both seen the harsh social and emotional penalties for any father who dares depart from the breadwinner role. We couldn't help but notice Ed's discomfort when we probed the subject.

How did this man come to his unconventional views about money, status, and his pivotal role as a parent?

"My mother's values may have rubbed off," Ed said. "She was not a very pretentious person. She was never that much concerned about making money. She always helped other people, too. She gave money to friends a number of times, to help them pay their house note. And also a black woman who baby-sat for me and cleaned house whom she gave money to regularly, and other things, too, over and above the pay."

Ed stared out the window of his shop into the backyard, where his boys and their friends would be coming that afternoon with their skateboards. He laughed. "Her house—my house when I was young—was much like our house today, where kids could come and destroy everything and feel at home. Our backyard was one of the few places we could go and kill the grass, play football, and high-jump. Her attitude was: You're only kids for a short time and this grass is gonna grow back. I think of that today when I see our backyard all trampled down.

"Stick around," he said. "You really ought to see these kids on their skateboards. They do unbelievable things—it scares me sometimes!"

In a way, saving time for each one of us—time for solitude— is a sort of last frontier. We're exploring the territory. Before we joined our lives, we had solitude in spades. But in the past few years we've saved free time for each other and haven't always left enough time for our individual selves away from each other. Some time, yes—but not enough.

In 1990 we spent some time apart. Frank hit some back-packing trails—first with an old Wesleyan friend, later by himself. Wanda had the house to herself for a week and later journeyed solo to California to be on hand—standing in the delivery room—for the birth of Jane's first baby, an alert, smiling, eight-pound redhead named Erik Stephen Robbins. When she wasn't helping her sister, she was able to take long walks and swims by herself.

In her book, *Disciplines for Discipleship*, Frank's sister-in-law, Patricia Webb Levering, a Quaker minister, writes: "The renewal aspect of solitude is particularly helpful in relationships. We find ourselves better able to be for others after we have had some time apart to be internally refreshed. Solitude of the heart creates an inner spaciousness, unhurriedness, and reflectiveness that leave room to be open to another person."

Patty knows whereof she speaks. Now in their middle forties, she and her husband, Ralph, regularly schedule time apart from each other, time for weekend retreats or just a few meditative solitary hours in the same house.

In this way Patty and Ralph have helped create and strengthen what we have also sought these last years living at the orchard: the ties of family and friends that blessedly bind.

CHAPTER ELEVEN

Living at Home

We've been writing this book in our base-ment office. Once a dungeonlike storage room, it's been a cozy space since 1987, when we installed new carpet, paneling, and lighting; put up colorful prints and maps of the world, the United States, and Carroll County; and cleaned grime from the high window that offers a view of the cherry trees east of our house. During the cold months, we work on twin Apple II computers in the toasty company of a woodstove, always happy to break out of the straitjacket of writing and fetch another log from the basement stash. And on the hottest summer days the office is a sanctuary of coolness, a place where two cats, too, find relief.

Every morning as we descend to work, near the foot of the cellar stairs we see the shadowy outlines of a rectangular box, perched above the floor on three apple crates and swathed in blankets. The box is six feet three inches long and two and a half feet wide. Though we can't see it for the blankets, we know very well what we are walking past. Someday it may yet perform the service for which it was designed. In the meantime it is a daily reminder that to march to our own drummer, we, too, have to be willing to defy convention.

An accomplished carpenter, Frank's grandfather, Ralph Levering, fashioned three coffins from pine boards he purchased at a lumber company in Mount Airy. It was not the custom of his community. But in 1940 when he was sixty-nine, Ralph thought the time had come. When he was done, each coffin had a fresh coat of chocolate-brown paint on the outside; each had four thick handles, two on each side. To secure the lid, each had four long screws with a heart at the top to be tightened by hand at each corner. When the lid was on tight, these hearts, visible at each corner of the coffin, would be the only adornment for the three plain caskets.

Ralph maintained that coffins, as well as funerals, should be simple and inexpensive. "Father believed that what money we had was a gift from God," Sam once told us, "and that we should not waste it on ourselves. There were very many useful ways in which money could be used—that helped other people, that helped make the world a better place."

When Sam's father died in 1945, the family laid his body in one of the coffins he had made, loaded the coffin onto the back of a truck, and buried it in the cemetery of Willow Hill Church a mile and a half from our home. A memorial service— silent, with people rising to speak when so moved—was held the same day. In 1961 the body of Clara Levering, Ralph's wife, was placed in the second coffin, trucked by the family to the church, and buried.

In the dark attic of Ralph and Clara's empty house, one coffin remained. Ralph had not made that pine box for either of his two sons, both of whom would be capable of making their own funeral arrangements. He had made it for his daughter, June.

As Sam remembers his older sister in her early adolescence, June was a quiet, studious girl, with long black hair and a bashful smile. Until the new apple orchard came into bearing, June played an active role in raising the chickens and gathering the eggs for income. Clara taught her three children in her home until they reached high school. At fourteen June was sent to Westtown, a Quaker boarding school in Philadelphia.

One night in 1922, when June was a senior, she had what she described to Frank in 1987 as a "breakdown." She had fallen in love with a young man named Eddie Wood, who worked at the school, and she thought about him constantly. Her love was unrequited. Following an erotic dream about Eddie, she had the breakdown that set the course for her life.

June was taken to an asylum for the mentally ill, run by Quakers. There, among other things, she was soaked in tubs of hot water to relax her nerves. After two months of treatments, without finishing school, she was escorted home on the train by her older brother, Griffith. Concerned that a return to Westtown would only lead to a second breakdown, her parents insisted that she remain at home and help Clara teach. According to Frank's father, Ralph and Clara attributed June's illness to a family history of mental trouble. Rather than sending June back into the world, her parents wanted to shelter her at home.

From this distance it will always be impossible to know what the right thing was for June. Within a year, still having dreams about the young man, June suffered another breakdown and was sent to the state hospital in Marion, Virginia, seventy miles away. For the rest of her life she alternated periods at Marion with time on the mountain, having been diagnosed schizophrenic and suffering repeated relapses. She never married; she never even dated. In the 1920s, with no training, June took up painting and sketching; her lifelike family portraits and austere renditions of orchard buildings and landscapes are family treasures. In the 1930s she joined the fundamentalist Apostolic Faith Church, and her painting abruptly ceased. The inspiration was gone, she said. When she wasn't in Marion, her days were filled with chores around the house and garden and Bible reading.

Before he died, Ralph asked Sam to promise that he would take care of June after Clara's death. From 1961 until 1987, with Miriam's help, Sam fulfilled that promise. When she wasn't in Marion, June lived with Frank's parents in the house where we now live. Musty and empty, the old homeplace up the hill concealed her coffin in a spiderwebbed corner of the attic.

For eleven months after we moved from California, we saw June often. To visit with her, you entered her domain in the downstairs bedroom in the Red House. In what had been her parents' bedroom, June sat small and hunchbacked on a rocking chair, her hair thin and gray, her bony hands trembling, her voice wispy, strangely ethereal. No longer was she hoeing the garden or walking her letters to friends to the mailbox. Her heart was beating sluggishly, her doctor said. Her ankles were swelling from poor circulation. Except to use the adjoining bathroom, she did not venture from her quarters. Sam and Miriam brought her meals into her room on trays. Scattered around the large room, with its high ceiling, tall windows, and full-length mirror on the bathroom door, were dusty stacks of Apostolic Faith literature and her Bible. She had all but withdrawn from this world. As Virginia's son, Jack Price, said after visiting her, June was going to "just slip away into thin air" one day soon.

In February of 1987 June agreed to spend time with Frank talking about family history, about her life. Every two or three days, giving her time in between to think about the next topic, Frank brought a tape recorder and stayed an hour—her limit before she tired. June was lucid and intense; sometimes she laughed merrily at a comic recollection; sometimes, as when she talked about her mental trouble or her father's funeral, her expression was almost frightening in the full flood of memory. In all, Frank spent twelve hours learning many things he'd never known about his family. After the twelfth hour he and his aunt agreed that they would stop for the time being, to resume their joint travel into the past if either felt the need.

On Wednesday, March 18, two weeks after the last session, Frank had a fever and spent the day in bed. That evening Wanda returned with Sam and Miriam from a day in Greensboro. Shortly after Wanda entered our house, the phone rang. "We've found June in her room," Miriam told Frank. "We think she's gone."

Virginia, a former nurse, arrived shortly ahead of us and took her pulse. "She's passed on," Virginia said. Behind her on the floor, June lay slumped against the mirror on the bathroom door that she had shattered as she fell. Shards of mirror glass lay around her on the floor.

Her heart had finally given out on her. A blustery March evening wind beat against the house, rattling the old windows. We sat together by the woodstove until Sam announced his intentions. He was the lone survivor of the family of five that had lived in the log cabin for two years until the Red House was finished. He would carry out his final responsibility to his parents and to his sister.

Early the next morning Sam called the county coroner in Hillsville and asked him to drive out to the orchard and confirm June's death. The coroner refused. Sam had to have the body brought to a funeral home, he said, where he would issue the death certificate. No, Sam said, he did not intend to deal with a funeral home. And wasn't the coroner being paid to go wherever was necessary to confirm a death? The coroner was indignant. Well then, he said, if Sam wasn't going to do the proper thing and use a funeral home, he would have to bring in the body to his office.

Garnet Dawson, along with his son and nephew, helped Frank carry the coffin down from the attic of the Red House. The four men lifted June's body into the sheet-lined coffin and loaded it onto the back of our open-air pickup. As Frank drove Wanda and Sam into Hillsville, his father brooded in silence. We parked in the lot behind the coroner's office, walked into the waiting room, and announced ourselves to the receptionist.

We waited. And waited. After half an hour Sam rose without warning and marched past the receptionist into the inner office. We heard heated voices. In a few moments Sam emerged, arms folded tight across his chest in one of his telltale signs of anger.

The coroner was behind him, his face flushed. "This isn't the way it's done," the coroner said. "You have to go through a funeral home."

Sam glared up at the much taller man, perhaps fifteen years his junior. "Show me the law," he said.

The coroner was mute. There was no law in Virginia that

said a body must be disposed of through a funeral home. "All right," he said. "You'll have to bring her in here."

Sam stared incredulously. As the coroner turned to step back into his office, Frank intervened, telling him that June was in a coffin and there were only three of us to carry it in, one being his seventy-nine-year-old father.

"Wait outside," the coroner snapped. "I'll be out."

We waited at the pickup. After fifteen minutes the coroner stepped crisply to the truck and we lifted the lid. He pulled back the sheet over her body and gave it a cursory glance, quickly took a pulse, then informed us that June was dead. We would need to return to his office to collect the death certificate and pay his fee. Without another word he marched back inside.

It was thirteen miles home, and despite the strangeness of it all and Sam's continuing anger, we were with him in spirit as well as on that winding country road. He was doing what he thought was the right thing.

The evening June died, Sam announced that he and his sister had agreed that she would be cremated. As he saw it, it was as simple a burial as one making use of the old coffin. It would cost a little more, but ashes would consume less space in the cemetery. Cremation would also allow time for more family members to gather for a memorial service.

Wanda called around and found what was by far the lowest price: a Greensboro, North Carolina, crematorium would do the work for two hundred dollars. Wanda secured a permit to transport the body out of state—no mean feat, as the woman who issued the permit was forced to call Richmond to verify procedure. Never in her six years on the job, she explained, had such a request come from an individual.

Sam rode with Frank the 150-mile round trip in the pickup.

A few miles from downtown Greensboro, the crematorium stood alone in a field across from a pasture. Frank backed the truck up to the loading dock of the two-story brick building, and two men wheeled the coffin inside. Frank helped them load the empty coffin back onto the truck. Sam and Frank drove home; June's ashes would return in a small box, via the U.S. Postal Service.

The following Sunday a memorial service was held at Willow Hill Moravian Church, where Sam's family is buried, and which his parents attended along with the Quaker meetings in Mount Airy. In June, when several of Frank's siblings who had missed the first service were visiting, a graveside service was held with only family members present. With a shovel, Frank buried June's ashes in the red clay beside the graves of her parents, brother, Griffith, and sister-in-law, Martha Leutsker Levering.

At the first service neighbors whom June had taught remembered her as a caring teacher. At her grave Sam spoke in a broken voice of his sister as a woman who had braved mental illness without complaint and unselfishly helped others in her family and community.

No doubt there was truth in those perceptions; there was also the lingering mystery of an outwardly gentle, inwardly stormy woman who had lived in the shadow of her parents and brothers. Yet in death, as in life, June was part of a distinct tradition that Sam had stubbornly honored. Simplicity and devotion to family and to one's idea of God, of what is spiritual and enduring, were at the core of the tradition that sank its taproot deep into the family's past.

Never more so than at the time of June's death, living here has exposed us to that tradition and forced us to consider how much we are or would like to be a part of it. It has caused us to think about how simplicity in its many forms can help one grow spiritually—spirituality defined as one's sense of belonging in creation, as connection with life outside oneself and with life's sources.

In the likely event that we are alive when any of them die, we do not wish to duplicate, with our parents, the peregrinations we had with June. Recently Frank's parents have declared their intentions to donate their bodies to a medical school, and we are pleased that friends have been asked to arrange the transport when the time comes. Still, we were moved by Sam's love for his sister, his grief, and his courage to be himself within the frame of his tradition. His actions have given us inspiration, a myth of defiance of narrow conformity, as we pass by Aunt June's coffin every day.

There are many other fitting ways to honor the dead, but this one we could gladly call our own. In the company of others who have seen more of life and death than we, whose religious faith is heartfelt, we felt ourselves being stretched out of our old selves toward the intuition of a more spiritual sense of life. Not only do possessions and the almighty pursuit of money, careers, and social acceptance darken the windows of perception; so does the refusal to acknowledge what is powerful, what is ultimately mystical, in one's own backyard. The simplicity with which June was laid to rest and remembered made her more immediate, more real; linked us—through her—to our own mortality and to the urgency of love that drives us as we live.

Still, as each generation has done here, we must live our own lives. Ralph and Clara drew definitive boundaries between right and wrong and established themselves as moral exemplars in a rough-hewn mountain community. They shielded their children from what they regarded as immoral influences, and the rules they taught them were strict: no smoking, no drinking, no premarital sex, no divorce, no luxury of any kind. They were active in the life of the community—in the church, in education.

Less involved in the immediate community, Sam and Miriam joined national organizations and helped create some of their own in a campaign for world peace. To them, Sam's parents often seemed overly judgmental, their mountain world too provincial. Still, with Sam and Miriam, sex roles at home were clearly defined. Until all but their last child was grown, Sam was the orchardist, Miriam the homemaker. In no uncertain terms they asked their children to be staunch Quakers like themselves, but—at least by the time Frank entered college—they balanced prohibition with the need for exploration.

Living our own lives in Virginia is a balancing act of its own, more intuitive at times than rational. What's right and wrong is not as clear to us as it apparently was for Ralph and Clara and as it is for both our sets of parents. Without the old absolutes to guide us, we feel our way toward answers that work for us on issues ranging from divorce to the use of alcohol and the nature of God, luxury, and feminism. One thing is certain: June's life stands as a haunting reminder of the price paid for failing to establish one's own identity, independent of received wisdom.

For us, a world without imagination would be a world without God; giving voice to the fanciful is a way of igniting the spark of divinity within.

On a Saturday night in October of 1987, we started a Halloween party tradition that we hope to carry on well into our second childhood. In addition to wanting to have a good time, we also wanted to open our house to our community.

For the festivities, Frank and Randall Dawson trucked the coffin down from the Red House attic, where it had been stored since June's death. They set the coffin on the apple crates on which it still rests. Wanda designed the invitations, most of which we hand-delivered to scores of startled neighbors within a five- or six-mile radius of our house. We mailed others to more distant friends. Because this was a first-time event, and because our neighbors are elaborately polite, if not always forthright, it was difficult to get a reading on just how many people would show for the "First Annual Levering Orchard Halloween Party." But with the help of our friends Bonni Kogen and her husband, Andrew Brodnick, from New York, and Frank's cousin Chris Wellons and his wife, Sandy Webbere, from Raleigh, we stocked up with homemade cookies, newly picked, caramel-coated apples, nuts, wine, and apple cider, hoping for at least a modest showing.

It was a balmy evening, with a gentle wind rustling what golden leaves remained on the cherry trees. Shortly before eight o'clock, the first guests drove under the pecan tree near the barn, where a huge "ghost"—a sheet with a straw-stuffed head—"floated" just above the car's windshield. Driving past our house, they parked on the open field below and—under a brilliant full moon—followed the path illuminated by candles in glass jars past two eerily lifelike Styrofoam "tombstones," which had once been used on a movie set. Glancing at the flickering jack-o'-lantern on the front porch, they entered the house, little knowing what was in store for them that evening.

Before the witching hour of midnight—when Frank's horrific movie, *Parasite*, was screened on the VCR for a roomful of night owls—what we estimated to be one hundred and fifty guests had entered into the spirit of the occasion. Many had enjoyed an audience with the mysterious Madame Petrovsky, a fortune-teller sequestered in a room off the hall, dressed in a long black veil, with ruby lips and forbidding eyebrows. Escorted by one of the hosts, each guest descended by candlelight into the basement as a tape played the sound of a heartbeat in the darkness. It was necessary, the host would say, to "pay respects to the deceased." As he or she opened the lid of the coffin, cousin Chris, in a homemade devil's costume, complete with horns and a pitchfork, lunged out of the coffin and sank his claws into human flesh.

Nor was this the last of the frights. Late in the evening Andrew gathered the crowd beside the tombstones at the edge of the yard, one of which read:

Dr. Ralph Levering
Born Feb. 27, 1947
Died Oct. 30, 1987

Gone to Be an Angle

As Andrew conducted a service for Frank's late, lamented brother and new "angle," a hand slowly wriggled out of the freshly spaded dirt beside the tombstone. As party guests shrank back, Frank staggered from the grave, his face ghoulish with berry-stained "blood." It had been a long wait—ten minutes lying stiff as a corpse and claustrophobic under the pile of branches that covered his face—but the effort was worth it. Shrieks of terror and delight followed.

None of these party stunts, we realize, rival Dante or Virginia Woolf as examples of the human imagination at its most transcendent. But they seemed to fit the down-home occasion. Neighbors and friends—who came as everything from a tube of toothpaste to Richard Nixon—played their roles to the hilt, having a great "frolic," as the mountain people say. Our neighbors just down the mountain, a couple in their early twenties who also have an orchard, came in homemade striped convict suits and went clanking around together throughout the evening, linked by a chain. Another young orchardist, thinking it the gracious thing to do, brought a jug of homemade moonshine as a gift, a portion of which our Manhattan friends carted back to the city as a memento of their Appalachian visit. Before they departed, many of the guests made sure they would be invited to the party the following year.

Without knowing if they would enjoy themselves, we were also delighted to see our neighbors in the cove reincarnated in their second childhoods. Later they all spoke fervently of what a fine thing it was to see the community together and to be able to catch up with neighbors they rarely took time to visit, as they had in the days before television.

Removing some false teeth to create the right snaggle-toothed effect, Virginia appeared on our doorstep as a witch in a black dress and hat she'd made herself; on a leash was her black cat, Delilah. Miriam basked for days in the afterglow of her success as Madame Petrovsky. Sam, whom we had feared would feel the chill of the demons of his own upbringing and take a dim view of the party, wore sandals and a white bathrobe and swung a kerosene lantern. Neighbors accustomed to his eccentricities had one more story for their collections. After peering at disquieted partygoers in the glow of the lantern, Sam told them he was the ancient Greek Diogenes, searching among them for one honest man.

On Sunday mornings beginning at nine, we aren't carrying a lantern as we sit with Sam, Miriam, and several other regulars in forty minutes of silent meeting in Mount Airy. If light comes, it's from within. But like Diogenes, we are searching—not for one honest man, but for the modicum of self-knowledge that mere mortals are granted.

Many Quakers would insist that simplicity in all of its aspects must come from a unified vision of the nature of God. In the life of Jesus, they would argue, are found the essential, eternal truths from which simplicity follows. Those who would simplify their lives must forge a binding relationship with God, much as Jesus did. Simplicity does not engender a more spiritual life; the spiritual life engenders simplicity.

For us, the search for meaning that is a necessary dimension of simplifying one's life need not follow in the footsteps of theology. The quest for a simpler life is itself an infinite journey toward God, harboring the growing sense not of transcendence, but of commitment to this earth in all of its—and our—imperfections.

As the Japanese poet Basho wrote, "Life is a journey, and the journey itself home." It is the search—the journey and not the destination, the questions more readily than the answers—that is most real for us. For us, spirituality is, first, the art of learning where you are, wherever that may be. As the American writer Annie Dillard put it in *Holy the Firm*, "Every day is a god." We live at the miraculous level of mundane existence, not in the hope of heaven or nirvana, not even in the mystical union with God that is the yearning, perhaps at times the reality, of the devout.

Our faith in the orchard has been tested. After the euphoria of our magnificent 1988 cherry crop, in 1989 when our fruit blossomed too early and late, killing frosts passed us over, we believed we had been favored with a "miracle," in Sam's words, to have cherries at all. So we proclaimed our "miracle crop" with a banner headline in our annual customer newsletter. Just maybe this would be the year in which we reduced orchard indebtedness to the lowest level in Frank's memory.

What we did not anticipate—especially after the drought of the previous summer, which had enabled us to stretch our normal four-week season to almost eight weeks—was monsoon-like rain. But rain came in sheets just two days before opening day and continued throughout June of 1989, pounding inch upon inch on our fragile cherries until a record fifteen inches were recorded for that month.

Miracle crop indeed! Not only were our pick-your-own customers put off by having to pick in slickers and umbrellas, but the fruit couldn't withstand the onslaught. Ripe cherries cracked open from the absorbed water, and many rotted. What's more, with only sporadic sunshine, the cherries that survived never fully sweetened.

Though our cherry set was close to that of the 1988 crop, our gross sales were only one-third of the previous year's. We tightened our belts even more and could only hope that 1990 would bring better luck.

As January 1990's warm weather failed to break, we grew anxious, wincing at the springlike temperatures that non-fruit growers in the region savored. When our cherry trees bloomed in March, the ever-optimistic Sam said we had a "fifty-fifty chance" of their making it through to bearing without killing cold. Then, on March 20, warned by the weatherman of an incoming blast of frigid air, we kept a sleepless vigil. It was a windy night—no amount of smudge pots (which we didn't have anyway) could have heated the air enough to help. At four A.M. Frank stared grimly for the umpteenth time at the thermometer on our north porch. The temperature read 25 degrees, then hung there for hours. After sunrise we trudged with Sam into the orchard, into the heart and soul of the business: the sweet cherry trees. From various sections of the orchard we broke off handfuls of twigs, gathering blossoms and buds. Later, when our samples had thawed, we cut into them with razor blades at the Red House. Rather than living green tissue, we sliced into the blighted brown of freeze-killed tissue. Very likely we would have no sweet cherries at all. Before the day was over, we learned that all the peaches, nectarines, and almost all the sour cherries and plums had been killed, too. Only the apples survived. We thought we'd hit bottom in 1989 with rain every day, but this luck was far worse.

But, we told ourselves—almost as optimistic as Sam or as a baseball manager in spring training—there's always next year. Now we're having a good fruit season—not spectacular but not bad. In poor years we're learning to cut our losses and put what nature gives us in a longer-term perspective. In good years we try simply to be grateful. Either way we don't forget our dependence on natural forces beyond our control. It's true— Leverings and now an Urbanska have been living here for more than eighty years. But so have wind, rain, warm sunlight, and killing cold.

. . .

It's August now, and creation gets hard to love. Whenever we work outside, we drip sweat. The sun stalks us, striding over the east ridge by eight-thirty and shooting into the cove. No wind brings relief, and this August there is no rain—only the dry heaves of distant thunder.

Deprived of long vistas in the late summer haze, we must choose the short ones. The world ends at the edge of the orchard. We rub our eyes and look at dew. In the ethereal light of dawn, it sheaths Walt Whitman's leaves of grass in a quicksilver sparkle. Even with the dry weather, the yard needs mowing; it's been a month now, almost. Cool to the touch, the first blades wet our bare feet. Dew oozes between the toes and drenches skin as we step. Our jeans dampen at the cuffs.

The full pour of August light, the heat of the day will dampen the concert. At this moment—with no human voices, no televisions blaring, no gears grinding on the mountain road—it's the birds' show, sound waves crisscrossing the cove from one island of forest to the other. "Maids, maids, maids, put on your teakettle," sings a hidden song sparrow. "Chewink, che-wink," offers a towhee. High in a tree somewhere a warbler cries, "See, see, see," but we don't see. We only hear.

Something's thrashing in the holly tree. It flashes from the serrated edge: a female cardinal on the wing, her body olive green and drab as an old sock. She rockets up the hill, swoops into the billowy green mountain ash beside the barn. She's invisible again. A limb throbs, like the broken surface of a pond when a frog's dived in.

These birds—that eat our cherries as well as seeds and insects—aren't alone in their love of the fruits of our labor.

Groundhogs strip the bark from young fruit trees, sometimes killing them, and need no invitation to dine on windfall fruit. Quite rare in the community when Frank was growing up, deer are now abundant and seem to love nothing more than grazing on the twigs of young fruit trees, stunting their growth. Wild turkeys have also made a comeback, though they are much too shy to invade the orchard. Early this spring, as we were descending our mountain from a climb, a flock exploded in front of us, plunging deeper into the forest in lumbering flight, like miniature cargo planes with red necks. Though we have often seen where they have been scratching the ground, it was our first glimpse of these four-feet-long birds that only a decade ago were unknown in Orchard Gap.

We step to the northern edge of the yard and walk a slow circle around the perimeter as the sky splashes more and more light on the palette. It's a Rousseau painting, weeds and all. Gone are the flowers of spring and early summer, virginal dashes of color in their neat beds. Here are the flowers of August, wild and domestic—a jungle riot, decadent and lush despite the lack of rain. The very names are sensual: althea, goldenglow, viola, cockle, milkweed, Japanese iris, bergamot, four-o'clock, hollyhock, pink lily. We lap up the profusion, the swirls of reds, blues, whites, yellows, and pinks spread five and ten feet deep beyond the yard, and try to see individuality: the spiky red petals of the bergamot with its long, square stem; the velvety white, pink, and magenta folds of the hollyhock petals with gilded outer edges.

We bring in phlox, slip it into a glass vase filled with water on the kitchen table. It's a simple and elegant bouquet—lavender petals bunched high on a long, slender stalk. We make coffee, eat cereal and homemade applesauce, and go to work.

When we sit down to dinner that evening, a few scattered petals lie curled on the tablecloth, the first casualties of domesticity.

August is the high season for vegetables. At noon the next day we peer into the haze from the front porch and thank God (and the Indians) for corn. It's not just the taste—the flavor of ripe ears that ten minutes before the first toothy crunch were still growing on the stalk. It's the beauty of corn rows a hundred feet from the kitchen stove, eight or nine feet high, leaves glistening, trapping a pool of dense emerald light in their shade. July thunderstorms made them tall. Now we disappear between two rows, brush silky cornstalk flesh, looking for the dark brown tassles that betray ripeness, and pick a dozen ears into a bucket. Then it's out into the sun—plucking blood-red tomatoes from staked vines, fresh lettuce (from the second planting, the first having gone leathery), and yellow squash tucked demurely beneath a tall canopy of broad, sandpapery leaves, little hairs on the squash that make it downy to the touch. We tug at the base of crimson stalks, and two beets appear, Christmas tree ornaments coated with dirt.

With August evenings comes pesto. Not every evening— it just seems that way. After jogging, Wanda goes out in the twilight to gather the glossy leaves from the basil plants, filling a two-cup measuring cup to the brim. A neighbor's cow lows from the foot of the mountain. A bobwhite rings out its name loud as a pistol shot.

Over by the cottage where Miriam's parents lived in their last years, Koh, the dog, is groundhog hunting again. Officially he's Sam and Miriam's dog—part collie, part shepherd, an adult dog with long tan-and-white fur and a handsome profile— named for T. T. B. Koh of Singapore, president of the Law of the Sea Conference in the early eighties. Unofficially he's the orchard mascot. Several years ago when jogging, we found him prostrated in the middle of the dirt road, his head scraping the ground. He had a collar but no tag, and when we petted him he followed us on to the church, then back home, where Frank's parents adopted him. Since no one claimed him, we determined that he was "set out," as the local saying goes— abandoned by someone on the side of the road. When we jog, which is most days, Koh invariably runs along, prancing down the same road on which we found him.

As Wanda kneels at the basil plants, Koh stiffens at one of the multiple entrances to the groundhog's underground den, his body arched forward, his long nose pointed at the hole. The groundhog's safe in his den. When Koh's not in the neighborhood, we often see the "whistlepig," as the mountain people call this creature the size of a large cat, standing on its hind legs surveying the world.

After ten minutes the basil leaves a pungent, minty scent on Wanda's hands. She walks them over to Virginia's and uses her food processor to blend the leaves with garlic, walnuts, Parmesan cheese, and olive oil into pesto sauce. Back in our kitchen, Frank has made a salad from the garden and cooked pasta.

We eat on the front porch, our plates in our laps. A mourning dove moans to the east, a high, lonesome lament. Way up on our mountain to the north, a hoot owl booms, its "Who? Who? Who?" resounding from the forest. The moon lifts over the ridge to the southeast, swimming yellow in the haze, just a few days short of full. A pair of bats flutter across its face, skitter and swoop in a crazy dance, their silhouettes jagged against the sky. In the fading twilight it's hard to get a close look at them—but then perhaps we shouldn't wish for it too strongly lest the wish come true.

The bats keep dancing, crisscrossing each other's paths. This is their party, not ours, and they'll carry on for as long as they damn well please. Like stunt pilots competing for attention, they careen out over the Damson plum trees at the edge of the yard, loop back toward the moon and the Windsor cherry, forty-nine years old and dying, limb by limb, in the east yard. Suddenly they veer back our way through the limbs of the white pine tree, and—instinctively—we duck. The air whiffles as they pass along the edge of the porch.

"I'm through with dinner," Wanda remarks.

"Same here," echoes her husband.

We go inside and clean up the kitchen. Night falls, and the kitchen casts a rim of light through the open screened windows onto the porch. We peer outside, hoping to see the bats, but find only the August moon.

"Guess they're gone," Frank says.

"They seem to be a pair, don't they?" Wanda says.

Having cut down more than half of our old Red Delicious apple trees, we're now down to maybe three thousand bushels. This year Garnet and Frank will pick the crop themselves. Shortly before Labor Day, when the apple season begins, they'll hook up the hydraulic lift to the back of the tractor and haul bins into the orchard on the old flatbed army truck. The tractor will move the bins from tree to tree, and a second tractor and lift—borrowed from a neighbor—will load the full bins into the truck for hauling to the packhouse.

Glenn Dawson and Sam will do the grading on the old Durand-Weyland grader. The smallest apples will fall through the holes in the sizing belt and go to the cider plant near Roanoke. Most will be sold retail out on the loading dock, where Sam, Glenn, and, at the busiest times, Wanda and Miriam will offer customers a selection among Red and Golden Delicious, Spartan, Fuji, Crispin Mutsu, Stayman Winesap, Granny Smith, and York Imperial.

In our unbiased opinion, the simple apple remains one of the Almighty's proudest inventions. By the time it's matured on a tree for five or six months, drinking in rain, air, and sunlight, an apple is no longer merely an apple. Like ourselves, an apple is a living thing. The freckles are called lenticels, and they are breathing pores by which the apple inhales. Until the time of consumption, an apple is alive and breathing. As our teeth bite into it, we hear the sharp report of thousands of living, breathing cells, their membranes crunched in a sound that conjures up the pure joy of partaking.

Unless our stars are crossed, sometime in the third week of October the apple harvest will be all but finished. The nights will be cool, but not yet cold enough for frost. The days will be unpredictable—some golden and drowsily warm, others brisk enough for a sweatshirt and light jacket. In the woods the poplars and maples and oaks and birches will be ablaze, but if it rains, the leaves will come swirling down until the trees wear a tattered look. And if we see no son or daughter or cousin of Hugo—the hurricane that in three hours huffed and puffed a thousand or more bushels from our trees in 1989— we will praise the gods of wind.

The last tree to be picked is always the old York Imperial. Two years ago in March we planted twenty young Yorks, but they haven't yet come into bearing, and this venerable giant remains our lone source for the lopsided, red and yellow apples that make tangy pies and are excellent keepers. The tree is east of the Red House a couple hundred yards, nestled against one of the rock walls that Frank's grandfather built along the contour of the hillside. Yellow-bellied sapsuckers, seven- or eight-inch-tall woodpeckers with red necks and caps, have drilled neat rows of holes in the trunk, extracting sap from the inner bark. But on a good year the old York tree with its sixty-foot wingspan still turns out thirty-five to forty bushels. Set out in 1911, it's the only remaining fruit tree planted by the orchard's founder.

Ralph Levering died on a Monday morning in May 1945, not long after the apple trees had shed their blossoms, three months before the bombs fell at Hiroshima. At seventy-four he felt chest pains on a Sunday evening, having returned the day before from a week-long college reunion in Maryville, Tennessee. He lay down on his bed in the same room where June would die forty-two years later. He would see the doctor in the morning.

On the eastern side of the Red House, the tall bedroom windows admitted the light of dawn, and Clara left the bed and entered the kitchen. "I hear the birds singing," she heard her husband say.

There are those who speak of the virtues of living in the moment. In that moment, one of his last on earth, Ralph was hearing the birds singing. He had asked for a glass of water. When Clara returned from the kitchen a few moments later, the man she had married in 1898, who had fathered her three children, who had brought her to this remote mountain community and shared her adult life, was dead.

We don't know where he is now, this man who found this place with his feet as well as his heart. But we feel his presence—in the barn and the house and the sheds he built, in the rock walls that haven't crumbled, in the York Imperial tree. And in the coffin that sits in our basement.

That coffin reminds us of how well we want to live in the time that we, too, are here. Not insulated by luxury, but in the beauty and truth of nature as it is. Not cut off from our community and the world community, but taking an active part in vital change. Not in abstinence, but in sufficiency. Not in fear of death, but in love of life. Not only as caretakers of tradition, but as tradition makers who can learn from the new insights of the present as well as the time-tested verities of the past.

Here in Virginia we have discovered that—though no one is ever free of contradictions—one *can* change the general direction of one's life, can make it simpler and more satisfying in a range of important respects. With us, because we found no quick fixes, because our lives hold the potential for as much complexity at the orchard as they had in Los Angeles, change has not happened overnight or without a small mountain of struggle. But we have changed, and we continue to change as we hone our desires and pursue goals that bring our lives and ideals into closer alignment.

In life here at the orchard, and in our travels, it is a joy to have learned that we are not alone in the quest not for more, but for better. While many Americans remain attached to traditional standards of material progress, others are examining their values, their priorities, their lifelong goals, and are choosing to measure gain not by what they have, but by who they are, by how they live.

The moon is full tonight. Long after darkness has fallen it peeks over the high east ridge, finds us on the porch as we sit listening to the frogs down the hill. Up the hill, Sam and Miriam's lights have gone out. So, too, have Virginia's to the east and, a half mile down the mountain, Garnet and Esther's lights as well. In these ancient mountains, old as time itself, almost, it's getting late.

"The sun," Thoreau wrote, "is but a morning star." On a night like this we imagine that we feel what that crusty old bachelor must have felt, the exuberance of new possibility, of seeing a richer way of living. We feel a fullness, like the moon's. We've worked all day, some at the computer, some in the sun. Now we sit on the porch and talk about nothing terribly important and fall silent, as married couples do, and talk again. We grow drowsy. The frogs croak. The moon glides higher, casting a silver sheen on the haze in the valley. Life is good. We want more of it, not less.

Tomorrow, as Garnet always says, we'll try it again.

FOR THE BEST IN PAPERBACKS, LOOK FOR THE

In every corner of the world, on every subject under the sun, Penguin represents quality and variety—the very best in publishing today.

For complete information about books available from Penguin—including Pelicans, Puffins, Peregrines, and Penguin Classics—and how to order them, write to us at the appropriate address below. Please note that for copyright reasons the selection of books varies from country to country.

In the United Kingdom: For a complete list of books available from Penguin in the U.K., please write to *Dept E.P., Penguin Books Ltd, Harmondsworth, Middlesex, UB7 0DA*.

In the United States: For a complete list of books available from Penguin in the U.S., please write to *Dept BA, Penguin*, Box 120, Bergenfield, New Jersey 07621-0120.

In Canada: For a complete list of books available from Penguin in Canada, please write to *Penguin Books Canada Ltd, 10 Alcorn Avenue, Suite 300, Toronto, Ontario, Canada M4V 3B2*.

In Australia: For a complete list of books available from Penguin in Australia, please write to the *Marketing Department, Penguin Books Ltd, P.O. Box 257, Ringwood, Victoria 3134*.

In New Zealand: For a complete list of books available from Penguin in New Zealand, please write to the *Marketing Department, Penguin Books (NZ) Ltd, Private Bag, Takapuna, Auckland 9*.

In India: For a complete list of books available from Penguin, please write to *Penguin Overseas Ltd, 706 Eros Apartments, 56 Nehru Place, New Delhi, 110019*.

In Holland: For a complete list of books available from Penguin in Holland, please write to *Penguin Books Nederland B.V., Postbus 195, NL-1380AD Weesp, Netherlands*.

In Germany: For a complete list of books available from Penguin, please write to *Penguin Books Ltd, Friedrichstrasse 10-12, D-6000 Frankfurt Main I, Federal Republic of Germany*.

In Spain: For a complete list of books available from Penguin in Spain, please write to *Longman, Penguin España, Calle San Nicolas 15, E-28013 Madrid, Spain*.

In Japan: For a complete list of books available from Penguin in Japan, please write to *Longman Penguin Japan Co Ltd, Yamaguchi Building, 2-12-9 Kanda Jimbocho, Chiyoda-Ku, Tokyo 101, Japan*.